Supporting Transgender Students

Second Edition

Support ing Trans gender Students

Understanding Gender Identity and Reshaping School Culture

Second Edition

Alex Myers

Foreword by E. Quincy McLaughlin

Cover Design by: Kevin Stone

Published by University of New Orleans Press

Library of Congress Cataloging-in-Publication Data

Names: Myers, Alex, author.

Title: Supporting transgender students, second edition : understanding
  gender identity and reshaping school culture / Alex Myers ; foreword by
  E. Quincy McLaughlin.

Description: Second edition. | New Orleans : University of New Orleans
  Press, 2024. | Includes bibliographical references and index.

Identifiers: LCCN 2024011406 (print) | LCCN 2024011407 (ebook) | ISBN
  9781608012619 (paperback) | ISBN 9781608012640 (ebook)

Subjects: LCSH: Transgender students--United States. | Gender identity in
  education--United States. | Sexual minority youth--Education--United
  States. | School environment--United States. | BISAC: EDUCATION /
  Inclusive Education | EDUCATION / Teaching / Subjects / Health &
  Sexuality

Classification: LCC LC2575 .M84 2024 (print) | LCC LC2575 (ebook) | DDC

  371.826/60973--dc23/eng/20240311

LC record available at https://lccn.loc.gov/2024011406

LC ebook record available at https://lccn.loc.gov/2024011407

This book is for the many transgender students who have fought to clear their own paths and make a road for others.

Table of Contents

FOREWORD

by E. Quincy McLaughlin

We school people remember well the first time a student or a parent or guardian requested support for their or their child's gender identity. Few things better reveal the character of a community than how it responds when a transgender or gender non-conforming (GNC) child and their family asks this of us.

When Alex Myers came out to his high school dean twenty-five years ago, teachers and administrators were on their own; there was little literature and no framework, just caring adults stumbling through and leaning on their foundational commitment to keep students safe.

I remember the first time I addressed a faculty about pronouns and shared the GLSEN Safe Space Kit. That was nearly ten years ago, when we had to remind faculty, staff, and students not to assume everyone in the classroom was heterosexual and not to assume one could know someone's sexual orientation or gender identity by looking at them. It's 2021 now, and although many of our schools have removed gendered pronouns from handbooks, created all-gender bathrooms, and modified administrative tasks to make name and pronoun changes more seamless, some schools still need a lot of help getting past the restrictive "boy or girl" binary.

This book is the help we need. It provides a guide for how we can help raise other people's children and keep them safe, specifically when we're working to support transgender and GNC students in our schools. It is about how to get from here to there, covering practicalities and their implementation; it shows us how to address systemic issues and modify the way our organizations communicate about gender altogether.

Most importantly, this book is written by Alex Myers, and he has a story to tell. A graduate of Phillips Exeter and Harvard, he was the first openly transgender student at both institutions. He now runs workshops and speaks at schools across the country about gender identity and supporting transgender students. It has been my pleasure to know Alex for many years both as a colleague and as a consultant in our efforts to design policies and facilities that are more gender-inclusive. Two of my own school communities are better for his work.

Our communities can get polarized quickly, even in their supportive responses and solutions. But gender is fluid and exists on a continuum for many of our students, and some of their gender identities will evolve throughout their years with us. Myers offers a way forward from wherever your school community is on this journey. If you 't know where to begin, Myers reminds us that all students benefit when a school initiates a gender audit guided by his good questions: Where do we make mention of gender in our school? Why do we want to highlight gender here? What is our purpose in seeking to know or control gender in this context? Although bathrooms and sports teams most often require interventions when we first begin to ask questions about gender in our schools, Myers calls our attention to an additional and broader set of concerns, such as the importance and life-saving ability of the proliferation of inclusive terminology and language.

Some of our schools have been engaged in this work of inclusion and belonging for years, and 2020 has coaxed others into recognizing the experiences of transgender people for the first time, most prominently through the election of a president who spoke for transgender rights during his campaign as well as at least eight transgender, non-binary, and GNC state candidates, including the nation's first openly transgender state senator.

However familiar you are with these issues, you wouldn't have opened this book if you didn't suspect your school needed its guidance, if you didn't believe there were transgender or non-binary students in your community or young people who have considered transitioning. Even if no student has yet asked to change their name or pronouns, you know there are those who need you to facilitate these possibilities in advance of their having to ask.

If you are just beginning this journey with your school or with a student, *Supporting Transgender Students* will reassure you that you can do the right thing. If your experience is like my own, you will worry that you won't think of everything, that you won't be able to build the necessary protection and affirmation quickly enough—and then you will discover Alex Myers and be relieved. Here is a fellow teacher, advisor, coach, and dorm head; he is a school keeper, a wise and generous guide who happens to also be a talented storyteller.

If you have the resources to host Alex Myers at your school, do it (you will enjoy the power of witnessing Alex tell his story to middle school students). If time, space, and travel prohibit that actual visit, this book is the best equivalent. Distribute copies to your faculty. Plan some professional development. Create a working group. Take a walk around the school with a questioning eleven-year-old in mind and keep them at the center of what you do.

In these pages, Alex Myers will help you to anticipate your students' needs and to prepare processes and answers in advance of students and their families needing them. But this book is about more than legal advisories and bathroom challenges. It's about nurturing and supporting *all* our students, including those who live inside and outside of our gender boxes and those who embrace and reject their assigned gender scripts. You will be better able to say to your students: *You can be who you are, you can do what you love, and we will be here to support you.*

We are, like Myers, school keepers charged with creating safe and supportive educational environments for all our students; we are charged with supporting and preparing the adults in our communities who care for children. As Myers writes, "Schools have a responsibility to protect the children within their care." Sensitive and astute, Myers is the fundamentally accessible guide our generation of school keepers needs now.

This book moves us from the discreet fulfillment of individual student requests to the complete adoption of cultural habits and practices that will accomplish our stated commitments to equity and inclusion. I have presented to hundreds of educators and dozens of schools on the dilemmas of creating safe and supportive school cultures that facilitate a child's healthy development. I well understand the complexities schools face today, and we are better when we draw on the work of school leaders like Alex Myers. He is one of our best teachers, and he understands what gets in the way of change.

Supporting Transgender Students sets a new standard for rethinking our gendered spaces and how they affect all our students. No school keeper, head of school, teacher, dean of students, division head, department chair, admission officer, college counselor, athletic director, librarian, chaplain, or coach should make any more changes to their school without reading this book.

Wherever you are in our collective effort to improve schools, the model Alex Myers offers here will help. Thank you for all that you are doing on behalf of our students and school communities. Keep it up. We'll get there together.

Enjoy reading.

E. Quincy McLaughlin
2021

E. Quincy McLaughlin is currently the Associate Head of School and Head of Upper School at Greenhills School in Ann Arbor, Michigan. A regular presenter at The Association of Boarding Schools, National Association of Independent Schools, and New York State Association of Independent Schools conferences, Quincy has served as a consultant to schools and nonprofits and provides a range of assessment, consulting, and training services. Quincy emphasizes best approaches to enhancing community life by creating safe, inclusive, and supportive learning environments for students and faculty.

INTRODUCTION TO THE SECOND EDITION

It's only been three years since *Supporting Transgender Students* first came out, but in that short time so much has changed in the fight for transgender rights and, particularly, in the realm of gender in schools. In turning back to this volume, I wanted to add information on school and public libraries, which have increasingly become targets of legislative action and are important sites for community building. I also wanted to update, where possible, legal landscape in which schools must operate. These past years have seen laws passed, school boards overturned, and principals and teachers fired in dozens of states, all over the question of gender in schools. Most notably, in Florida, laws now make it illegal for educators to discuss gender and sexuality with students younger than third grade and assert tight restrictions on what content is "age appropriate" and permissible in older grades.[a]

Legislation like this makes inclusion harder and creates a hostile environment for transgender students and their parents. As these laws spread, teachers are being fired or disciplined for showing movies, reading books, and displaying artworks—works as mainstream as Michelangelo's *David* have resulted in termination.[b] Often, the teachers comment when they hear the complaint from a parent or administrator is: *I had no idea that this would be a problem.* Or: *I never mentioned transgender identity.* These laws create confusion and sow fear, making silence feel like the only safe option. But silence can be deadly for LGBTQ+ youth.

Beyond schools, transgender individuals, particularly transgender children, have been the subject of debate and discussion that has, in eighteen states as of this writing, led to laws restricting or banning their access to gender affirming care, from being called by their chosen name and pronouns, and being able to access the medications, surgeries, and support that allow them to fully become the people they know themselves to be. Another twelve states are currently considering such legislation, and the situation continues to evolve.[a] Sadly, it doesn't take more than a cursory glance at the headlines to know that a new edition of this book is needed.

As I will state again and again, given these realities, some of the strategies and changes I propose throughout the book will be legally impossible for some schools, depending on their jurisdiction. What is always possible—and more important than ever—is identifying ways that your school can minimize the harmful impact of such regulations, of transphobia and bigotry in general, on your transgender and gender non-conforming students and offer them full-throated support wherever and however you can.

When I wrote the first draft of *Supporting Transgender Students*, I composed with the feeling that the wind was at my back. Yes, there were many pockets of resistance, reluctance, and occasional refusal, but most schools I worked with were approaching the work, even if grudgingly, with the attitude that it had to be done. Now, though, my stance is much more defensive—much more aware that the ground is shifting under my feet or, in some cases, has fallen away entirely. Instead of building, we are retrenching. This is a familiar position, unfortunately, for civil rights work.

I have been working with schools to support transgender and queer students since 1995. In that almost-thirty-year span, I have seen ebbs and flows. I have witnessed legislative and school board interest fluctuate from hostility to engagement and back again. Early on in my work, as students (mostly in high school) came out (mostly as gay), the impulse from administrators, board members, and the surrounding communities was to keep things quiet, to not make it a big deal. This was matched on the national level with the military's "Don't Ask, Don't Tell" policy for gay troops. Supporting trans and queer students, when it was done, was done in private organizations: closed support groups and confidential clubs. The first wave of my work with schools was to get them to open those doors, put words in print, say things out loud: to acknowledge that they had queer and trans students and to begin thinking of them as visibly, audibly, and physically present in their communities.

In the years that the battle for marriage equality was fought on the state and national level,[1] a related struggle was going on in schools around queer and trans students. Were these students "different" in some meaningful way from their straight and cis peers? Did supporting queer and trans students mean suggesting that they assimilate? Did being successful as a queer or trans person mean passing, covering, being accepted by straight culture? Just as the states and the nation grappled with the question of whether "gay marriage" was or could be or should be the same as "marriage,"[2] so too schools and students wrestled with the idea of acceptance and accommodation for queer and trans students. Like the country, and like much of the queer community, in 2015, many schools and educators were leaning toward the idea that so long as queer and trans students "followed the rules" (aka, behaved according to the established [straight] cultural standards), they could be out.

But real inclusion is much more radical than that.

Back in 2016 and 2017, drafts of early chapters of this book took the form of speeches and talks delivered at education conferences or to school boards. In those years, I was helping schools acknowledge the students they had who were struggling to understand and express themselves, to find a place to belong in hallways and classrooms that were designed according to a very limited idea of gender and sexuality. I didn't feel like I was delivering a controversial message, and I hope that many of you, who go on to read the rest of this book, agree.

My main argument was and is: don't force students to conform to expectations that are set by people who don't understand who the students are. Or, to put it more specifically, don't set schools up so that only

---

1 The culminating years of struggle for this right were 2004 to 2015. However, for those interested in history and wanting to have a fuller context of queer civil rights, looking at the earlier work on this front in the 1990s (what culminated in the Defense of Marriage Act in 1996) as well as the very early efforts in mid-century America, offers a clearer arc of this work. Only considering the final decade of this effort feeds into the argument that gay rights have come "quickly" and "easily"— true in comparison to the struggles of other marginalized communities, but also not completely accurate. The longer view also helps to explain the current moment and all its fluctuations, and all the legislation that has been put in place around LGBTQ+ identities and lives.

2 Early efforts for civil rights around marriage led to civil unions and same-sex unions, a sort of "separate but equal" situation that preserved the word "marriage" for heterosexual couples. Understanding this history helpfully reinforces the importance of language in the work for LGBTQ+ rights. When does "marriage" need an adjective in front of it? When does "woman"? And what do these words alone, by themselves, imply?

straight, White, able-bodied, cisgender, Christian boys can be successful, praised, respected, and comfortable. Educating students based on who administrators wish them to be, versus who they actually are, creates a culture of assimilation and oppression. When administrators and school policies are set up to police students' identities and to force students to dress and behave based on oppressive, exclusionary social hierarchies, education is impossible. Even more, students are at risk of harm.

Work toward inclusion gained traction and then momentum. In 2018 and 2019, I was delivering talks across the country and even around the world—schools from every region in this country were reaching out to do work on gender inclusion. This work was often being done in concert with, or on tracks parallel to, responses to the #MeToo movement and the Black Lives Matter movement. Inclusion, disruption, racial justice, and institutional accountability were all being talked about in ways that finally felt like real change instead of just window dressing.

So, I suppose it shouldn't be surprising that the backlash came hard and fast. It is a truism often spoken in equity and inclusion work that when you're accustomed to privilege, equality feels like oppression. Instead of perceiving the work around inclusion as addressing profound inequities, many people in power read the situation as a loss of their rights, their power, and their control. This is the situation we are facing now, in 2024: a retrenchment, and the drawing of stark lines. The transgender student is no longer someone to be tolerated, let alone included. In fact, to some, the transgender student—the transgender person—is not a person at all, but an ideological pawn. More and more legislation is being written and passed across the country that restricts the activities and limits the bodily autonomy of transgender individuals in schools and beyond.

For the moment, it is possible for cisgender liberal people to look at the situation and feel a sort of distant pity and perhaps wonder— why is it that transgender people are being so picked on? But transgender people are just the easiest target. We are not the end goal. I fear that the rights that are being stripped from us will soon be taken from others. Indeed, it is not a far leap from the restrictions of access to medical care and procedures for transgender youth and adults to the unfolding restrictions around abortion. The question is not what medical procedures transgender people should have access to, but, rather, who should get to make decisions about other people's bodies and healthcare. These are not transgender rights, but human rights.

This is what makes a new version of this volume critical: the need to take into account the new language, the new approaches, and the unfortunately growing number of challenges around supporting transgender students, and to protect the humanity and well-being of those students.

NOTES

a. Parental Rights in Education, H.B. 1557, FL State Leg. (2022).

b. Associated Press, "Principal resigns after complaints on 'David' statue nudity," *The Associated Press*, March 24, 2023, https://apnews. com/article/florida-censorship-david-statue-nudity-michelange-lo-84bba40d47339eff7770ec58fcb23dd1.

c. "State Action Center," *National Center for Transgender Equality,* accessed July 10, 2023, https://transequality.org/state-action-center.

PROLOGUE

August 1995: I approached the imminent start of the school year with more than my usual degree of excitement and anxiety. Standing in my mother's sewing room on the second floor of my childhood home in Paris, Maine, I gripped the phone as I dialed the number for Phillips Exeter Academy. In two short weeks, I was due to return for my senior year. I was a student in good standing, a varsity athlete in ice hockey and lacrosse, president of the Jewish Student Organization, first tuba in the concert band. I also was—or had been—a girl.

That's why I had the phone in my hand, and that's why my hand was shaking as I listened to the buzz on the other end of the line.

"Phillips Exeter," the raspy voice of our beloved operator answered. I could picture her sitting at her massive wooden desk, the high windows behind her letting in slants of summer light, in Jeremiah Smith Hall, the administrative building in the center of Exeter's academic quad. The big potted ficus tree to the side.

"Dean of Students?" I said. My voice crept up high with nerves, and I pushed it down to gruffness. "Please."

"Hello?" the dean said after I'd been switched over. "This is Alex Myers. I'm a senior. . . ." I paused, waiting to see if the dean would give an indication of recognition. "I live in Hoyt Hall. . . ."

"Oh! Alice! Of course. I thought you said Alex."

"I did," I replied. "That's why I'm calling. I changed my name, and I wanted to let you know that. And I also . . . I'm coming back to school as a boy this year."

A long pause ensued. "What do you mean by that?" said the dean.

"I mean I want to be a boy."

I pressed the handset of the phone against my ear. I have never been good at conflict or at speaking back to authority. My general MO at Exeter

xi

had been to follow the rules and avoid all interaction with the deans so that I wouldn't have to have difficult conversations. It had worked for three years of high school, but it wouldn't now. I had to say something.

"All my life, I've felt like a boy, even though I was a girl. This summer, I came out as transgender, and now I want to live as a boy."

An even longer pause.

"Well," the dean said at last, "that will present a few challenges."

I could tell he was trying to be humorous, to inject a little levity. "Probably," I agreed.

"Let me call you back tomorrow," he replied, and hung up.

Over the next few days, the dean called back and forth, speaking with me and my mother. What did I want? What did the school feel was possible? What would be safe? What would be comfortable?[3] What should teachers be told, and who should tell them? Could they change my name on the rosters? Would I still be able to play on girls' sports teams? How about live in the girls' dorm? The questions went on and on with no ready answers in sight.

I did know what I wanted, at least in a very general sense. I wanted to be a boy. I wanted to pass, to have other students and teachers call me "he" and "Alex." But I wasn't sure how to get there. Neither was the school. They'd never gone through this before; they'd never even imagined this scenario. It was 1995. The word "transgender" was pretty much brand new.[4]

In the end, there was a lot of discussion and a lot of compromise. I returned to live in the girls' dorm where I'd resided the previous three school years. When I called my roommate to tell her I'd be coming back as a boy, she said she didn't want to live with me. So, I got a single. A quick resolution that didn't address my roommate's fears nor how I felt about her rejection of me. I worried that others in the dorm would feel the same, that I would be ostracized. When I asked the deans if I could come back early

---

3 There is a profound difference between safety and comfort, though many students and some administrators use these terms interchangeably. This difference—and the importance of articulating this difference in discussions of civil rights and identity—will be discussed later.

4 The term "transgender" was coined in 1965 and used in psychological works, but it didn't replace the term "transsexual" for many years. In the mid-1980s, transgender became more commonly used within the LGBTQ+ community, eventually spilling over into more frequent usage in all channels in the early 1990s. Terminology and the history of that terminology— particularly as it relates to the medicalization of identities—is very important when it comes to inclusion and will be discussed at length later on.

and meet with the student leaders in my dorm as well as the dorm faculty, just to explain to them what was going on and give them a little help in case they were asked questions about me, the deans said no—they didn't want to make a big deal of this. This was my first hint at how they wanted to handle my transition: keep it quiet, don't make a fuss. There was a sense, a slight undercurrent, that I might be doing this "for attention," a reaction that I thoroughly resented. I knew that I was going to be more visible on campus—more notorious—but really, all I craved was a sense of belonging.

They did put "Alex" on the rosters instead of "Alice." And they said it was no problem if I followed boys' dress code—coat and tie to class. Other than that, I was on my own.

As the summer drew to a close, my mother took me shopping for a blue blazer, a couple of dress shirts, and a few ties. My father donated a few of his old ties as well. Everything else I already had in my wardrobe; I'd more or less been dressing in boys' clothes for years. I got a trim at the barber's, thinking that my new hairstyle would probably be the biggest shock to my classmates. For three years, I'd had bushy brown hair pulled back in a ponytail. Now, I had it buzzed to a number three on the sides, with about two inches of length on top. I cannot describe to you the bliss of the haircut that removed my ponytail: the lifting of a real and meta-phorical weight from my neck. Nor can I effectively convey the deep sat-isfaction of watching the barber's clippers trim the edges of my hair as I stared at my reflection, finally, finally seeing something that looked like my imagined version of myself after years of gazing at a near stranger.

When I got to my dorm on move-in day, my mother went to meet with the college counseling office. I grabbed a box of books from the back of our car and started walking it up the stairs to my room. As I headed up, someone's mother was coming down, and she stood aside on the landing to let me pass.

"Aren't you nice," she said as I walked by. "Are you helping your sister move in?"

"No," I replied. "I live here."

Her eyes widened as she sputtered, "I didn't know the dorms were co-ed!" She hurried down the stairs.

I imagined her trotting across campus to the dean of students' office. I hoped they had a lot of fun answering her questions.

That day, in that stairwell, I had a profound realization about gender. Up until that moment, I had been so full of doubt. Here I was, returning to a two-hundred-plus-year-old institution that had been founded as an all-boys school, that had grudgingly let girls in twenty-five years prior, that still had *Venite pueri ut viri sitis,* meaning, "Boys, come here, that you might be made men,"[5] carved above the entrance to the main academic building. Here I was, feeling trapped by who I'd been in the past—unable to escape being known as a girl. Trapped in the dorm—on campus, the first questions everyone asked was "Where are you from?" and "What dorm are you in?" Usually, the answer automatically identified whether you were a boy or girl. Trapped on my sports teams, which functioned in much the same way. Everything seemed to keep me defined as a girl.

And yet. Despite the obvious context of the dormitory, that woman in the stairwell had thought I was a boy. I was convincing enough in my appearance and presentation that she recalibrated her understanding of the space rather than recalibrating her understanding of me. This is what gender is and how gender works. I'd been feeling it my whole life—the sense that I knew I was a boy or, rather, that I knew I wasn't a girl. But I couldn't figure out why what I felt wasn't obvious to others. That's because gender is both internal (identity) and external (expression). I felt, I knew, I understood. But as a little kid I hadn't been able to translate that knowledge of self to the outside—and, when I did, I was often labeled a tomboy. That was better than being a girl, but it wasn't exactly accurate.

Coming out as transgender had allowed me to not just understand myself but explain and express that self to others. As much as gender is deeply internal, it is also simultaneously about perception, about the outside. In a sense, gender is about interaction, how we present ourselves to the world. That woman read me as a boy. Why? Because of my haircut and my clothes. Because of how I moved my body. It was all in how I looked, and how her perception of me aligned with her predetermined notions of gender, of boyness. She certainly had no idea of my anatomy beneath my clothes, but she didn't have to ask me "What are you?" So much of our daily experience of other people's gender is incred-

---

5 In celebration of its first twenty-five years of coeducation, Exeter had an additional inscription carved that spoke to *pueri et puellae* (boys and girls). This just underscored, for me, the inescapability of the binary in language and in culture. Both inscriptions remain in place today.

ibly superficial. Our own experience of gender—particularly if we are transgender—is deeply internal and private. This contradiction is part of what makes gender complex and, to me, wonderful.

I remember making it to my room, setting down the box of books, and letting a smile spread across my face: I could do this.

It's now twenty-five years later and I'm still calling dean of students' offices to talk about gender. Amazingly enough, the set of questions they ask has remained more or less the same as it was when I first came out. Twenty-five years later and across this country, indeed, around the world, many schools are just now responding to their first transgender student coming out. Or, perhaps, they are looking at a school across town or down the road who has its first openly transgender student, and they are thinking: *We better figure out what we're going to do in that situation.*

More and more students are coming out as transgender or gender non-conforming (GNC).[6] They are coming out at younger ages. There are a variety of reasons for these trends: there is a much greater presence of transgender figures in the media, and the conversation around these figures is much more positive. Students now have a variety of models of what it means to be transgender available to them. More students can find a person who articulates a feeling that they share—*I never felt like a girl or a boy; I always wanted to wear my sister's dresses; I hated having to put on a swimsuit*—and arrive at new self-understanding because of that. In movies, in literature, on social media, there are more and more positive and diverse depictions of transgender people. These depictions affect families and teachers as well, making them more aware of the possibility that a child might begin to question their gender and more attuned to what GNC behavior and expression might look like.

Yet, schools still struggle with how to handle transgender and GNC students, and parents and guardians of transgender and GNC

---

6 Throughout, I will use these two terms, transgender and gender non-conforming, to stand for the range of gender identity and expression terms applied to and by trans people. I understand transgender to be a big umbrella term. But I also understand that many people do not like the idea of a "shift" or the implication of the binary that this term might suggest. Many people, people whom I would describe as transgender, are non-binary—they don't want to reassign as the "opposite" gender. To capture this, I use the term gender non-conforming (GNC). I am aware that not everyone likes this term: Students I work with use non-binary, agender, gender expansive, and other terms. I'm streamlining things for simplicity and clarity. I don't mean to erase anyone's self-understanding.

children still struggle with how to get schools to accommodate their children's needs. It's those same roadblocks I faced twenty-five years ago. What team should they play on? What bathroom should they use? What name do we put on the roster? Schools also have to consider how to respond to students whose parents/guardians don't want them to transition—or, given the incoming wave of reactionary, anti-trans legislation, when state law prohibits them from doing so. Under those circumstances, how can schools offer appropriate support to students while adhering to relevant policies and laws? In a moment when some state laws seek to literally criminalize parents and guardians, educators, physicians, and librarians who attempt to connect transgender and GNC children with supportive resources and care, how can schools provide shelter from these tensions?

In the midst of such turmoil and sensationalizing, it's also important to be clear about the purpose of schools in the first place. Parents and guardians of transgender and GNC children have to monitor how much their child is doing to educate others, rather than getting an education themselves. It's also the case that gender, and enriching collective understandings of gender, isn't only supportive to transgender and GNC students. How, then, can schools instill an inclusive, expansive, progressive culture of gender for the entire student body?

Beyond schools, these same questions can seem overwhelming to civic institutions like churches, summer camps, or neighborhood recreational sports leagues: how do we as a society move to a more equitable and informed position when it comes to transgender and GNC kids and gender competency? How do we balance respect for individuals with the need to share common space? There are so many factors to consider that reform can feel daunting or even impossible.

Many schools or other institutions simply handle each student who is transitioning on a case-by-case basis; this tends to feel more manageable than system or policy-level change. After all, statistically speaking, it is unlikely that a school would ever be overwhelmed by a massive number of transgender students such that they couldn't respond to students' needs on a case-by-case basis.[7]

---

7 Counting transgender people is complex, and the statistics are always changing. In 2022,

And yet, such a response is inadequate. It may not be inadequate for the individual student, but it is inadequate for the institution, for the broader student population, and for the culture at large. Keeping accommodations for transgender and GNC students at an individual level largely keeps those students "off the books"—unofficial. Parents and guardians, too, can feel more comfortable with a "one-on-one" approach. Some parents and guardians might prefer this approach because it keeps things quiet; many parents and guardians of transgender or GNC students grapple with their own transphobia when their child comes out. They may feel embarrassed by their child's transition, and the "one-on-one" approach generally keeps things less public.

Other parents and guardians of transgender and GNC kids worry about their child becoming a focal point, standing out for the wrong reason. But though this concern is quite valid, parents and guardians should be leery of asking for exceptions to rules and policies, or what amounts to "special treatment," for their children rather than working with schools to design a policy that is fair and effective for all students.

Moreover, the one-at-a-time approach means that real systemic change—a true shift in school culture—will never happen. Schools need to change signage and facilities, policies, and guidelines. But schools also need to train and encourage teachers to do the work of gender inclusion in their classrooms and clubs and teams. This means committing to making gender part of the curriculum, something that is taught, discussed, and understood.

This book argues that it is time to make official, sanctioned space for transgender and GNC students in terms of school policy, guidelines, best practices, and facilities. The days of making things up ad hoc as specific situations arise should be relegated to the past on the level of policy, law, and rhetoric, across the US, especially as coordinated attacks on trans rights mount. Transgender and GNC students are present in significant numbers, in a persistent and consistent manner, such that it is time for schools and other institutions to tackle the question of how to not just address these students individually but

estimates for the adult population in the US ranged from 0.3% to 5.1%, depending on age group, with an average of 1.6% of the adult population overall identifying as transgender or non-binary. (See note *a*.)

also within the larger context of overall school life and culture in general. Though, as an educator, my focus in this book will be on schools, teachers, students, and families, the philosophy and approach that I describe are equally applicable to a variety of civic institutions and, indeed, to any person who is wrestling to understand just what gender is and why it should matter to them.

Gender is far from the only politicized vector of identity that impacts educational environments. Gender exists in addition to—and is itself shaped by—race, class, religion, nationality, dis/ability, and other aspects of identity. All of these forces inform classroom power dynamics and shape the social interactions that students take part in every day. These are the forces that gave our educational institutions the structure, shape, and values that they have today. As educators, parents, and guardians, we need to open our eyes and see the impact and effect of these identities. We cannot pretend that all students are the same. For example, we cannot believe that an institution designed by and for White men will serve a Black girl as well as it serves a White boy. We need to interrogate our systems, examine our practices, and make visible those key aspects of identity that our society encourages us to ignore or take for granted. We need to do so in our classrooms by actively teaching first ourselves and then our students how to talk about their own identities and the identities of others. Gender is not the only factor at play by any means, but it is the one that will be the focus of this book.[8]

I will put forward the case that by helping support transgender and GNC students, schools can create a more positive, open, equitable culture for all students—regardless of gender identity. Some schools, particularly private schools, will find it easier to make such changes to their facilities, practices, and policies. Some schools will be prevented by law from putting any overt gender policies in place. I have worked

---

8 I should note, also, that though I list these identity categories and therefore make them seem distinct, they do, in fact, overlap and intersect—and people existing at these intersections often experience compounded marginalization. Transgender Black women, for instance, are some of the most marginalized and vulnerable individuals in our society today. Schools need to understand that students have multiple identities that are in conversation, and sometimes in conflict, with each other. Does a school give space for a student to be both Black and a girl? Or does a student have to pick and choose between these? Both gay and Jewish? And so on.

with schools in both situations and will try, throughout this book, to indicate how a school can still advocate and make space for gender inclusion, even if it finds itself constrained by laws or by the politics and culture of its governing board and donors.

This book is not a cry for parents and guardians to become social justice warriors, nor for transgender and GNC students to become activists (unless that's what they feel called to do!). Rather, this book is meant to offer support and encouragement to embrace a rational and reasonable re-examination of how gender drives so many of our policies and practices, as well as practical tips for transforming those policies and practices where necessary for the well-being of students.

This is a book about schools and students and how gender influences, consciously and subconsciously, the policies and practices of every single school. But even more, this is a book about gender and society. Every single one of us has a gender identity; every one of us has a variety of gender expressions. Many of us go through our days largely unaware of our own gender and only passingly aware of others'. By allowing gender to be this passive presence in our lives, we are succumbing to a hierarchical structure put in place centuries ago. This book is a call to question the assumptions we all have around gender, a call to become aware and responsible, a call to consider not just transgender identities, but whatever our own gender may be, and how that shapes our world.

NOTES

a. Anna Brown, "About 5% of young adults in the U.S. say their gender is different from their sex assigned at birth," *Pew Research Center*, last modified June 7, 2022, https://pewrsr.ch/4d8XtNU.

CHAPTER ONE:

WHAT IS GENDER AND WHY DO WE NEED TO TALK ABOUT IT?

More than twenty years have passed since I moved into my single in the girls' dorm at Exeter, and I am back at the Academy, this time as an Instructor of English. It is 2015, and as I walk around the campus and the town, I run across a few of the teachers I had for science, mathematics, and history. Some are retired now, but many are still teaching at the Academy. Some don't recognize me, but once I introduce myself, I can see the spark of memory flare up: "Oh! Alex! *Of course,* I remember *you.*"

As a teacher, I have uttered these same words to former students, passing off a small lie in the name of making the student feel cherished. But in these cases, I am fairly certain my former teachers remember me pretty well, or at least they remember one aspect about me: all of them watched me transition. And now I am standing in front of them, a man. Many of them probably doubted I would end up like this; many of them thought I was acting out or going through a phase. Some of them even told me that to my face when I was their student.

But here I am, a member of the faculty of Phillips Exeter Academy, returned to the fold. After a few sputtered remembrances, the first question from my teachers is: "So, what's changed at the Academy? What's stayed the same?" It'll be a few months before I can answer this adequately, but my initial feeling is: not very much. And, mostly, that's good. The academics are still strong; the students are still hardworking; the faculty is still caring; the school is still dynamic, bursting with energy. But not very much has changed around social justice—especially gender. Boys and girls are housed separately, play on separate sports teams, but in those separate spaces, the expectations and culture are incredibly different. Though Exeter—like most schools—may not make explicit rules that dictate what boys and girls can respectively do, that's the effect in practice. We create and maintain separate boy cultures and girl cultures—with grave repercussions for all genders, repercussions that last well beyond high school.

Indeed, everything I have just said about Exeter applies to society more broadly. In twenty-plus years of being out as transgender, I have seen some change (it has been hard-fought, and I am deeply appreciative of it),[1] but mostly things have stayed the same. In 1997, when I was a sophomore at Harvard, the now defunct ABC news-digest show *Primetime Live* interviewed me. They wanted a human-interest story: the first openly transgender student at Harvard. On the whole, the show's angle was positive. They wanted to get the basics across: How did I know I was a boy? What did being transgender mean for my future? How had my family and friends reacted when I came out? They interviewed a variety of people at Harvard and beyond, most of them supportive, including psychologists who discussed whether being transgender was a mental illness.[2]

In 2015, I was interviewed by *PBS NewsHour*. Caitlyn Jenner was coming out on network television that week, and PBS wanted to get involved in covering transgender identity. I sat down with the news anchor for an interview—and faced almost the exact same questions that *Primetime Live* had asked me eighteen years earlier. Both interviews were mostly focused on establishing that transgender people were normal, that we lived real lives, that we suffered and deserved basic civil rights. I had hoped that in eighteen years, we might have advanced to consider more nuanced questions about gender—getting beyond the fascination with medical transition, looking at transgender as more than a shift from one end of the binary to the other, considering the non-binary richness of gender expression or how the understanding of gender has shifted over time.

But the conversation has advanced only incrementally. When the PBS

1 There are now over a dozen states that include "gender identity" in their non-discrimination clauses, and many more municipalities that do the same, for instance.

2 Gender identity dysphoria was the official diagnosis in the DSM until 2013. Gender dysphoria remains as a diagnosis; more on this later in the chapter. (See note *a*.)

piece aired, the only difference from the ABC interview was the absence of the psychologists (and I had a bit more gray hair). Given the increase in the volume of news coverage and other discourse around the subject of transgender identity, why is it that these topics remain so baffling? Why is it that we struggle to understand the basics of terminology, the fundamentals of the concept—not just for schools but for society more broadly?

In part, I think this is because gender itself remains an elusive concept for many people. Gender is invisible to them as individual identity yet hypervisible as it functions in society. This is the crucial paradox that we have to understand if we are to make our schools and our culture more equitable and inclusive. As gender has become part of the public discourse, and thereby has been rendered visible to those who hadn't considered it before, an all too predictable negative reaction has formed.

This can be seen most clearly in the use of the phrase "gender ideology," a term that has cropped up and been employed by anti-trans politicians and activists. By deeming gender an "ideology," these groups want to suggest that gender is "just" an idea, a set of beliefs arbitrarily held by some.[3] Though this phrase is meant to be derogatory or dismissive, there is truth in it. Gender is, in part, a set of beliefs; multiple ideologies around gender have always existed and likely always will. For that matter, homophobia and transphobia can also be described as gender ideologies. The goal of transgender advocacy—the goal of the methods and approaches detailed in this book—is simply to make the mainstream ideology of gender an inclusive, equitable one. Schools play an instrumental role in that shift.

THE COMPLEXITY OF GENDER

The question "What is gender?" provokes a complex and never-ending discussion. There is a universe of texts that attempt to answer this question medically, psychologically, spiritually, culturally, and theoretically. In twenty-five years of trying to, first, understand my own gender

---

3   The implicit (and sometimes explicit) opposing position is that gender is biological, innate, determined, and set. That is, the insistence that anatomical sex at birth is the determining factor for all aspects of gender—there is no "belief" possible. Anatomical sex and its relation to gender will be discussed in other places in this book.

identity and, second, explain myself (and gender in general) to others, I have come to a simple conclusion: I cannot define gender. But I can explain how it works in society and why it is important for everyone to understand the social functions of gender.

The best place to start explaining gender is with the story I told in the prologue: the woman in the stairwell of the girls' dorm. She took me to be a boy despite the obvious context. She "read" me. That's arguably the most typical way that gender works in society. Gender is one means by which we classify and understand another person. Like other classification schemes, it is useful to us because, in part, gender is external. We usually don't have to ask any questions to get a read on whether a person is a boy or a girl: that information is telegraphed through clothing or hairstyle.

However, there certainly are many times that we cannot perceive whether a person is a boy or a girl. And it is in these interactions that the true power of gender begins to reveal itself. Such ambiguity isn't always a product of a person deliberately trying to be androgynous, blend genders, or exempt themselves from gender. How many times have you seen the following (or done the following yourself): A baby lies in a stroller, blanket tucked to its chin, little woolly cap pulled down on its forehead. "Ooooo," coos the passer-by. "How cute! Is it a boy or a girl?"

We like to know—in fact, we often insist on knowing—what gender a person is. We get very uncomfortable when we can't discern gender and even more so when a person refuses to tell us.[4] What difference could it possibly make whether the baby in the stroller is a boy or a girl? And what are we really asking?[5]

The answer is that we feel a need to know so that we can categorize and appropriately respond to that individual. If we are told the baby is a boy, we might point out the ways he resembles his father or say he looks strong. If the baby's a girl, we might praise her beauty, delicacy, or sweetness. We will say these things regardless of how the baby actually looks or acts. Our responses are shaped by preconceived expectations

4 The truth of this is captured in the *Saturday Night Live* sketches featuring the character Pat in the 1990s.

5 Many people tend to conflate sex and gender. When I work with students (or teachers) and ask them explain how they know they are a boy or a girl, the most common answer I get concerns anatomy. But sex and gender are not the same thing, though they are related. We will explore the differences and overlaps later in the chapter.

around gender and by the reflexive desire to adhere to the social code. And, conversely, the baby—as it grows and continues to get this feedback—will come to embody, disrupt, complicate, or reject the associations that people put on it around its gender. We create this feedback loop for ourselves and others throughout our lives, sometimes subconsciously and sometimes very deliberately. It is put upon us by others and then, in turn, becomes deeply internalized, so that we begin to impose it on ourselves. The social conditioning process of gender has long been a fact of human society, though it varies through individual, cultural, and historical approaches.

When we think about the social functionality of gender, it is clear that most of our interactions with gender are very superficial, based on the outside—this is what is usually called "gender expression." It's one's clothes and one's hairstyle. The makeup and accessories someone decides to wear, or the lack thereof. The walk, the talk, the body language, the affect used when speaking or writing texts and emails. Gender is, to terribly paraphrase Judith Butler, performance.[6] Gender is a presentation we make to others in order to be "read" in the way we want to be.

However, gender is also intensely internal. Let me provide a bookend to that story of the mother who encountered me in my girls' dormitory the fall of my senior year. Flash forward eight months, to May, to lilacs blooming and graduation about to occur. Exeter, like many high schools, has a tradition of senior superlatives (Most Likely to Succeed, Best Smile, and so on). In the spring of my senior year—having survived (and at many times even enjoyed) a year of being out as transgender on campus—I was running a stealth campaign for a senior superlative: Most Changed Since Freshman Year. To be honest, I thought I was a shoo-in.

But the votes were tallied, and I didn't get it. That evening, as I read through the school newspaper's reporting on who had received the superlatives, I jabbed at the picture of the boy who had won "Most Changed." Sure, he'd started the ninth grade as a seventy-pound shrimp, not even five feet tall, and ended up as a massive crew jock, but still. I was reading the paper with my best friend, Lexi, and I said to her,

---

6 For a full read, see Judith Butler's pioneering *Gender Trouble* and their many follow-up essays, interviews, etc.

"I can't believe I didn't get it."

She gave me her characteristic smirk. "You're such an idiot," she replied. "You haven't changed at all."

In the moment, I thought she was being snarky and sarcastic (such was our normal mode of interaction). But ever since she said that, I've been thinking about it. And it took me a while to see how right she was.

At the time, I was fixated (as many transgender people who first come out are) on the idea of transition, the idea that I was leaving behind a name and identity that had never felt right and becoming something new. It felt like major transformation, caterpillar-to-butterfly scale. But since then, the longer I have been out, the more time I have had to reflect and understand and simply be (rather than become), the more I understand what Lexi meant.

She meant that, despite all the external shifts, the name, the hair, the pronouns, I was still very much the person I had always been. My externality prior to my coming out—my presentation as a butch or jocky or tomboy-ish girl—was no more a commentary on self than my current external presentation as a boy. Both were simply an attempted translation of a deeper self, the part of the self that might best be called a gender identity. And that aspect of my identity hadn't changed one bit—the only difference was the language I used to describe myself.

*   *   *

I can remember being four years old and having an old friend of my father's ask me, "What do you want to be when you grow up?" And I told him: "I want to be a boy." I knew even then it was what I was meant to be.

I knew I was a boy from as early as I can remember.[7] And I quickly learned that if I insisted that I was, in fact, a boy, people would become annoyed or alarmed. So, I learned not to say it. But I knew I was.

---

7   This is true for me. It is true for many transgender people. But not all. It's also a streamlining of my story. It can be dangerous to champion this narrative, since many transgender people don't come to an awareness or an ability to articulate their sense of self until much later in life. They may get a feeling that something is "wrong" or doesn't "fit" about who they are, but not put it in terms of gender. For me, I was aware very young of feeling like, or wanting to be, a boy. I should also note that many kids have cross-gender feelings without actually being transgender.

How did I know? I felt it.

That is an entirely accurate and entirely inadequate answer. It is an answer, I have found, that enrages audiences. What, many people have asked in response to my assertion, is to keep a person from saying, *Well, I feel like a toaster oven?* Or, *I feel like I'm really twenty-one, not sixteen?* Why are these invalid things to say, while a transgender person's assertion that they feel like a certain gender is something that ought to be respected?

That is a question that can only be answered with an exploration of where gender identity comes from. Gender expression—that outside performance—is socially constructed, subject to change from time period to time period and from place to place. Gender identity—that internal feeling of self—comes from something inherent. Something biological, something innate, something psychological.

Both transgender people and gay[8] people share a similar history of having been classified as either having a mental illness or as making a transgressive and unnecessary lifestyle choice at different points in time. I think that, broadly speaking, both gay people and transgender people have realized that talking about mental illness or lifestyle choice is a way that many in the mainstream try to gain control over and make themselves feel comfortable with a difference that is truly innate. Where does gayness or transgender identity come from? I don't know. Studies are inconclusive. Is it genetic? Epigenetic?[9] I don't know. And, to be honest, I'm not particularly interested in getting to the bottom of the "problem."

What I do know is that I am this way and that many other people are this way and, yes, we are different from how the majority of people understand their gender identity. But that does not make us "wrong" or "made up." Nor does it mean that we should be fixed. A search for a "gay gene" or a "transgender gene" will not help us understand the most salient aspects of gender identity. The fact that many within the

---

8 I'm using "gay" here as shorthand for LGBQ+ sexual/romantic attraction identities; I know that is not correct, but it is simpler.

9 There have been a lot of studies, many of them inconclusive. A few studies seem to show genetic linkages, particularly for gay men, but also suggest that there are a variety of possible genetic pathways that lead to gay individuals. It is also true that many animals—not just humans—have individuals within their populations that engage in same-sex sexual interactions. Is this the same as being gay? No. But it does suggest that there is a biological basis to same-sex attraction.

LGBTQ+ community promote this search just points to a desire to justify and explain, to, in Kenji Yoshino's word, "cover" our identity.[10]

Transgender people and gay people also share a similar history of mainstream culture—particularly the medical establishment and religious groups (not to mention more vigilante forms of violence)—trying to "fix" them. Whether it is electroshock, castration, hormone treatments, or conversion therapy, there is well over a century of documented attempts to "correct" gay and transgender individuals. Studies and interviews with those who have survived these attempts show conclusively that trying to make gay and transgender people into straight and cisgender[11] people will result in depressed, non-functioning, and/or suicidal individuals.

So, yes, I feel that I am a boy. It feels right to me when I am addressed as "he." That is the extent to which I can explain and justify my gender identity. And I would challenge any cisgender person to do better than that with their own comprehension of their gender.[12]

The words we are taught and the words we create for ourselves allow us both to make sense of who we are internally and to generate understanding in others. That may sound very convoluted (as many things around gender can), but it is important to realize the power of language in this sense.

When we are young, in particular, there can be a scarcity of words and an abundance of concepts. We don't know what to call things; we lack the vocabulary to explain, even though we may understand or feel something deeply. As we grow older, we get more words—but these words come with connotations and associations and rules and limita-

---

10 Yoshino's book *Covering* is an excellent examination of how marginalized identities accommodate themselves within mainstream culture. Covering is, in a way, a sort of apology for who we are as gay or transgender individuals.

11 Cisgender is a relatively new term for someone whose birth sex aligns with their gender identity in the socially expected way: a female who identifies as a girl; a male who identifies as a boy. In short, someone who is not transgender or gender non-conforming. We have a tendency only to label the "other." In earlier conversations, then, we would be left with transgender people and "normal" people, phrasing that is clearly problematic. "Cisgender" both addresses this problem and serves as a reminder: Everyone has both a sex and a gender identity.

12 Usually, as mentioned earlier, when a cisgender person is asked to explain their gender identity ("How do you know you're a boy?"), that person makes reference to genitalia. But being a boy is not as simple as having a penis. If a chromosomally, genetically, physiologically "perfect" male who identifies as a boy were to undergo some horrific accident resulting in complete castration . . . would that person suddenly no longer be a boy? Is a woman-identified female who gets a hysterectomy or a double mastectomy less of a woman? Of course not.

tions. This word is "right" for us, that word isn't "proper" . . . and so on. A child who is questioning their gender may try out words to see if they feel good and to see what reaction they get.

Schools play a major role in reinforcing traditional language around gender and in enforcing proper behavior through gender expectations. It is still unfortunately common to hear teachers (and other adults) utter phrases like "Girls should be nice" or "Boys need to run around a lot." And if it isn't said, it's often implied. The words "girl" and "boy"—without room for any other possibility of gender identity—come with a vast array of connotations relating to behavior, hobbies, character, and capacities.

Schools, with their interest in enforcing "good" behavior, often rely on gendered language to express their expectations. By doing so, cis girls and boys are confined to rigid labels not terribly distant from the expectations of the pre-feminist era, even though many people nowadays would disagree with traditional gender stereotypes. Trans and GNC students, meanwhile, are left outside of language altogether, deprived of meaningful words to describe themselves and uncertain of where they belong and what is "right" for them to be. Such prescribed language forecloses discovery, authenticity, and connection for all students.

When we aren't given language to describe ourselves, we have to come up with our own. Further complicating this situation is the reality that adults—and other children—who hear new or alternative terms for gender often react with skepticism and a sense that since a term is unfamiliar to them, it isn't any good.

Every generation of adolescents creates its own language for a wide range of reasons, and this is particularly true around LGBTQ+ identity: There is a delightful array of terminology. I call it delightful, but I know that many find it vexing and confusing. Labels come and go rapidly, and it is absolutely fine not to know what "pansexual" or "agender" means when you hear someone use it for the first time. But the proper response to your ignorance should be to acquire more information and understanding, not to say, *I don't know that word, so it can't be any good*.

Pronouns are an excellent example of how language can be expanded and repurposed to support understanding of gender and self but also cause a lot of (unnecessary) consternation. "Gender neutral" pronouns are not new; use of alternate pronouns to "he" and "she" goes back to the nineteenth century.[13] But recently "they" as a singular pronoun has gained ascendency, being used by trans, non-binary, and GNC individuals alike to convey their identity through language.

Just as with other areas of trans and GNC identity, there has been predictable backlash to "they." Often, this takes the form of claiming grammatical incorrectness: people will insist that "they" is always plural or assert that it is impossible to conjugate correctly or clearly with a singular "they."[14] The truth is, people are uncomfortable with change, afraid of making mistakes, or are simply transphobic. "They" is a wonderful way of asserting identity in language that all English speakers already know and use.

In fact, pronouns have come to play an increasingly prominent role in asserting identity. It has become commonplace in many circles to include pronouns in an email signature, for instance, or to put them on name tags. Again, I see this as a wonderful way to share with people a bit of who we are and how we wish to be understood.[15] Some people also use more than one pronoun—he/they, for instance—or saying "any pronoun is fine." Sometimes using new pronouns is a form of exploration, trying out how it feels to be referred to in this way. Other times, a person might adopt "they" as a pronoun in an act of solidarity, indicating that they are in support of a range of self-expression and understand that gender isn't limited to the binary. Critics will read these instances as an indication of "contagion,"[16] the spread of ideas that they are more

---

13 The 2020 book *What's Your Pronoun?: Beyond He and She* by Dennis Baron is an excellent history of pronouns in the English language.

14 It is easy to debunk all these arguments: Use of the singular "they" goes back to Chaucer. Moreover, we all use "they" as a singular pronoun in casual conversation, such as "Hey, someone left their cell phone on the table." As far as verbs go, we all use "you" as both a singular and plural pronoun and manage to conjugate verbs along with that pronoun just fine. "You are right," for instance, can refer to a single person or a group of people. Context is what clarifies. . . . The same goes for "they."

15 The common position of pronouns, coming right after a person's name, means that they have displaced the honorifics that used to go there (PhD, JD, etc.). I, for one, would much rather know someone's pronouns than their degrees.

16 I frequently hear this complaint about elementary and middle school classrooms: One kid starts using "they" and suddenly all their friends do too. That's not a bad thing. They aren't being "copycats" so much as trying to show support, perhaps, or wanting to experiment— both of which are great things for children and adolescents to do.

comfortable having silenced. Language is powerful. Pronouns, in partic-ular, because of their ubiquity, are an important way for trans and GNC individuals to make themselves visible and legible.

When I was a child, I had just two gender words available to me: boy and girl. My brother was a boy and I was a girl. This was reinforced to me in various ways. It was explained biologically. It was enforced through clothing. And when I asserted what I felt—"I want to be a boy!"—I was told that I was not one. When I tried to behave as I wanted to, rough-housing, or refusing to wear a dress, I was told: "Girls don't do that."

Somewhere early on, I acquired the word tomboy. I loved this word. It seemed to capture the in-betweenness that I felt. The not-quite-girl and not-quite-boy self that I harbored within me. *Tomboy*. I used it as an excuse. Why did I not act like other girls? Because I was a tomboy.

I outgrew that word, sadly. Somewhere around puberty, tomboy became no longer possible. Now what was I? When I looked around the rural Maine town where my family lived, there weren't any exam-ples of women who modeled what I wanted to grow up and become. Not to disparage the women of that town, but their lives seemed impos-sible to me. It wasn't until I went off to prep school that I acquired new language and understanding.

At prep school, I met my first openly gay people. There was an English teacher, Ms. Robinson, who was out as a lesbian. The first time I saw her walk across campus, I just about melted. She wore jeans and cowboy boots and a flannel shirt. She had short hair, a boyish cut, and little silver hoop earrings. She wore no makeup. She walked with the easy stride of a young man. My immediate thought was, *I want to be her.*

It took me a good chunk of my ninth-grade year to come out as a lesbian, but eventually I told my close friends and my brother. "Lesbian," like tomboy, was a word that was helpful in explaining to myself and to others why I wasn't like other girls. Language has tre-mendous power to define and explain—and to restrict and confine. Lesbian translated a part of myself that let me say, *I don't want to make myself sexually attractive to straight boys. I don't want to be a stereotypi-cal woman.* But, like many labels, it also chafed.

Over the next couple of years, I became active and involved in gay rights groups and LGBT youth social groups. I met lots of other lesbians. Some of them were very similar to me: butch, former tomboys. And others were profoundly dissimilar: makeup wearing, dress loving. For years, I just assumed that the other butch lesbians were like me: they thought of themselves as boys, and being a butch lesbian was the closest they could get to that. It took me some time to realize, but the truth was that I was dissimilar to all of these lesbians in one fundamental way: I didn't want to be a woman.

In my junior year in high school, I went to a gay pride march in Boston. A couple friends and I had made a bedsheet banner proclaiming the existence of the Exeter Gay/Straight Alliance. The parade organizers placed us right behind the Lesbian Avengers, most of whom had shaved heads, lots of piercings, and plenty of tattoos. Many of them were also bare chested, with just duct tape over their nipples.

Marching along, the Avengers would every so often turn around to chat with us, and pretty soon they were cajoling us to join their group. My friends, two girls from school who were out as bisexual, were quite happy to do so. But I remember thinking, *No way*. I didn't want to take off my shirt; I wasn't proud of my breasts. And as I walked along, chatting with these women who looked more like boys than I did, I began to realize that, fundamentally, I was very different from other lesbians. I wanted to be a boy. I understood myself to be a boy. They were women and proud of it; they just didn't want to be bound by socially expected gender or sexual norms.

Once again, I had lost a word that had been useful in translating some part of myself. It wasn't until I met actual transgender people and got to know them well that I would finally arrive at a new level of self-understanding and acquire a term that I have cherished (and struggled with) for over two decades now.

All of this is gender: there's no easy definition. Gender is how we understand self and how we live that self in the world. Gender is one way—perhaps the primary way—that we sort people in society. If schools only engage gender on the level of boys and girls—if those are the only terms that are used in rules, on signage, and in classrooms—then students will be very circumscribed in their ability to understand and express themselves.

Even though it can be messy, it is crucial to give students access to expansive language and concepts when it comes to gender.

OTHER KEY TERMS

Besides gender identity and gender expression, there are two other components related to gender that I have alluded to: biological sex, which is also referred to as anatomical sex, sex assigned at birth, and sexual orientation. These four aspects are interrelated in a complex and fascinating way. To me, they are all stars that make up the constellation that we understand to be gender: separate, distinct, but coherent together. Let me try to explain biological sex[17] and sexual orientation on their own and then explain what these two aspects have to do with gender.

Biological sex is usually determined at birth, according to the baby's external genitalia. When we talk about biological sex, we are really talking about more than just external genitalia. Biological sex also includes chromosomes, hormone levels, internal genitalia, and secondary sex characteristics (facial hair, muscle/fat ratio, body hair, etc.). But these attributes are not so visible at birth, and therefore, external genitalia are used to make that initial determination. Some people reading this paragraph might wish I'd stop dancing around this definition and simply pin things down: "If there's a penis, it's a boy!" But it isn't that simple, and that desire to make it that simple has caused a lot of problems.

Most babies born around the world display "standard"[18] external

---

17   The current preferred term in much of the transgender community is "sex assigned at birth." In usage, this often emerges as, for instance, describing someone as "assigned female at birth." I think this framing is extremely helpful to capture the larger concept of biological sex, particularly the cultural context. "Assigned female at birth" reminds us that some aspects of identity are ascribed by others (in this case, the doctor, the state). It also reminds us that identity has a temporal setting, "at birth," with the implication that it can change. For these reasons and more, I think this is excellent terminology to utilize. However, for this chapter and elsewhere in the book (and in my daily spoken language as well), I will use "biological sex." This term feels more accurate because some of the relevance of "assigned female at birth" is limited—that was the statement at birth, yes, but what's your identity now? Are you taking hormones? Have you had surgery? Do you understand your body differently than it was understood at birth? All these aspects matter and aren't captured by what's "assigned at birth." I also prefer "biological" to anatomical because anatomy refers to structures—body and organs, essentially—but sex includes hormones, chromosomes, and other non-structural components.

18   I try to avoid the word "normal," which implies a positive judgment. Rather, I use "standard" or "common" whenever possible. Again, language is important.

genitalia, and in a vast majority of these cases, those external genitalia accurately indicate a corresponding set of chromosomes and internal genitalia that "match" the external. For instance, vulva and vagina on the outside, XX chromosomes, ovaries, and uterus on the inside: female. However, some babies display what are often called ambiguous external genitalia (elements of both male and female genitalia). These individuals are deemed "intersex"[19] and, like transgender and gay individuals in the past, they are often subjected to "corrective" surgical procedures. Quite often, these surgeries are done almost immediately after the delivery is over, often without giving the parents or guardians a chance to understand and meaningfully consent to the procedures. (And, needless to say, without the consent of the child.) There is a rush to make things "right," to standardize ambiguous external anatomy. These surgeries are still shockingly common, though the intersex movement has made some progress in leading the medical profession to better practices.

There are many debates over how to count the number of intersex individuals in the general population. Traditionally, the medical establishment counts only those who have surgery to "normalize" their genitalia, which yields a count of one in one thousand births. However, intersex advocates have argued that the number should include a wider range of individuals with chromosomal and anatomical differences that don't require surgery, which yields a count of one in one hundred births.[20][b] However you count the numbers, it is important to realize that intersex is also more than just those born with ambiguous external genitalia; a child can also be born with standard external genitalia and later find out they have internal genitalia that don't "match." So, for instance, a baby is born with a vulva and vagina and is sexed female. At puberty, the child's body doesn't mature as expected, and tests reveal that the child has undescended testes instead of ovaries.

How is this relevant to understanding gender as a whole? This matters because the foundation of our societal insistence on a gender binary

---

19 Here again, language: "Intersex" replaced the term "hermaphrodite." Intersex people have always existed, and different cultures and time periods have different terminology and understandings of what their "mixed" nature means.

20 An important concept to absorb, in the background of these numbers, is that there are important conceptual questions to ask: Who gets to define these metrics and terms? Why does medical intervention get privileged as the benchmark of identity?

rests on the idea of a biological or anatomical binary. "God made humans male and female" is meant to imply that there are only two ways to be, and those ways are determined at birth through what our bodies manifest. This is false on many levels . . . and even its literal assertion is incorrect. Human bodies are not neatly binary at birth or at any other time.

None of this is meant to suggest that intersex individuals are automatically transgender or GNC. Some intersex people are, and many are not. Biological sex, whether male, female, or intersex, does not determine gender identity or gender expression; it does, however, have a relationship to gender identity and expression. Some aspects of gender expression, such as growing a beard, depend upon having the biological capacity to do so, for instance. But there is no inherent correspondence between biological sex and gender expression, nor between gender expression and gender identity. These pieces move independently of each other, with varying degrees of harmony and conflict.

This harmony and conflict is partially described by "gender dysphoria," another key term to understand around transgender identity. Gender dysphoria is the feeling of conflict between one's anatomical sex and one's gender identity. This feeling of conflict can lead to distress, anxiety, and, in some cases, self-harm. Many transgender people experience gender dysphoria—which is often summarized as feeling they are in the wrong body—but not all do. Gender dysphoria is not a requirement for being transgender.

It is also important to understand that the dysphoria can lead to depression and anxiety—not because the dysphoria itself causes mental illness, but because society still largely regards people who experience dysphoria as "wrong" or "abnormal" in some way, instead of promoting gender competency and ensuring that such individuals have options and support. Gender identity disorder, like homosexuality, used to be listed by the American Psychiatric Association as a mental illness. That is no longer the case. But individuals who experience gender dysphoria can go through real suffering and pain as they figure out how to resolve the sense of conflict they feel between their body and their mind. Understanding dysphoria is very important for those who want to support transgender students.

In my work with schools, I make it a practice to always pair a discussion of gender dysphoria with a discussion of gender euphoria—the feeling of excitement or delight when the clothing or the makeup or the hairstyle delivers a sense of rightness or belonging in your own body. Too often, when we share stories of LGBTQ+ experience, they are full of trauma and emphasize the difficulty and danger of these identities. In working with adolescents, it is important to acknowledge the reality of this—the rates of suicide, the frequency of homelessness, and so on—but also to emphasize that coming out doesn't just mean depression and trauma.

The euphoria story I often share about coming out is this: not long after cutting my hair short and changing my name, I went with my family to a diner and the waitress came over and asked me, "What can I get you, young man?"

The utter elation at those few words—the realization that I didn't have to "correct" her or feign embarrassment, that I could simply nod and acknowledge that, yes, that was me. For other trans people I know, it's putting on makeup and looking at themselves in the mirror or wearing a certain outfit. Essentially, it is the feeling of rightness, okayness, selfness that is deeply affirming and empowering.

These poles of experience are not isolated to trans or GNC people—rather, they can be experienced by anyone, including cisgender individuals who face feelings of alienation over the expectation of conforming to gender. Whether it's a matter of being expected to have certain interests, to wear certain clothes, or to play certain roles, the moment when any person steps away from a gender norm and into a more authentic expression of self can be euphoric.

Just as the binary idea of gender is rooted in the assumption of binary human genitalia, much of the distrust and misunderstanding of transgender and GNC people, as well as outright transphobia, stem from the insistence that anatomical sex determines gender identity. This insistence, arguably, is at the root not only of transphobia, but misogyny and the subjugation of women as well. To believe that biology is destiny, and then to further imbue that biology with behavioral or personality traits (to have a uterus means you are motherly and nurturing, for instance) is both to conflate gender with sex and to set up social hierarchies and power dynamics based on that conflation.

A lot of gender-based oppression stems from assumptions made about how someone with a female body "ought" to act. A lot of transphobia stems from the insistence that a physical body reveals more "truth" than a person's mind. It is true that most people in this world are cisgender—that is, the majority of people who are anatomically male identify as men and the majority of people who are anatomically female identify as women. That makes this alignment—cisgender identity—prominent, common, and typical. It does not make it right; it does not make it destined.

But to people who are cisgender, it can certainly seem like the world works this way. The gender-anatomical sex binary, if you believe in it, creates a very clear set of hierarchies and expectations. It organizes the world—usually—in a way that gives cisgender men the most power. Much of the violence against non-binary and GNC people comes from those who wish to protect a system that works well for them, that entrenches and reinforces their position at the top of the hierarchy. But gender and sex are not the same thing, and there is no tidy or "proper" configuration of sex to gender identity, nor gender identity to gender expression, let alone gender expression to biological sex. And we find the same relationship (or lack thereof) with sexual orientation.

Sexual orientation refers to romantic and sexual attraction and relies, in part, on the gender identity and expression of the people involved. Let's take the example of a woman who is attracted to other women. This person might define herself as a lesbian. Her being a woman (gender identity), plus the gender identity of the people to whom she's attracted (also women), is the basis for the label lesbian (sexual orientation). She could add to that by saying she's a woman who's attracted to butch women—that's referring to gender identity (woman) as well as gender expression (butch). She could also add that she's a woman (gender identity) with a female body (biological sex) who is attracted to butch (gender expression) women (gender identity) of any biological sex (that is, female, male, or intersex).[21] And so on.

---

21 This last parenthetical is particularly important to pause on. It is unfortunately very common to hear people assert that trans women aren't "real" women. This position is advocated by several groups of radical feminists and has recently been taken up and amplified by celebrities, such as J.K. Rowling. This is an instance of transphobia that has a lot of layers

Our sexual orientation doesn't define our gender identity, nor does it define our gender expression. For instance, straight men can both find a wide range of gender expressions in women attractive and have a wide range of gender expression themselves. Yet there is an undeniable linkage between sexual orientation and gender expression. To be specific, within the queer community, there has long been a significant number of gay men who are "effeminate"[22] and a significant number of lesbians who are butch in both appearance and behavior. Of course, not all gay men and lesbians display these gender expressions, but many do.

Why is this? Does being a lesbian "make" a woman more inclined to be butch? Or, if a woman is a lesbian, does she simply feel more able to express that aspect of herself? The answer could also be something else entirely. Consider that on its own, sexual preference is largely invisible. One usually can't tell if a person is queer or straight as they walk down the street. But a gay man's feminine affect could be a way of signaling to others that he is gay. That is, after all, part of gender expression's function in society: to communicate some (otherwise hidden) aspect of inner self to the outside world.

Some parents, guardians, and educators feel a great deal of hesitation about approaching the topic of gender because of its connection to sexual orientation. When I work with elementary school teachers and students, there's a reluctance to talk about gender because "the students are too young." When I dig into this belief with adults, I find that what they mean is that, in their estimation, the students aren't ready to learn about sexual intimacy. That may well be the case, but at any rate, it's a whole other subject; educators can talk about aspects of

---

to it, but it boils down to the same conflation of anatomical sex and gender identity that I discussed above. To say that trans women aren't "real" women is to imply that what keeps them from being real is their anatomy. You can easily find arguments that talk about how trans women were raised as boys/men and so absorbed lessons about privilege, etc. These arguments dress their transphobia in language that appears to be about gender expression (i.e., the teaching of gender, the cultural interpretation), but their assumptions are predicated on the belief that someone born male (biological sex) can never escape that "destiny" of maleness, that their identity will always be determined by that.

22 Here's another piece of vocabulary to watch. "Effeminate" denotes feminine behavior in men that is inappropriate. Yet, I still hear this word deployed as if it is a neutral adjective. There's a significant difference between describing a person as feminine, which *is* neutral, and effeminate.

gender without talking about sexual intimacy.[23] This is one more reason why parents, guardians, and educators need to understand the difference between gender identity and sexual orientation, between biological sex and sexual orientation.

When it comes to gender and biological sex, I do not think that children can be too young to talk about it. From an early age, children should be taught about their bodies, and how to refer to all the parts of their bodies, and who should and should not touch their bodies, etc. Age-appropriate discussions of biological sex are essential for healthy development for a number of reasons.

The same is true of gender. Indeed, many transgender children are aware early on of their gender identity—or are aware that the way they feel about their gender (and/or about their body) doesn't line up with how many other people feel. It is fairly common for transgender children to begin to talk or act in ways that reveal their feelings about their gender as early as four or five years old. This might take the form of a direct question: "When do I get to be a girl?" Or it might take the form of imaginative play, wearing costumes and taking on new names.

Yes, these can also be the behavior and questions of cisgender children. After all, most people's gender identities are more complex than labels suggest. And children, who have expansive imaginations and are trying to play through the complex world they see around them, naturally and appropriately will want to "try on" different identities. This sort of play is healthy for kids of all gender identities. The psychological rule of thumb for transgender children is persistent, consistent, insistent. A child who is transgender will not easily abandon lines of questioning and behavior around gender.[24]

By the time children are old enough to enter kindergarten, they will already have absorbed many lessons about gender from the world around them. They may be starting to have questions and ideas of their own. To say

---

23 Sometimes the word "sex" is the root of the problem, since "sex" can be shorthand for biological sex as well as shorthand for sexual intercourse.

24 That said, again, there is no single "right" way to be a transgender person. There are many transgender people who didn't begin to talk about or act on their transgender identity until adulthood. That doesn't mean they are "faking it"—it could be a question of safety or repression. And it could be a case of natural development. There isn't a "proper" timeline for any of this.

that elementary schools shouldn't teach kids about gender at all—which is what is happening in many state legislatures in this moment, as blueprinted by Florida's 2022 "Don't Say Gay" bill—is to abandon them to educate each other or to pick up lessons from the environment around them. Schools can and should give students vocabulary and a conceptual understanding of gender and biological sex early on instead. As is often the case in educational institutions, it is the adults' discomfort around the topic, rather than the students' needs, that drives the restrictions in the curriculum.

Indeed, the official name of Florida's H.B. 1557 is "Parental Rights in Education," legislation meant "to reinforce fundamental right of parents to make decisions regarding upbringing & control of their children."[d] But no parent has the ability to control who their child is or will become, and approaching development from such a stance, rather than a stance of curiosity and encouragement, is likely to result in alienation, resentment, or worse. Fortunately, there are many good models for education around biological sex, gender, and identity in elementary school classrooms that are widely available, should educators be legally permitted to apply them.

There's a lot in my list of definitions around gender that isn't certain. There's a lot that overlaps and perhaps even contradicts. To lay it out once more: Biological sex (male/ female/intersex), gender identity (man [or boy]/woman [or girl]/transgender/non-binary)[25], gender expression (masculine/feminine/non-conforming/agender/fluid), and sexual orientation (straight/queer/bisexual/lesbian/gay/asexual/pansexual)[26] are four different categories. Each individual has four different markers, one in each of these spaces. Some of these aspects of identity are easily visible and readable while others are entirely hidden. As we consider taking steps to support transgender and GNC students, we need to be very clear what we are talking about: biological sex or

25 Here I am using transgender as a marker for gender identity. "Transgender" is a word with lots of utilizations. It can be an umbrella term, a general category under which other terms like non-binary, genderqueer, and agender fall. It can also be what I call a matrix term, a term used to describe the alignment of biological sex and gender: Someone who is transgender has a gender identity that does not align in the socially/culturally expected manner with their sex. And, transgender can be a term that describes someone's gender identity.

26 None of the lists within the parentheses are exhaustive. There are an abundance of glossaries geared to different constituencies (media, children, educators, medical professionals) to be found online.

gender identity? Both? We need to make sure our language is accurate and inclusive.

WHAT IS GENDER-AFFIRMING CARE?

A few of the previous sections have referred to "gender-affirming care," and for anyone who has paid attention to recent headlines around state legislation, this term is not a new one. In considering how best to support transgender students—whether as a teacher, caregiver, or administrator—gender-affirming care is an important piece of the puzzle. Like many terms in and around the transgender and GNC community, it has a range of definitions and is often (willfully) misunderstood.

Language is so important to all aspects of identity, and this term is no different. Dial back the clock to the 1980s and you'd hear talk show discussions of "sex changes." That term gradually began to be replaced by "gender-reassignment surgery" and now by the larger category of "gender-affirming care." This shift is an interesting one that highlights how our cultural attitudes toward gender have developed. The term "sex change" emphasizes only the anatomical and highlights the "transition," which feeds the dominant narrative about transgender people. I call this narrative the "caterpillar to butterfly" storyline, where we begin as one thing and then have a massive change into something else.

Certainly, there are transgender people whose storylines fit this trope, but for many of us, this storyline isn't accurate and is quite harmful. First of all, the idea of a "sex change" reinforces the binary—from one sex to the other. Second, the very word "change" suggests that you were one thing and now you are another. This plays into the misconception that transgender people are duplicitous, having a "before" self and an "after" self, rather than getting to exist as a single (albeit complex) entity.

By expanding beyond "surgery" and into "care," the new terminology acknowledges that many aspects of care aren't medical interventions at all—an important shift in understanding what it is that transgender and GNC people need. So, what is gender-affirming care?

In the broadest sense, this term refers to practitioners—doctors, mental health counselors, massage therapists, and others—approaching clients and patients in a way that acknowledges that individual's understanding of their gender, rather than imposing a "scientific" or "legal" expectation of what their gender ought to be. If that feels like a convoluted explanation of what should be a simple interaction, then let me share a scene with you, a scene that has played out in my own life many times.

In college and graduate school, I was living as a guy and passed fairly well. I wasn't taking hormones and had not had any surgery, and all my official documents still listed my sex assigned at birth, female. When I would go to the university health clinic, I'd usually get through reception without much hassle and then wait in the examining room for the doctor to come in. They would often ask what was wrong, engage with me for a bit, then refer to my file. Then, the moment would come when they would say something like, "It says here you're female." And from there on, it was my job to explain to them that, yes, I was female and, yes, I lived as a guy, and no, that wasn't actually why I was in the office today. Then, usually a handful more questions from the doctor, some flubbed pronouns, and me sitting there wondering if I had strep throat and deeply skeptical of whether I could trust this person with my body.

So, on a fundamental level, gender-affirming care means that practitioners—anyone who is going to care for an individual—should use the name and pronouns that the individual has elected to use, and affirm that person's gender, regardless of what is on the legal or medical paperwork.

While people still tend to make a direct connection between gender-affirming care and surgery, there's a lot more that goes into this care. After all, few schools will be in a position to enable a student's medical transition. But that doesn't mean they can't provide or connect the student to gender-affirming care. At the current moment, Alabama, Arkansas, Texas, and Arizona all have laws in place restricting or criminalizing gender-affirming care for minors and over a dozen other states are considering such legislation. These laws name surgery, hormones, and puberty blockers as illegal. They fly in the face of established medical opinion and do real harm to youth who are seeking treatment for gender dysphoria at a critical juncture—pre-puberty—in their lives.

But there are also other important aspects of gender-affirming care that aren't criminalized in these states, that are rarely singled out by lawmakers, and that schools can help connect students to. For instance, speech and behavioral therapists can play a huge role in mitigating dysphoria in both adolescents and adults. Many transgender people have a dislike or even aversion to their voices—too high, too low, it doesn't sound like how they think they should sound. Speech therapy can be a powerful part of gender-affirming care as individuals learn to modulate, control, and inflect their voice to match their self-perception. Many schools work regularly with speech therapists to support a variety of student needs, so identifying practitioners who provide this gender-affirming care can be a wonderful resource.

While not all transgender and GNC individuals include surgery or hormones as a part of their transition, many do rely on mental health support from trained and experienced counselors. This, too, can be a resource, a part of gender-affirming care, that schools can help students connect to. Having a mental health therapist who is gender-affirming and can provide alternatives to medical procedures is lifesaving—particularly in states where the medical interventions have been criminalized or in family situations that aren't supportive of medical transition.

Another aspect of gender-affirming care that schools can provide is allyship. Being an ally means supporting a peer, colleague, student, or other community member by being in conversation with them about what they need and want. It doesn't mean acting on behalf of others but rather, acting with them.[27] Being an ally of a transgender person starts with affirming that person's gender and journey, even as it is ongoing and unfolding. It might also mean advocating for that person's rights in big or small ways—correcting someone who uses the wrong pronoun or showing up at a rally. It fundamentally means listening to that person, asking them how things are going, offering to support them in a variety of ways, and affirming them. Teaching and modeling good allyship is an important way for schools to be inclusive communities.

These new practices of allyship and gender-affirming care demonstrate a growing acknowledgment that many transgender and GNC

---

27 I find it a helpful reminder that no one gets to give themself the title of "ally." It can only be conferred by someone else.

youth feel trapped. Sometimes that is a physical feeling—trapped in a body that doesn't feel right, that doesn't feel like theirs. Other times it is more emotional or situational—trapped in a family or town or school that doesn't understand them, or trapped by expectations around dress and behavior that won't let them be themselves. Gender-affirming care means providing a space for these students to explore and explain these feelings and get some relief.

BUILDING BELONGING

The real work for schools and other social institutions, such as churches, summer camps, youth groups, comes in here. An identity such as gay-ness can have profound implications on a person's sense of belonging. But, unlike gender, sexual orientation is not something we use to sort students—at least not overtly. There are no signs hanging in public places instructing gay people to use this toilet or lesbians to go to that changing room. But there are signs all over the place that say where boys and girls should go. Almost every adult carries a little piece of plastic around with them that declares whether they are M or F.[28] Every day, implicitly and explicitly, we are sorted into places, roles, and situations based on gen-der. This is why schools and other institutions should address, not just transgender students, but the overall ways in which gender creates and sustains culture and social environments.

Whether you are a parent, a guardian, a student, a teacher, or an administrator; whether you have a transgender grandchild, a classroom with students who are questioning their identities, or have never heard the term "gender non-conforming" before opening this volume, this book is meant to help you—and it is meant to help you help others. The most important step, becoming aware, has already begun. Though it is hugely important to affirm that transgender identity is real, not a

---

28   The M or F on a driver's license is meant to be a statement on biological sex, at least that is my understanding. When I was eighteen, I had legally changed my name to Alex. I went to get a new license and—with my short hair and new name—the clerk took me to be a boy. I hadn't checked either the M or F box on the forms, but the license I was issued said "M." The clerk made a judgment based on my gender expression—which just reinforces how many assumptions we make based on gender expression and how, though we insist on conflating biological sex with gender identity, the two are not the same thing. At eighteen, I had not undertaken any kind of medical reassignment and was entirely female.

phase or a "state of mind," awareness is not just about acknowledging others; awareness is about acknowledging yourself. Each of us must be aware of how gender works in our own life—how we have used our gender identity and expression to gain advantages, and how gender has, in turn, also limited our experience in the world.

In the following chapters, I will use schools to demonstrate how to accomplish both understanding and positive change. Most of my work as an educator and advocate has been with schools. But I have also worked with summer camps, church groups, and a variety of workplaces. The ideas and steps that I outline here are applicable to all these environments and others as well. I will start with a sense of how to lay the groundwork for a successful plan and then walk through the steps of how to create a culture that dismantles the negative aspects of gender hierarchy, that is welcoming to a wide variety of gender expressions, and that makes more people feel comfortable and supported.

NEXT STEPS

REFLECT

1. Get comfortable with terminology. Look at diagrams like "The Genderbread Person" and engage in some journaling or thought about yourself and the diagram. What words do you use to describe your own gender identity? Gender expression?

2. Look at the terminology used in this chapter or refer to glossaries such as those provided by the Transgender Legal Defense & Education Fund (TLDEF), the Human Rights Campaign (HRC), and GLSEN (formerly the Gay, Lesbian & Straight Education Network). Then spend some time journaling about these words. What terms do you use to refer to yourself? What words make you feel "good" about your gender? What words make you uncomfortable? Why?

RESEARCH

1. Watch a movie or television show that has a positive presentation of a transgender person. Bonus: Look for one that was written by, was directed by, or stars a transgender person.

2. Read articles and essays about (and/or written by) transgender people. Challenge: Try to find and read articles written for a transgender audience rather than for a cisgender audience (them.us and PinkNews, for example).

3. Listen to a TED talk or other speech by a transgender person—try to find one that isn't only about coming out or traumatic experiences.

4. Familiarize yourself with the ongoing surge of anti-trans legislation, especially if it's taking place in your state. What restrictions are being imposed on trans and GNC people in your community, and what can you do to help counteract that and support your local trans community?

ACT

1. Reach out to a colleague, friend, or family member and discuss gender. Have a conversation in which you can practice using this new terminology.

2. Attend a workshop, seminar, rally, or other event that has to do with LGBTQ+ identity. Pay attention to the language that is used and, if possible, engage in conversation that lets you practice using new terminology.

NOTES

a. American Psychiatric Association, "What is Gender Dysphoria?," *American Psychiatric Association*, accessed March 4, 2024, https://www.psychiatry.org/patients-families/gender-dysphoria/what-is-gender-dysphoria.

b. ISNA, "How common is intersex?," *Intersex Society of North America*, accessed July 10, 2023, https://isna.org/faq/frequency/.

c. Carrie Macmillan, "Expertise with Kids Questioning Their Gender Identity," *Yale Medicine,* January 23, 2019, https://bit.ly/49BLhlI.

d. Parental Rights in Education, H.B. 1557, FL State Leg. (2022).

CHAPTER TWO:

HOW TO GET STARTED . . . AND WHY

A few years ago, I was invited to participate in a senior administrative meeting at a prep school. I was at the school to address the student body about gender identity. The administration wanted me to give some perspective on the changes they were considering to accommodate transgender students—their first transgender student had come out a few months before in the middle of the academic year.

Of course, the first question that the administrators wanted to address concerned bathrooms.[1] I sat at the table in the deans' office and listened as the deans and directors tossed out some options.

"We could designate the bathroom near the front desk as gender neutral."

"That's pretty far from the classrooms."

"What if we renovate a bathroom on each floor of the academic building?"

"That's too expensive. . . ."

They quickly shifted from bathrooms to locker rooms. The student in question had to take a mandatory PE class, and all students were required to change into gym clothes.

"He can't use the girls' locker room, can he?"

"Can't he just change in the bathroom?"

"Right, but which bathroom?"

"So, do we build a new locker room? Whichever room this kid uses, it's going to be a problem."

One of the deans, who'd been scribbling notes on a legal pad for

---

1 It's always bathrooms.

the whole meeting, looked over what he'd written. "We're going to be eviscerated," he pronounced.

Another dean nodded. "I can't see us justifying all these changes simply for one person. Making all these special accommodations is going to bring a lot of criticism."

Heads turned to face me, perhaps expecting me to pounce on this somewhat insensitive remark, to reply with a quick "Social justice for one is social justice for all!" sort of truism.

But instead, I nodded. "You absolutely shouldn't make changes for just one person."

THE BIGGER PICTURE

As I've said earlier, transgender and gender non-conforming (GNC) people will never be the majority at a school or within society. We won't even be a substantial minority. And while I do believe that granting access for a minority is extremely important,[2] arguing for massive shifts in school facilities and policies to accommodate a small number of students sets everyone up to lose. Framing the issue in terms of "special" accommodation often produces the wrong sort of result, period.

For instance, when an institution considers best practices for transgender people in restrooms, a workplace or school might be thinking of just one person. The logical solution therefore appears to be creating a single-user restroom. There. That person has a private place they can use. For so many reasons, this solution is inadequate and problematic.[3] It is crucial not to begin the planning phase or begin outreach to constituents by focusing on the transgender and GNC individuals. The framing of the argument needs to be shifted to a much broader scope to make the changes effective as well as palatable to the school population (students, faculty, and families) in general.

I once visited another school that had just had its first GNC student come out late in the winter of the student's senior year; the student used they/them/their pronouns and understood themself to

---

2　The ADA makes this case better than I ever could.

3　The specifics of this scenario will be looked at in Chapter Six.

be genderfluid and non-binary. I arrived and gave a talk to the whole school community and then met with several smaller student groups to take questions and talk through their concerns.

As I spoke with the students, they quickly raised concerns around the graduation dress code and how accommodations around gender would affect that. Historically, the senior class wore caps and gowns in the school's colors at graduation: boys in maroon robes and girls in white robes. When the GNC student had come out, the school immediately spotted the trouble: Asking the student to dress in either maroon or white would be shoving them into a category that didn't respect their gender identity.

When I arrived on the campus, the administration was still determining a resolution to this situation. Would everyone wear a mix of maroon and white? Would maroon robes and white robes be assigned at random? Would robes be abandoned all together?

The proposed solutions didn't matter, though. What I found as I talked to students was a profound sense of resentment from the cisgender students: a beloved tradition was being taken away. But what about the one GNC student? They were almost in tears when they spoke to me. All of this was their fault, they felt. If the graduation dress code was changed and their peers were upset about it, they would be to blame.

The student explained, "I told the deans that I didn't care. Or that I would wear both maroon and white. I don't mind being the only one who has to change. But the teachers want to make it comfortable for everyone."

The administration's gesture had the right motive, I think. Maybe there were other students in the graduating class (or in future graduating classes) who were uncomfortable with the dress code, who didn't want their graduation presented in such starkly binary terms, or who didn't understand themselves to be a girl or a boy. Regardless of the motive, the effect was one of singling out an already vulnerable student and making their identity even more controversial. Additionally, the proposed changes created the sense that accommodating transgender and GNC students meant "taking away" practices, privileges, and traditions from the school community.[4]

---

4 I'll talk more about dress codes in other chapters.

This response is sadly quite familiar. When accommodations are made for minority students, the majority often perceives that they are "losing" a right, prompting a backlash and resistance to implementing new guidelines or practices. This negative reaction reinforces how essential it is to frame these changes: schools, workplaces, summer camps must educate the majority, not just accommodate the minority. To quote once again that classic social justice axiom: "When you're accustomed to privilege, equality feels like oppression." This is the truth that teachers and counselors and parents and guardians and administrators must grapple with first.

Even as I agree with the above truism, I would simultaneously maintain that if the work of inclusion is done well, it benefits everyone, not just the marginalized community. Inclusion does not have to be a zero-sum game. Addressing major changes to a school's facilities or policies shouldn't be couched in terms of, "We have to do this because of the transgender students."[5] Rather, changes should be considered in terms of the overall school culture. What facilities feel inadequate? What spaces on campus create problems? What are the times or places where girls on campus feel unwelcome, vulnerable, or marginalized? When do boys feel pressured to participate in (or silently witness) violent or hateful acts, or suppress their emotional range?[6]

When I pose these questions to schools, in many cases, the places that are named as "problem spots" on campuses are the single-gender spaces: locker rooms, sports teams, dormitories, bathrooms.[7] In many cases, the practices that bolster and prop up these problem spots are the ones that reinforce the gender binary and its attendant value judgments. For example, a school that has a dress code of a coat and tie for boys and "modest" tops and "appropriate"-length skirts for girls sends the message that boys are professionals and girls are distractions. This message, communicated from the administration implicitly, fil-

---

5 Ideally, it shouldn't be done in response to transgender students at all. That's often more than half the problem: If a school waits for a kid to come out to make these changes, the pressure on that student is tremendous.

6 This list is not meant to be exhaustive but rather to provide examples of the sorts of questions that a school might ask to assess its larger culture around gender.

7 I will expand on all these areas and more in the following chapter.

ters down into how girls and boys perceive themselves and how they learn to treat each other on that campus and in their adult lives.

Dress codes might seem like a school-specific topic, but the principles laid out above are applicable to a wide range of other areas. For instance, in the workplace, standards of dress, if not a formal corporate dress code, remain intact. In some workplaces this can extend to the expectation that a woman should wear makeup or maintain other special grooming standards. Beyond anything that is an established rule, the unwritten set of social expectations (and so much of gender is unwritten social expectations) around clothing is extensive. If a woman wants to be taken seriously in a professional context, she will often opt for a more masculine-styled suit. But careful! She can't look *too* masculine, so she will often temper that suit with a feminine touch, whether that is a scarf, or nail polish, or heels.

The point here is not to try and adjudicate what people should or should not wear, but to make people conscious of the decisions they feel compelled to make and the gender-based reasons behind those decisions. Such an awareness can then empower people to articulate why they want or don't want to wear certain accessories or articles of clothing and to challenge the unspoken expectations. Laying the proper foundation for cultural changes around gender means that we are talking not just about the right of a GNC individual to blend masculine and feminine articles of clothing, but for all of us to examine, question, and reevaluate our own expectations around what we wear and what we expect others to wear—our own expectations around gender, conformity, and self-expression.

It is unlikely for a school to be successful in undertaking cultural change if pressure comes from outside or from smaller internal groups. So, the change must come from inside and work with a broad coalition. The work can start on an individual level: teachers, administrators, and parents and guardians (as much as they can be drawn in) who are committed to reading, talking, listening, questioning, and learning about gender, identity, and inclusion.

Given how far-reaching gender's implications are for each and every one of us, I like to challenge schools and social institutions with a simple question: Why not start big? Why not look at tackling the broader issues that are problematic for *all* students at a school and, in the process of doing so, also address the needs of transgender and GNC students? Every student has a gender identity and a gender expression. Some students will go through their lives never questioning these and, frankly, not giving them much thought. And that's fine. But many students will wrestle with these questions—not just transgender students. Girls will wonder: "If I wear this to class, will the teacher or the other students take me seriously?" Boys will wonder: "If I hang out with these people, will everyone think I'm gay?"[8]

These sorts of questions will pervade their lives, continuing into their professional careers. The reality of this makes it even more important for parents, guardians, teachers, and leaders of youth groups to understand gender, to create conversations that help children understand gender, and to tackle the challenge of addressing their own assumptions, policies, guidelines, and facilities around gender. Learning how to talk about gender broadly, to name the ways in which it influences our actions, improves relationships all around. Stripping away the stereotypes that envelop femininity and masculinity helps us to interact with each other as humans first.

Gender identity and gender expression are part of everyone's lives. Restrictive enforcement of the binary has a negative effect on many individuals. This doesn't mean that the binary needs to be dismantled or that everyone ought to be androgynous. But it does mean that gender—everyone's gender, not just that of transgender and GNC students—needs to be carefully considered when creating facilities, policies, and best practices in a school or other institution or within a family.

So, yes, schools should undertake the project of gender inclusion because the work of inclusion can have a positive impact on all students by helping them understand how gender works and how the hierarchy of gender influences them. There's also another compelling reason for schools to become gender inclusive: transgender and GNC

---

8 Phrases like this emphasize the connection between gender and sexual orientation. The two are not the same, but they are related. Part of how we understand gender (and express gender) is through our sexuality. That is, being "a man" is traditionally in part defined through sexual conquest of women. So, by virtue of being gay, a man might be seen as less "manly."

youth are an incredibly at-risk population. In public schools and private schools, with preteens and teenagers, study after study finds that transgender and GNC children face an increased risk of being bullied and harassed at school and suffer much higher rates of depression and anxiety than their peers. They have a higher rate of suicidal ideation, suicide attempts, and, sadly, a higher rate of death by suicide than other children of the same age.[9] These statistics are ignored and denied by pundits and organizations seeking to legislate transness out of existence. The work to restrict access to gender-affirming care being done in dozens of state legislatures across the country will only heighten the dysphoria, anxiety, and depression that many transgender individuals experience. In fact, in a 2021 survey on mental health in LGBTQ youth, conducted by the Trevor Project, 94% of the nearly 35,000 respondents reported that recent political activity in the US had negatively affected their mental health in the past year.[a]

Schools have a responsibility to protect the children within their care. It isn't enough to offer a general stress and anxiety course or to have rules about bullying and harassment. When the structure, facilities, and policies of the school itself set up an environment that denies the existence of GNC students or that makes the daily life of a transgender student hypervisible (i.e., they always have to use a single bathroom, they are the only one who changes in a separate locker room, etc.), then the school itself is complicit in marginalizing these students and creating further stress and anxiety in their lives. This phenomenon of hypervisibility is only exacerbated by the rise in vitriolic discourse around trans rights, and the limiting of those rights, including youths' right to access gender affirming care, is a very real additional source of chronic stress.

On the other hand, small changes can produce meaningful positive outcomes for transgender and GNC students. When I work with schools, students often report back to me that encountering minor changes—the option of filling in their own gender identity instead of only having M/F on a form, a bathroom sign that reads "all gender" instead of "boys" or "girls"—provides a small boost of affirmation,

9 The Trevor Project has compiled many sobering statistics about LGBTQ+ youth and suicide and is a vocal critic of emerging legislation that harms transgender and GNC youth. Visit their website for more information.

enough to remind them, in the course of school day full of microaggressions, that someone cares and the school has thought about them. Indeed, schools have an ethical obligation to serve these students well and create an environment that recognizes and supports their needs to the full extent of the school's legal ability.

PUTTING BIG CHANGES IN CONTEXT

Of course, making the big moves that I'm pushing for isn't easy for any institution, which is why setting up the proper framework is so important. The motivations vary when schools do make big moves. Sometimes, it's money: the move feels financially necessary. They might feel the need to stay competitive with rival schools or to keep up with the times and current educational trends. The best moves are the ones made with the student body's needs as the primary target and with the school's core mission as the central focus.

Often when schools make big moves, it can feel that the institution is shifting away from what it has always been. It becomes incumbent on schools to approach major change through the lens of their mission and vision—to make sure that whatever new facility, policy, or curriculum is being added that it helps the school direct its energy to its mission and creates a more focused and coherent culture rather than diffusing the school's purpose.

When I came out to the Exeter administration as a teen in 1995, their questions and concerns were immediate. I was giving them two weeks of notice, and they needed to figure out where I was going to live—evaluation of the bigger picture did not seem relevant from their point of view. Today, I work with many schools that have responded similarly: a student comes out (self-identifies) as transgender or GNC, the school springs into action (or is reluctantly dragged into action) and addresses the immediate, daily concerns of that student—and those discrete concerns only.

I also work with schools who haven't yet had an openly transgender student on their campuses. They look at peer and rival schools, the trends in adolescents across the country, and sense that sooner or later (likely sooner) they will have an openly transgender or GNC student in their community. The school may be aware that they have students on campus who are questioning their gender or playing and experimenting with their gender expression. The staff wants to make sure there is space within their rules and classrooms for these students to do so. They want to be sure to handle *all* their students well.

For both types of circumstance, I suggest the same approach. Whether you have been responding to the needs of transgender individuals for twenty years or not at all, the best place to start by examining the organization's mission. When I begin work around school-wide policies and practices on gender, I first ask the administration to gather all their mission and vision statements. The mission reflects what a school is as well as what a school wants to be.

Mission and vision statements should be written in both an accurate and an aspirational manner. When a school is contemplating a major change, it is crucial that it consider whether it is stepping away from its mission or simply reengaging with its mission. The former can be a challenging process, one that needs input from trustees, alumni, boards of governors, and other constituencies; the latter can be a largely affirming and energizing process. So, who should do the examining? Who puts this review process into motion?

In later chapters, I will suggest the formation of a gender task force, ideally a group of educators, administrators, and students in charge of spearheading the work of gender inclusion. It may be that such a task force could undertake this initial work of examining the mission. The impetus to begin might come from elsewhere: it may be a transgender student or that student's family. It may be an administrator who has attended a conference. It may be a group from the faculty who has heard students' need for this work.

I recommend reading this whole book before convening a task force in order to have information about all the pieces of the puzzle before beginning the work of gender inclusion in earnest. In reality, every school's process will unfold differently. Here, I've started with the school's mission rather than with the process of forming a task force, because I believe that rooting the inclusion process in the heart of the school's purpose is a crucial first step for each school. The mission statement of a school also isn't typically restricted by the laws that govern the curriculum. Bans such as Florida's "Don't Say Gay" law apply directly to classroom content. The mission and values of a school exist outside of that realm and can be a great place to do meaningful work toward inclusion.

Every school and institution draws its mission statement from a different source. For some, it comes from the founders and exists as a historical document. For others, the mission is constantly being revised and updated. Many schools have divided their mission statements amongst various departments, so that athletics and academics and residential life might all have separate missions. Digging through some of the more historically rooted schools, one finds original founding statements such as:

"Promoting virtue and useful knowledge among the rising generations." (Berwick)

"A shrine from which boys and girls shall take the highest inspirations for better and grander lives." (Loomis Chaffee)

"Above all, it is expected that the attention of instructors to the disposition of the minds and morals of the youth under their charge will exceed every other care." (Exeter)

In beginning to do work around gender and school culture, schools should reach back historically and simultaneously reach out broadly to current constituencies.

How can a school be true to its founders' intentions *and* be relevant and purposeful in today's world? By couching cultural shifts in their historical institutional missions, thereby embedding the past in their evolution and encouraging a positive sense of ownership over the work of gender inclusion. That way, these shifts seem not so much like profound changes as a reengagement with the schools' core principles. To engage successfully with the present moment, a school must be able to look both forward and backward.

For instance, from these historical documents, one might draw out the idea of "minds and morals of youth," "better and grander lives," and "virtue and useful knowledge." Start here—keep the basic premise on which the school was founded. Admit that the language is archaic, yet the ideas are still relevant. All three of these historical phrases place the ethical, psychological, emotional, and intellectual development of students at the very core of the school's purpose. If, as presented in the first chapter, gender is one of the primary ways that an individual understands both self and the world, then teaching, planning, and building programs around gender should be central to any school's mission. By articulating this, it helps a school to begin a program of change that feels rooted rather than radical.

This advice isn't just for schools. The process outlined above is an incredibly helpful way to approach difficult conversations for parents, guardians, or individuals who want to support transgender youth or transgender community members in civic or communal contexts. I've often encounter resistance along the lines of "the way we've been running things is fine" in local governments and civic organizations. The best counter is to point right back to the organization's core principles. If you are working with a parks and recreation department, for example, what's their charge or charter? A typical municipal mission statement will read something like, "Our goal is to provide programs and venues for young people of all backgrounds to participate and enjoy a variety of recreational programs while maintaining a safe, wholesome environment." Pointing to "safe" and "all backgrounds" would be a good place to start a conversation.

This doesn't mean it will be easy; what one person might regard as safe for a transgender child, another might view as unsafe for a cisgender child.[10] Even if conflict arises, by focusing on the school's mission roots the conversation, not in an individual's identity, but in a broader social context and mission.

BEYOND NON-DISCRIMINATION CLAUSES

I came of age as a transgender person in the mid-1990s, a time when non-discrimination clauses were one of the top priorities of the LGBT

---

10 See Chapter Ten for more information on conflict resolution and self-education.

civil rights struggle. In the fall of 1996, when I arrived at Harvard University, I was the first openly transgender student in that college's history. My being out at Harvard began before I was even accepted to the school. I signed up to interview with a Harvard alumnus in the winter of my senior year at Exeter. The interview took place in Exeter Library and since I came straight from class wearing a blazer and tie. He was an older man, probably retired. We sat down and began talking about my class, The Worldly Philosophers, a course on the history of economics.

We talked for about half an hour, at which point the interviewer gave a little jump: "We're nearly out of time," he said, "and there are a few questions I'm supposed to ask you." He pulled out a file folder that the college counseling office had prepared for him. It had my transcript and other pertinent information, including a sheet he drew out and studied, his brows knitting. "They have you down here as *Alice*," he said.

For a moment, I considered explaining that my parents had been huge fans of Alice Cooper or coming up with some other excuse. I knew that wouldn't work. Instead, I said, "That's right. Alice is my legal name. But I go by Alex. I was born and raised as a girl and came out as transgender and started living as a guy a few months ago."

It was a speech I was getting good at giving; I had used it on dozens and dozens of peers and teachers already that year. Usually, the person I spoke to would ask something: What does transgender mean? How did you know? Are you going to have surgery?

But this time, the interviewer just looked at me, gaping. His mouth opened and closed as if no words could possibly fit this moment. Finally, he shuffled the pages of the folder together.

"This interview is over," he said.

I left thinking that it hadn't ended very well. The next day I went to my college counselor and told him what had happened.

"Let's see what Harvard does," he advised. "If we don't hear anything from them in a couple of days, I'll contact them."

Now I know that this is a textbook case of transphobia. No doubt the interviewer felt that he'd been deceived, that I was playing a joke on him. He could have felt that gender ought to be a certain way and in a certain alignment with biological sex. This is also a textbook case of how schools unintentionally follow their own rules—using a student's legal name on files, for instance—without considering the precarious position they might be putting a student into. At the time, however, I didn't feel empowered to protest or do anything other than what my college counselor suggested. Sit tight and hope for the best. And I was fortunate that I was sitting in a place of utmost privilege: I had a college counselor. I had an institution that supported me.

As it turned out, within the next week, my college counselor heard from the Harvard admissions office: they'd send down a new interviewer. This time I went to the library and met with a younger woman, an associate director of admissions at Harvard, who began by apologizing for the previous interviewer—apparently he had written up a scathing report of our meeting—and telling me that he would no longer be doing interviews for the college. I thanked her, and we began our conversation.

This was not my first time experiencing discrimination based on my gender identity. I'd been refused service at restaurants already, but this was the first instance of encountering an institution that made the right choice in addressing discrimination. As I walked back to my dorm from this interview—feeling much better than I had after the previous one—I realized that they had done the right thing even though they had no legal obligation to do so. The thought heartened me: the college had a strong ethical sense. On the other hand, it scared me: when would I next be discriminated against with no legal recourse?

When I did arrive at Harvard the following year, I wasn't sure how out I wanted to be at first. Maybe I just wanted to live as a guy and have no one know anything about my past.[11] But within the first few months of living on campus—in a single room on a men's hallway, sharing a bathroom with guys—I came out to friends and classmates and got active in the college's association of bisexual, gay, lesbian, and transgender students, the Bisexual, Gay, Lesbian, Transgender, and Supporters Alliance, or BGLTSA. They added the T when I joined.

In those few months, I discovered that though I was very happy being addressed as "he" and being treated as a boy, it felt like I was hiding something, keeping a secret from the people around me. The presence of

11 This is known as "going stealth" in much of the trans community.

this secret weighed on me. I worried that people might find out or suspect, and that by trying to hide this part of my past, I would end up not being able to be close to anyone. I realized that I would be happier and more honest if I shared my transgender identity with others. I came out and got involved.

In BGLTSA we looked at what needed to change at the university and soon settled on asking the college to amend its non-discrimination clause to include the phrase "gender identity." I was simultaneously working with an off-campus group whose aim was for the city of Cambridge to update its non-discrimination clause in the same way—a push that was then occurring in cities across the country. It seemed like the logical place to start getting legal protections for transgender people. The non-discrimination clauses already included sex, gender, and sexual orientation, as well as race, ethnicity, religion, and many other categories. Sexual orientation was the most recent addition, and that inclusion had been hard-won in many cases—so, too, was the fight for gender identity.

Harvard didn't add gender identity to their non-discrimination clause until 2010. By that time, I was already well launched on a career as a high school teacher. When *The Harvard Crimson* emailed me and asked for a comment, I was taken aback. "They *just* added it?" I asked myself in disbelief. It felt oddly like a hollow moment, almost of defeat. It took thirteen years to add the phrase gender identity and the college had already graduated dozens of transgender students.

The city of Cambridge, on the other hand, changed their non-discrimination policy quickly: by 1997 the language regarding gender identity was added. It was a victory. I felt proud of having worked to help make the change, but living in Cambridge over the next three years, I still experienced a lot of intolerance based on gender. Friends who were androgynous or GNC were kicked out of bathrooms. We all had slurs yelled at us from passing cars. One night, we were threatened and then chased out of a subway station by a group shouting homophobic language.

Perhaps it is this experience that has led me to shift my approach and focus on mission statements as a first step toward gender inclusivity. Many schools have started with the non-discrimination clause in their work to support transgender students. It feels right: it feels visible and meaningful. It's simple—you just have to add a couple of words to an already existing statement. But too often, that gesture is meaningless. Yes, the school makes gender expression a "protected class," but the school hasn't done any of the work to understand how gender affects the lives of its students—or how to protect transgender and GNC students as a "class." Gender identity feels like an add-on or an afterthought when fighting for its inclusion in non-discrimination clauses—a late arrival at a party already well underway.

Adding phrases to a non-discrimination clause can provide some legal protections. But it won't change cultural understanding and practices. Institutions that want to do more than provide window dressing, the ostensible sense of change, need to dig into the core of their identity and acknowledge the ways that they are shaped historically and presently by gender. It isn't enough to simply state one's values; they must be lived as well.

The changes in the following chapters will concern policy, signage, and rules. I will also address culture, curriculum, and training. The two prongs cannot be separated. Just as adjustments shouldn't be made *just* for transgender and GNC students, so, too, this work cannot be done by *just some* faculty and administrators. Every teacher is responsible for the culture around gender in their classroom, on their team, or in the club they advise. If you're a teacher and you think gender doesn't apply to your area of teaching, then you need to spend some more time reading, thinking, discussing, and learning. Schools must create not just non-discrimination clauses and gender inclusive policies but institutional cultures that invite, encourage, and require faculty to do the work every day in every space.

NEXT STEPS

REFLECT

1. Pick a public space: an airport, a museum, a stadium, or a school. Walk around and notice all the gender, from the overt signage on restrooms to the more subtle mentions in artwork, advertisements, perhaps even the other people present as well. When you have moved through the space, reflect and journal about what gender you saw, how that made you feel. What you didn't see represented in gender. Whether anything made you feel understood, or if anything made you feel resentful regarding gender.

RESEARCH

1. Familiarize yourself with the legal status of transgender people in your state, locality, and school. Look at non-discrimination clauses and the language they contain. Bonus: consider the history of these laws. When did they change and why? Are they under any current threats?

2. Research the mission and vision statement(s) of your school. Look at founding documents and more recent updates. Comb over the language that feels relevant and speaks both to heritage and the present moment. Locate phrases that bear on the idea of inclusion.

ACT

1. Gather a group of colleagues, friends, and allies. Do this work with others. Talk about what you hope to do. Find people who are enthusiastic and interested. Educate each other. Make part of that education an awareness of the legislation and activism currently occurring in your area and state. Make sure you know the arguments that are currently in the news for your region and be able to articulate your own position.

2. Talk to a decision-maker. This might be an administrator, a member of the school board, or a trustee. Choose someone who is likely to be at least open-minded and hopefully an enthusiastic supporter. Run some initial ideas by this person and get honest feedback about how the larger board or administration would respond to what you are thinking about.

3. Continue to research, refine, and seek advice. Build a network of allies and interested parties. Make people feel included as you seek their opinions. When you have sufficient language, buy-in, and interest, work with decision-makers to initiate the process of making change. The rest of the book will delve into the specifics of this initiation, which will start taking shape for your school's specific situation once the conversation gets going.

NOTES

a. The Trevor Project, "National Survey on LGBTQ Youth Mental Health 2021," *The Trevor Project*, last modified 2021, accessed February 23, 2024, https://www.thetrevorproject.org/survey-2021/?section=Introduction.

CHAPTER THREE:

TAKING STOCK THROUGH A GENDER AUDIT

When I work with schools on forming gender inclusive communities, I like to use the metaphor of a dinner party. Imagine that the work your school has done for the mission or vision statement is you writing up an old-fashioned, paper invitation. Here, in clear, flowing script, you are stating what you offer. As you admit children (if you are a private or charter school) or matriculate them (as a public school), you are offering them this invitation. Picture that: sending out a card that says, "Welcome! Come to my house for a delicious dinner!"

Once the invitation is sent, many schools feel that the work of inclusion is done: they've welcomed a widely diverse group of students. If you were actually hosting a dinner party, what other obligations would you have? Let's say that on the day of the party, you unlock your front door and hang a sign with a bunch of balloons that reads "Come on in!" You set out a spread of wonderful food on your dining room table. Isn't that welcoming and inclusive?

What if you invited someone who has a terrible allergy to shellfish or peanuts? Who can't digest lactose? Did you ask about dietary preferences? Did you label all the food on your table? If the students—your guests, perhaps meeting you (an authority figure) for the first time—have the courage to ask you which foods are safe for them to eat, do you even know exactly what you are serving them? Or have you invited them into your home and furnished them with food that could make them ill or even kill them?[1]

---

1   This is focusing on the idea of inclusion for those who even make it in. You could extend this scenario and talk about how the people you've invited are even *getting* to your house—are you on a public transit line?

Many people might consider this metaphor and reply with a sort of shrug: If you have a food allergy, it's your responsibility to speak up for yourself, and probably, if you want to be safe and well fed, you should bring your own food. And I can agree with a fraction of this sentiment. It's good to teach children with allergies (and other needs) to be self-advocates. But this is a *dinner party*, and you're the *host*. Or, to leave the metaphor aside: This is a school, and you're the teacher or administrator. You have said in your mission statement that every child will be nurtured and cared for and helped to be their best selves—you have an obligation. If you issue that invitation, you better have the right food clearly labeled on your table, ready *before* the student asks. If they have questions or concerns about what you are offering, as host, you should be gracious and accommodating.

This has long been a baffling situation for me. Almost every school I work with wants to have as diverse a student body as possible—a wide variety of backgrounds, races, religions, talents, hobbies, ethnicities, and so on. The lesson of diversity has, by and large, sunk in for educational institutions. But what happens after that invitation has been sent to a varied crowd? What happens after a school has opened its arms wide and said, "The more difference, the better!" All too often, the school then narrows that breadth and offers only one possible way to be accepted, one narrow path to being "in good standing" or "successful" or "popular" or "at the top."

If you believe in diversity and inclusion, you must create a school that not only admits students who are quite different, but that also helps, encourages, and enables them to become *even more different*. This open-ended attitude of hospitality is even more important when the world beyond the school is hostile to certain students explicitly because of who they are.

The takeaway I want to emphasize from my dinner party metaphor is that the student shouldn't have to ask for what they need. A lot of the time, when a student comes out as LGBTQ+, the first response is a teacher or administrator asking, "What do you need?" That feels like a kind and helpful response, but the student probably doesn't know what they need because they may have never had it before. If they do know, they may well not be in the position to ask for it. At the moment of coming out, they are likely feeling extremely vulnerable and wanting to be as little of a burden as possible. Where the student with the peanut allergy has very visible and clear needs to an administrator, a transgender student's needs might not seem as pressing to the same adult.

Transphobia and internalized bias might make even a well-intentioned adult dismiss the requests of a transgender or gender non-conforming (GNC) student, whether they see that student as "playacting" or as "overly sensitive." (I have heard both critiques from administrators about students—or their caregivers.) Even the most forward-looking teachers and administrators can have a hard time imagining what a truly gender-inclusive school looks like. Transphobia, and other deep-seated biases, can cause a profound myopia. For the administrator who is comfortable or privileged in their gender (or race, etc.), it is hard to see and impossible to feel the compelling need to create profound change for the sake of inclusion. Then, the question that they're so quick to ask—"What do you need?"—is an empty one: the student is often not able to provide an answer, and the adult is often not prepared to address or imagine those needs.

The goal of the chapters ahead is to get schools to be able to flip that question around. Instead of asking students "What do you need?" schools should be able to say, "Here's how we can help support you." And be ready with a range of offerings—from facilities, to policies, to practices, to resources—that are already in place. That's what it means to be an inclusive organization: you don't just open the door and welcome diverse students; you prepare your school and change the institution so that it has anticipated the needs of the students who will come through that door. In a nutshell, you can't invite people to a dinner party and then poison them—and if that is your goal, you definitely shouldn't be hosting. If an institution wants to be truly inclusive, it must consider the needs of the students who attend and be prepared, anticipating what they will require before they ever come through the door.

At the same time, the work of inclusion is not a "one-and-done" sort of project. Our understanding of identity and self, our needs as individuals and as communities, changes over time. Some administrators and teachers will find this frustrating. They'll want to send out a committee, figure out what needs to be adjusted, and then make the changes.

Done. But inclusion doesn't work like that. Rather, a school is putting a response system in place—a set of practices that are flexible, adjustable, and recursive. The best inclusive practices build a space for reflection and recalibration so that a school is continually changing, adapting, and re-shaping itself around its current students, families, and employees.

This approach to inclusion requires a range of preparatory measures to work with student needs around financial support, anti-racism, religious practices, and so on. For a school that wants to address gender inclusion, the best place to start is with a gender audit.

As I mentioned with regard to the work around the school's mission in the previous chapter, the question of *who* does this work is pertinent. In subsequent chapters, I will discuss forming a gender inclusion task force, and for some schools, the task force is the group that should undertake this audit. However, other schools won't set up a committee or empower a task force until after the audit is done. Just as the mission statement provides the foundation, the audit provides the structure of the work to be done. I set the following steps out as preliminary to forming a task force—akin to sending an expeditionary force out to map the terrain so that others can more easily follow.

So, who is doing this audit? It could be an administrator and a couple of interested teachers; it could be a partnership of a family (likely one who has a transgender child) and some teachers. It could be the school's Gay-Straight Alliance. The gender audit is a self-diagnostic tool meant to give the school a sense of the work it has to do toward becoming fully inclusive and welcoming to students of all gender identities and expressions, as well as becoming prepared to respond to students who are questioning their gender.

FIRST QUESTIONS

An audit begins with the seemingly simple question: Where do we make mention of gender in our school?

The first time I worked with a school on a gender audit, they began with a list on a whiteboard. The initial items came quickly: signs on restrooms and locker rooms, language about sports teams, reference to a girls' dress code and a boys' dress code. Then a slower phase, as one teacher offered: "Don't we put gender on rosters?" And another added, "I think we have certain prizes that go to a boy and a girl." And then the registrar noted that gender was marked on transcripts, and the college counselor said that financial aid forms had gender check boxes . . . and soon we realized that gender was noted all over the place, in multiple databases as well as in public signage, not to mention in all manner of publications—from internal rulebooks to external marketing pieces.

This school's reality mirrors the reality of society at large. Think for a moment of how often you are asked what your gender is. There are many legal forms that require this to be stated, many places—from gyms and yoga studios to gas station restrooms—that have spaces designated by gender. If you apply for a credit card, go to donate blood, or take a survey online, you will be asked for your gender. That's a wide range of interactions that ask for this information. Pause for a moment and consider: Why do they need to know? Whose interest is served by having this information? Is it for your safety?

Whenever I conduct a gender audit with a school, I think back to my personal experiences with forms that require me to check a box and how. No matter how much I ponder it, I cannot figure out why we think we need to notate gender where we do. When I first came out in 1995, all my paperwork registered me as female. My transition was a social one,[2] meaning that I cut my hair short and changed my name and pronouns. And by "changed my name," I mean, I asked people to call me Alex instead of Alice. Any more "official" transition at that time felt impossible—and that isn't just a factor of it having been the mid-1990s.

Most students today would feel that same amount of impossibility. If students want to legally change their name or gender marker, if they want to undergo medical transition,[3] the process can be daunting. It is expensive, time-consuming, and requires parental/guardian permission if the student is a minor. Additionally, some state laws are making it even more difficult to change certain documents or obtain specific medical interventions. An ongoing wave of legislation has banned gen-

---

2 Though that language wasn't in use then.

3 These are all big ifs.

der-affirming care for minors, in some cases criminalizing the parents or medical providers who support this care.

When I turned eighteen, I could begin the legal transition on my own. For me, that meant officially changing my name. I was a resident of Maine, the state where I'd been born, and went to probate court to complete the process.[4] Once that part was complete, I took my documentation to the DMV and got a new license, one that said Alex Myers. It still said F under sex. A year later, I moved to Massachusetts as a college student and soon declared my residency there. Back to the DMV: I filled out the paperwork, had my picture taken, and handed over my Maine license. The clerk looked at everything and squinted at me. I felt my stomach drop—I could just sense that a big, gender-loaded, probably insulting statement was heading my way. But all she said was, "You look awfully young." I did, if I was read as being a boy—I was almost nineteen, but I didn't have a single whisker. On a good day, I looked about fifteen.

In short order, I was given a new license, and, to my great surprise, it had M under sex. I hadn't asked for that, hadn't filled in the "wrong" box. I'd even handed over the license that had me listed as F. But the clerk had looked at me, taken in my short hair and clothes and made a determination: M. As I joked to a friend later that day: easiest sex change ever.[5] Joking aside, I share this anecdote to point out that schools, governments, and institutions ask for people to state their "gender" all the time. What do we think we're asking for? And why do we think we need that information?

This is the second set of questions schools should ask of their own practices as they undertake the audit: Why do we want to highlight gender here? What is our purpose in seeking to know or control gender in this context? And beyond these questions, there's another, perhaps more basic tenet that needs to be considered: What are we actually marking or noticing or insisting on when we designate gender?

And the answer to that question is usually: We're not sure. Or the

---

4 We'll look at this story and names in a later chapter.

5 "Sex change" is not the preferred term now—"reassignment surgery" or "gender affirmation surgery" are much better. Also, I should note that having information listed incorrectly on a state or federal issued ID is a felony. I did not ask for the change; I did not know that having incorrect information was a felony, and when I learned of this (years later!), I sought to remedy the situation.

answer could be several different things. Let's take a couple of examples. If the school nurse has medical records on a student, that record is likely to note M or F. In this instance, that is likely a notation that indicates sex designated at birth: whether the person, based on external genitalia, was deemed to be male or female. Medical records are legal documents and have to record the sex designated at birth (or, to be more accurate, the sex designated on the birth certificate).[6]

In another instance, let's suppose a student goes to meet a math tutor for the first time. When the math tutor pulls up that student's file, what information do they see? The student's legal name? The student's legal (birth certificate-designated) sex? Why? What does that teacher or coach need to know about the student? I would argue that what's more helpful are designations that the student might *choose* rather than what has been *chosen* for the student.[7] For instance, the tutor should see the name the student goes by and the pronouns the student uses . . . not the legal name they do not use. Moreover, a math tutor has no possible need to know the anatomical sex of a student, so why do we put it on many of our school transcripts, rosters, and so on? Sex appears in these places out of rote habit; it has been done this way and so we continue to do it this way. But when we designate a space a girls' locker room, for instance, what are we asking about?

To be honest, I love to ask this question of schools. It is often a great way to ease teachers and administrators into understanding the difference(s) between biological sex, gender identity, and gender expression. So, let's walk through it.

If you put up a sign that says "Girls' Locker Room," what is the basis of your differentiation? The purportedly correct answer, or at least the intended measure, is biological sex. To be very blunt, schools want to be

---

6 This is an important distinction. Some states allow birth certificates to be altered after gender reassignment while others do not. Some states will only issue an "amended" birth certificate, meaning that the certificate will always indicate that the sex marker was changed.

7 Recent legislation has curtailed schools' ability to support students' chosen name and pronouns in certain instances; more on this in later chapters. With this example, though, I'll point out that getting rid of gender on paperwork/databases/signage when it isn't required is still a good, harm-reductive practice that prevents active mis-gendering of students, whatever the law requires. In cases where full-throated gender affirmation is made impossible by state mandate, the fewer times gender is codified into school paperwork, the fewer times trans and GNC students stand to be mis-gendered as a byproduct of bureaucracy.

sure that there are penises in one room, separate from the room in which there are vaginas. Push this even further in conversation, and you will soon arrive at a lot of fears about sexual assault, predatory behavior (usually boys/men preying on girls/women), and safety. These are difficult and fraught topics to discuss, and so, despite the #MeToo movement's inroads toward mainstreaming conversations about sexual violence in various institutional contexts, schools usually don't discuss them, preferring to leave them implied by long ossified rules and norms. But if schools want to understand how gender informs our educational practices and shapes our educational institutions, we need to open this conversation up. I will delve into more depth of how to handle locker rooms, restrooms, and the questions of safety and privacy in later chapters, but for now, I want to focus on the process of auditing spaces and policies.

At first glance, engaging in conversation about sexual assault in schools doesn't seem to have much to do with supporting transgender and GNC students. But I assure you, it does.[8] As you enter the gender audit, you will need to create the time and space to have difficult conversations about the relationship between school policy, school spaces, and common perceptions of safety. These subjects in turn will require those in the conversation to unpack their deeply held beliefs around gender.

As I will explain in later sections, schools need to build time into their professional development calendar so that all teachers and administrators can practice reading, thinking, and talking about gender in small, peer-led groups where they can safely test out their understanding. Any school undertaking the work of gender inclusion is likely to encounter resistance, so it is best to plan for it and address it patiently, through education and conversation rather than confrontation. You can't rush to transform a school's culture with signage and rules. The faculty, administrators, parents and guardians, and students need to be educated along the way, and education in this arena often involves a lot of unlearning.

Which brings us back to the girls' locker room, a space that is single

---

8 Look no further than "bathroom bills" and the conversations about sexual assault that surround them. Almost always, the number one concern raised about letting boys (whether that term is being used to refer to cisgender boys or [transphobically] to transgender girls) use the girls' bathroom is that the boys will sexually harass or assault the girls. I'll discuss this rhetoric more in Chapter Six.

gender designated usually because schools want to keep male bodies separate from female bodies. But who's actually checking this, on an anatomical basis? (The answer is no one, I hope!) A monitoring gym teacher does not actually know the biological sex of the people who enter a girls' locker room. It's not protocol to ask for certification of such (nor should it be). Instead, the people who enter girls' locker rooms are people who look like girls, who are thought to be girls, and who are understood by the community to be girls. In other words, this is a designation based on a mixture of gender identity and gender expression in social practice, even though the intention is to base admittance on biological sex.

Let's suppose that a school, citing safety concerns as they are framed above, doubles down on biological sex as the differentiating factor and tells students and families: anyone who is designated male at birth must use the boys' locker room. If that school has a transgender girl in its student body, they are then requiring that girl to go into a boys' locker room to change. Is she going to be safe there? If she transitioned before arriving at the school and no one except the upper administration and school nurse (those who might have access to documents stating sex assigned at birth) know she is male, does this policy of segregation based on anatomical sex actually keep all students safe?

Clearly not. A 2019 study published by the journal *Pediatrics* found a positive correlation between the enforcement of gender-exclusionary school restroom/locker room policies for transgender and non-binary students and instances of sexual assault against those students; this correlation was strongest for the trans girls. The study, based on a survey of over 3,600 transgender and GNC American adolescents, found that trans girls who were restricted from using the girls' restroom at school were 2.49 times likelier to be sexually assaulted than trans girls who permitted to do so.[a]

Separating based on biology works only when schools have entirely cisgender, heterosexual students. And I would argue they don't even work well then: bullying and harassment are still more likely to occur in these segregated spaces even if everyone is cisgender and straight. There is no proof that segregating spaces according to a binary notion of sex automatically makes anyone safer, physically, emotionally, or sexually—and this approach is not the only way for schools to address these very real concerns.

NAVIGATING GENDER

If biological sex can't be the differentiating factor, schools should determine who belongs in which spaces on students' identities and expressions—the social manifestations of their gender. Identity and expression seem much more salient than anatomy: they are the aspects of a person's being that actually impact the school community. They are the aspects that students of all genders bring to their classes and extracurriculars, the markers by which teachers, administrators, and peers recognize them.

My questions to schools at this point then become: Who is the ultimate arbiter of a student's gender? Who gets to say who is a girl and who is a boy? A parent or guardian might fill out the form that goes to the nurse's office. A student might say they are non-binary. A peer might object to "that boy" being allowed into the girls' locker room. A school board might decree that, identity and social experience aside, gender is designated by the sex assigned on a birth certificate. But which input is most weighted? Who gets to determine identity, and what's the school's role in that process?

Again, recent legislation has stepped in to provide (some) resolutions here. In several states, laws make it impossible for a student to assert new names, pronouns, and gender identity without their caregivers being notified of the requested change by the school.[b] In those cases, for the legal standing of the school, that input must be factored in. But in truth, the school itself is in no position to declare someone to be a boy or a girl. While documented governmental recognition is often a protective factor for transgender, GNC, and other marginalized people, even the state does not have the authority to declare any person's gender. Only that individual can assert their gender identity.

Remember that gender has two components: outward expression and inward understanding. Some children will have a good degree of control over their expression; others' parents and guardians will govern how they dress and style their hair. But every individual has intuitive awareness of who they are: their identity. Some may not have the words to articulate their feelings; some may know but be afraid to say; some may be questioning and doubting what they feel; and many will be ready to assert exactly how they understand themselves. A minor child is under the legal control of their parents or guardian, but a child—given most schools' stated missions of instilling agency and self-determination in their students—should still be able to say who they understand themself to be.

If a school doesn't have the authority to be the arbiter of identity, then why is the school encoding gender in so many of its policies, signs, organizations, and documents?

Here again we wind up at that second step of the gender audit. After you've found all the places where your school mentions gender, you should ask: Why? To what end? The answers might not be readily apparent, but finding clarity is essential. That clarification process entails questioning assumptions about gender and social spaces that we've been trained to take for granted. These assumptions are often rooted in transphobia and heteronormativity—even if we don't realize it, even if we consciously oppose those forces. If the answers to your question of "why?" turn out to rely on specious or exclusionary principles, let that awareness guide the subsequent outcomes of and conversation around the gender audit.

As I've said before, my goal in doing work around gender inclusion is not to create an androgynous world where everyone has identical pudding-bowl haircuts and wears gray smocks. Rather, it is to make sure that we understand gender and see it in its full range of varieties, not just in cis-centric, binary terms. In asking *Why?* and *To what end?*, the desired answer is not to eradicate gender; the goal is to be aware of the actual complexity of the matter, to be inclusive of all gender identities, not just those that fit into standard notions of gender, and to only include this information in institutional records when it actually aids the mission of the school.

Almost six years after getting that M-marked Massachusetts license, I started taking testosterone. After a year of hormone treatment, my doctor wrote a letter stating that I had reassigned my gender medically. This letter allowed me to change my birth certificate in the state of Maine to read "Record of a Live Birth: Male." I wanted to have this documentation; given only two options,[9] I felt that Male was more accurate than Female. . . . But it was also complicated and still is for me. I present as a masculine person; most people look at me and assume I am a guy: I pass. But I don't understand myself to be a man, and I don't want to undergo any more of a medical transition—I don't want surgery of any kind. So, though I take testosterone and therefore have facial hair, male pattern baldness, a lower voice, and so on, I remain mostly female in body. This feels right to me; this is who I am. But databases and application forms and identification documents don't seem to have the right spaces for me and for many transgender people.

What do we think we know about people when we think we know their gender? What assumptions do we make? What biases do we bring? What permissions do we grant, and what privileges do we deny? Gender is shorthand. Gender is a shortcut. Gender lets us treat other human beings as less than full individuals, and that's a terrible thing. On the other hand, gender can be an opportunity to explore and express and experiment. So many people—cis and trans—experience gender as a set of rules and expectations that restrict and confine them. Questioning instead of accepting is a crucial part of an education, and a crucial step toward autonomy and freethinking.

Hopefully, doing the audit will let schools begin to understand and absorb this reality and then consider how to change their culture. Because, although right now in most institutions and in many social interactions, gender functions as I've described above, it doesn't have to. Gender should be a robust way to express self, not a set of rules used to limit self. We need to teach our students (and ourselves) more language, more concepts, more narratives around all types of gender.[10]

---

9 Maine and many other states now offer an X or non-binary designation for driver's licenses and other official, identifying documentation. For a current, comprehensive overview of these policies by US state or territory, see note *c*.

10 The author Viet Than Nguyen has written and spoken eloquently about "narrative scarcity" when it comes to the stories told by and about Asian and Asian American people. (See note *d*.) I think this concept applies to wide range of marginalized groups. There is certainly a great deal of narrative scarcity around LGBTQ+ folks of all races—the dominant storyline is still "coming out." Even more, where gender is concerned, I would say there is narrative scarcity and also language scarcity: a lack of usable, meaningful, positive, and permitted terms to refer to the full range and experience of gender.

FROM AUDIT TO ACTION

Once the school has completed the gender audit and taken stock of what its rules, guidelines, signage, and so on are around gender, it should consider the question of when these practices serve the students and when they don't; the school also needs to know when these designations are legally required and when they are optional. Schools will find that there are times when it is legally required to note a person's biological sex: medical forms, financial forms, official school transcripts. In most cases, the notation here needs to match the sex stated on the individual's birth certificate. There's not much room to wiggle around these requirements. In some cases, a school might not even have control over how the forms are written.[11]

But outside of these formal cases, noting gender is usually optional. After completing a gender audit, schools might notice places where language is easy and desirable to fix. Instead of text in marketing material saying, "Boys and girls at XYZ School enjoy small class sizes," the school might revise to, "Students at XYZ school enjoy small class sizes." This is a minor change that moves away from binary gender language and keeps things focused on academics.

In other places, it can be trickier—or more illuminating, depending on how you want to see it. For instance, at schools with separate dress codes for boys and girls, it might seem harder to replace that binary language with just the word "students." Notice that! When you conduct an audit and hit a spot where you aren't *legally* required to state gender but still have a gut reaction of *we should* or even *we must*, you should pause and once again ask: Why? These are usually the spots where a substantial conversation is required, where conformity to gender roles is still expected, or where people—teachers, parents, guardians, students— might have deep implicit bias (generally unfounded) about safety.

An audit might also highlight spots where there is neither a legal requirement nor a felt need to disclose gender, but where the required editing goes beyond a simple tweak. One common such scenario is when schools list students' gender, which is usually actually biological sex, on

---

11 Some scholarship application forms (or college application forms) might ask students to designate "gender" and offer only "male" and "female" as options. Others might have a write-in space. Others might refer to this as "sex;" there is little consistency.

a class roster or in a school directory. The reason typically given for this practice is the norm of "gender balancing" classes and student bodies—that is, maintaining an equal number of boys and girls. That is often a well-intentioned goal, but it's one that can be achieved at the administrative level; it doesn't need to be noted on the roster the teacher sees.

Typically, certain individuals within a school need to have access to private information about students' biological sex, such as a school nurse or, in this case, the registrar. It is incumbent upon these people to deal with this information appropriately and discreetly: here, looking at the M/F field in the students' records and making sure there's an equal number in each class section.[12] When the roster leaves the registrar's hands, it can be wiped clear of that private information about biological sex. The classroom teacher can trust that the class has been balanced (just as the teacher trusts that each student on that roster has been immunized without needing to see immunization records). Not everyone has a right to know a student's biological sex.

Another defense of this roster designation is that it allows the teacher to know what pronoun to use and, so, in theory, should be a good thing for transgender and GNC students. Talking this perception through can be a great way to start raising awareness about assumptions. If you see someone designated F on a roster, you are going to expect to see a feminine person who uses "she" as a pronoun. But these might be incorrect assumptions; as we've seen, a student's reported biological sex might not have anything to do with their gender identity or pronouns. A teacher might like the reassurance of knowing what a student "really" is, according to their roster, but if you have a GNC student in your classroom, you are likely making incorrect assumptions based on what the roster designates. Pronouns are better clarified within the relational context of a classroom or other school-based group (and, sadly, within the bounds of relevant state law) than inferred from a piece of paper.[13]

---

12 It is true that just sorting students on the basis of male or female markers will not achieve *gender* balance. If a school only allows for binary designation, any student who is GNC or non-binary won't be visible. Moreover, if a student who is biologically male has socially transitioned and is living as a girl, that student would likely still be designated M in school records. However, this desire for balance and diversity can be addressed in several other ways, as will be discussed later.

13 More thoughts on navigating this in Chapter Five.

In short, there's no reason to include this information on class rosters, and many reasons not to. In this scenario and others, schools should be empowered to apply more radical edits to their protocol and messaging.

There is no question that what I'm advocating for here is a minor shift (removing gender from rosters) and also simultaneously a major shift (teachers accepting that they might not be able to "read" or make assumptions about their students' gender and, indeed, in some cases shouldn't). These are not easy shifts to make, and teachers will need support and training to be able to fundamentally change some of their classroom practices. It takes time, it takes effort, and it takes education. Perhaps this is a good moment to return to the metaphor I engaged earlier, the dinner party. A teacher is inviting students into a space, playing host, as it were. Within the classroom, a social contract exists; in some schools it is explicit and in some schools it is implicit. The classroom is the teacher's space, the teacher's "home," and the students ought to respect that. But the teacher has invited the student in and is the host; the teacher has an obligation to welcome the students as they are.

For instance, it is quite possible, even likely, that a teacher will be uncomfortable or unfamiliar with using "they" as a singular pronoun. But once a teacher learns that a student uses "they" as a pronoun, it becomes incumbent on that teacher to use that pronoun correctly and fluently in conversation.[14] A teacher can't just say, "That's grammatically incorrect," or, "It makes me uncomfortable to use 'they' to refer to you." Whose comfort is this about? Who is in charge? Who is the host?

At the end of a gender audit, it is important to give space to absorbing the information and planning the stages of how change will happen. When I work with schools on audits, the usual reaction is a stunned shock at just how often gender is mentioned. It can feel overwhelming, especially when schools use multiple databases and rely on gender markers to autofill pronouns in emails and other forms. There are lots of little pieces as well as big, concrete (literally concrete, in the case of some

---

14 Ideally, teachers have a chance to get used to using "they" as a singular pronoun before such a student enters their classroom. For many, this is an adjustment that takes practice, and the early, frequent mistakes should be worked out before a student might be hurt or offended by misgendering. I often suggest that people practice on their pets: Imagine your dog has come out as non-binary and now uses "they." That gives you a chance around the house to practice referring to your dog with the right pronoun and apologizing and catching yourself when you slip up.

facilities) spaces. The idea of making meaningful change can feel utterly impossible. The next few chapters are going to break down the process into different areas, with the goal of making broader change feasible.

NEXT STEPS

REFLECT

1. Do some thinking and journaling on your own use of gendered terminology, your daily encounters with signage, forms, and other reminders of gender. Think of this as a gender audit of your own life. From when you get up to when you go to bed, where is gender present in your life? Where is it positive? Where is it negative? Where do you control it and where is it imposed by others?

RESEARCH

1. Gather and explore the materials your school produces, from the website to the handbook to the human resources intake forms. Get a sense of where gender appears, what terminology is used, and how much material is out there that you'll need to consider.

ACT

1. Gather a small group of interested parties: administrators, teachers, board members, parents/guardians, students, alumni. Meet to go over goals and intentions and review terminology. Divide the group (if you have enough members) into areas to research all the mentions and implementation of gender at your school (such as online material, infrastructure, print material, etc.).

1. Set a timeline for the research. Compile the findings in a usable fashion and reconvene your group to review the findings.

2. Sort what you have discovered into helpful categories that will enable you to move forward with the work. This might be, for instance, short-term goals and long-term goals.

3. Spend time digesting the findings of the audit. Examine all the language that's used, consider who the stakeholders are (athletic department, school nurse) for certain forms and facilities that utilize gendered language. Talk through possible changes and do some research: visit or talk with peer schools and see what their signage looks like, for instance. Crosspollinate ideas about possible changes and solutions wherever possible.

NEXT STEPS

4. Identify what restrictions, whether at the state, local, or district level, if any are relevant to the policies and messaging the group would like to change. Brainstorm about harm-reduction possibilities your school can explore, such as removing unmandated mentions of biological sex from institutional documents, while still adhering to applicable laws.

5. Discuss in your group what feels plausible to begin with, in terms of time, money, and buy-in. Discuss the work, both logistical and cultural, that needs to be done in order to also achieve the longer-term goals.

6. Consider who you need to work with to accomplish your goals and what training and education will be needed to make this work possible. Schedule time to provide information sessions and share the results of your gender audit. This could be a good opportunity to reconnect the broader school community with your school's mission and why the gender audit itself is part and parcel of carrying it out.

NOTES

a. Gabriel R. Murchison et al., "School Restroom and Locker Room Restrictions and Sexual Assault Risk Among Transgender Youth," *Pediatrics* 143, no. 6 (June 2019): 1–10, https://doi.org/10.1542/peds.2018-2902.

b. Eesha Pendharkar, "Pronouns for Trans, Nonbinary Students: The States With Laws That Restrict Them in Schools," *Education Week*, June 14, 2023, https://www.edweek.org/leadership/pronouns-for-trans-nonbinary-students-the-states-with-laws-that-restrict-them-in-schools/2023/06.

c. "Identity Document Laws and Policies," *Movement Advance Project*, last modified February 28, 2024, https://www.lgbtmap.org/equality-maps/identity_documents.

d. Jennifer Lee and Karthick Ramakrishnan, "From Narrative Scarcity to Research Plenitude for Asian Americans," *RSF: The Russell Sage Foundation Journal of the Social Sciences* 7, no. 2 (2021): 1, https://doi.org/10.7758/rsf.2021.7.2.01.

CHAPTER FOUR:
MAKING THE FIRST MOVE

In working toward institutional change, it is important to recognize two seemingly contradictory things: It can take time for institutions to enact significant change, and institutions—even large and old institutions—are capable of making sweeping changes, sometimes very quickly.

Once you have completed a gender audit and have a sense of the whole picture of gender at your school, you should prioritize and organize the work you have to do:

Prioritize: look to the changes that will make the most positive impact for students in need.

Organize: consider how much time and money (and other resources) will be required for each change.

But before you make your to-do lists and prepare to wrangle some new policies, you need to think about your school realistically. An adage that I live by in this work is: Culture will eat strategy for lunch every day. As a teacher and administrator, I know that I can create a rule or policy—clearly written and with great intentions—and it will not make a bit of difference in affecting student behavior unless I have done work to help students and teachers understand the need for this new policy and buy in to the change that is being made.

WHO'S WITH US?

Right alongside adjustments in language, policies, and facilities, you need to do the work to educate your students, teachers, parents and guardians, and staff. You need to make sure they understand the relationship between gender and your school's culture. You need to invite them into the conversation and provide them with information and the chance to discuss that information. For any change to be effective, they need to be part of it, rather than responding to it after the fact. Nothing will make a policy less popular (or even possible) than springing it as a surprise on people. What your school will allow, support, and encourage regarding gender and identity should be clearly written and articulated to families, faculty, and students in advance of the start of the school year.

In the paragraph above, I keep saying "you"—who am I talking to? Who is going to do this work of changing school culture and policy? When I started doing this work, it was often the first out transgender student who led the charge. Or, if they had supportive families, it was their parents and guardians. Sometimes, a school would have one or two out queer faculty members who would spearhead the work toward gender inclusion.

But let me be clear: I'm not talking to any of those groups when I say "you." It is unfair to ask a newly out transgender student (or even a student who has been out for a couple of years) to organize the work that will make a school welcoming to them. That is too much of a burden; it is the proverbial pulling oneself up by one's bootstraps, which the laws of physics tell us is utterly impossible. Nor should we wait for parents and guardians to push for change. It is sadly rare for transgender and gender non-conforming (GNC) students to have supportive caregivers, and those who do are extremely fortunate.[1] Some states' current or pending legislation actively discourages family support of trans and GNC youth; in 2022, Texas Governor Greg Abbott went so far as to suggest that parents who seek gender-affirming care for their children should be investigated by the Texas Department of Family Protective Services.[b] But even very supportive parents and guardians often want to protect their child from extra attention and don't want to "make a scene"—and even if they would, most caregivers don't have the bandwidth to advocate on a consistent or ongoing basis.

---

1   Homelessness is a serious problem for LBGTQ+ youth who are rejected by their families and even more so for youth who are not cisgender. According to a 2022 report by the Trevor Project, 34% of the transgender, non-binary, or gender questioning youth surveyed had experienced or were currently experiencing housing instability, compared to 23% of the surveyed cisgender, queer respondents. (See note *a*.)

As far as putting this work on LGBTQ+ staff and faculty, well, I'm going to guess that they already have full-time jobs. Unless their contracts are different from their straight and cisgender peers, there's no need to give them extra work because of who they are. This happens all too often to faculty of color and faculty belonging to other marginalized groups at schools; officially or unofficially, they end up offering "sensitivity" instruction to their colleagues as well as support for students who share their identities, all on top of their actual jobs and all without effecting structural change.

As discussed earlier, I usually recommend that a school wanting to undertake the work of gender inclusion form up a small task force. Depending on the school culture, this might include students and parents and guardians, or it might be made up of faculty and administrators; it could also include an outside consultant or alumni. The group should consist of people who are interested in doing this work—who want to see it succeed.[2] It is fine if the participants don't know much about gender, so long as they are truly open to learning and believe in the purpose of the group: to promote gender inclusion. Ideally, the group would include at least one transgender or GNC person (I also subscribe to the motto "Nothing about us without us"). It would also ideally include an administrator who can make change—someone who sits on a governing board or has access to meetings at which decisions are made. Without this, the task force runs the risk of doing a lot of hard work and then finding none of it enacted.

Alongside this task force, I recommend forming focus groups early and often and staying in communication with the school's various constituencies. No one likes to be surprised by changes; everyone appreciates having their feedback sought. Give all students, families, teachers, and administrators a chance to listen and respond to proposed changes, to ask questions and make suggestions. Offer the groups at varying times of the day/week so that people with a diversity of schedules can attend. Answer doubts and confusion with opportunities for education. Listen carefully to groups who have hesitations about

2 Resist the call for a "diversity of opinions" about the proper role of gender in schools—there is a place in this process for dissent and disagreement, but the gender inclusion task force is not that place. See instead focus groups.

the work you are doing. Engage with people who disagree. You don't have to bend to their demands, but you are likely to have more success if they feel that they are heard. Some of these focus groups might also serve as spaces where colleagues can begin to educate themselves and work through some of their biases, assumptions, and discomfort around transgender people and gender in general.

If the focus groups are run well, they will be difficult, brave spaces.[3] What I mean by this is that they will be places where people learn, and learning most often involves a degree of discomfort. Discomfort is not the same thing as a lack of safety. For the discomfort to be productive and educational, each focus group should include a leader who is trained in facilitation, and care should be taken to consider the power dynamics in each group. Are there senior faculty members and rookie faculty members in the same group? Are some families major donors and others with children on full scholarship? I'm not suggesting that everyone needs to be "the same" (that's an impossibility) but that the facilitator needs to be aware of the background dynamics and make sure that—at least within the space of the focus group—all group members are able to speak up, to be heard, and to be respected.

Even with a facilitator, these spaces are likely to spark difficult interactions. It is crucial to set ground rules and some common shared values and expectations. It is crucial for the facilitator to be a person who can name problematic behaviors and offer gentle correction and commentary. So, once again, a common dynamic at school is for the person who is advocating for change to be themselves in a marginalized group and/or to be a junior faculty member. Asking such a person to facilitate a conversation sets them up to be vulnerable and potentially unsafe. Before forming focus groups, schools should be sure they have well trained facilitators.[4]

Another brave space that administrators need to be ready to enter is difficult conversations with non-supportive parents. In recent years, more families have felt emboldened and have been given talking points

---

3 See John Palfrey's *Safe Spaces, Brave Spaces: Diversity and Free Expression in Education.* This book is powerful in suggesting how to speak into and through difficult moments rather than insisting on shutting down discussion in the name of safety.

4 Any school undertaking diversity, equity, and inclusion work would be well served by training faculty, administrators, and students in these skills. There are excellent resources available through books, websites, conferences, and consultants.

from news coverage to raise concerns about schools supporting transgender students. I've seen this happen in public schools and private schools, in areas that are liberal and in areas that are conservative. Most often, parents are raising a specter. That is, there hasn't been an actual event that has been problematic. But a parent might come to a school and say: "I've heard that some schools are letting boys into girls' locker rooms. What's this school's policy?" Or they might name a practice that is in place and call it problematic: "My child says that her classmate changed names and pronouns and the teachers support it. That's grooming."

In the face of such commentary, schools often want to calm, placate, and keep the issue quiet. This tendency is what has led to the years and years of handling transgender students off the books, so to speak. But in the current moment, with so much news coverage and legislative action around transgender students, there is no more keeping quiet and trying to manage things silently. School administrators need to be ready to listen to concerns from parents and guardians and to explain school policy and its reasoning. Administrators should be ready to offer options and solutions that allow for inclusion.[5] It is incumbent on administrators to anticipate the resistance, learn the language of the moment, and be ready to reply with answers that center support for all students.

HITTING THE GROUND RUNNING—WITH A PLAN

You've got your mission statement, you've formed your task force and focus groups, and you have your gender audit in hand. Now, you need to be realistic. I like to plot changes on a timeline of "within this school year" to "never." (Well, if I'm being optimistic rather than cynical, "never" would be "a long time from now.") While larger-scale changes may be seductive, it is so important to identify work that can be done in a short time frame—what I like to call low-hanging fruit. Nothing energizes a group like seeing change happen in real time—and nothing makes a movement fizzle, or fester, like running out of momentum because the initial goals were too monumental.

5   For instance, at schools where parents oppose having a girls' locker room or restroom that is open to usage by transgender girls, a school administrator should be ready to offer a single-user bathroom or a changing space that can be used by the cisgender student whose family is concerned.

Ideally, the first work done by the task force can be enacted in a short time span and is visible to most of the community. Depending on your school, this might be a display of books in your library to show what's available on the topic of gender identity. It might mean organizing an event, like a service for the Transgender Day of Remembrance, and hanging up posters to advertise. It might be forming an affinity group to offer a safe space to transgender and GNC students—and making sure that students and faculty are aware that the group exists. All this is to say, the first step doesn't have to *change* anything. The first step should heighten awareness, should serve as an invitation of some kind, and should prompt conversation.

Here's another example of a first step. One school I've worked with decided to redesign the well-known Genderbread Person, a popular graphic that uses a gingerbread cookie figure to describe the elements of gender: expression, identity, anatomical sex, and sexual/romantic attraction.[6] The school took the "person" in the image and replaced it with the school mascot, so that the new image would be immediately familiar and intriguing to the student body. They adjusted some of the text to make the terminology and explanations age appropriate. And then they made a lot of copies.

Before hanging them up, though, the group offered a couple of informational sessions to explain the posters. They brought them to a staff meeting and shared them at a student council session. They wrote an op-ed for the school newspaper, which printed the image as well and sent a brief note home in the family newsletter. In short, they opened up opportunities for education and discussion—they raised awareness.

Other times, identifying viable short-term projects can mean breaking larger work down into small steps. For instance, if your school only has binary-designated restrooms, converting them to all-gender restrooms might seem nearly impossible: in addition to the support of the administration, it would require renovation, which takes both time and money. So, what can you do with the restrooms you currently have? Is there signage you can hang to clearly redefine who can use that

---

6 You can find this graphic online in multiple iterations. Make sure you reference the most updated version. It is also illuminating to go back to version 1.0 and trace how the language and understanding has changed. For the most recent version of the graphic, see note *c*.

space[7] and how that space ought to be used? Are there opportunities to educate the community about gender-designated spaces and discuss all students' safety and comfort? You might not be able to change the infrastructure, but you can change the attitude and understanding of that space.[8]

CULTURE-BUILDING

Patience is required when doing work to build an inclusive community. There will be setbacks and there will be pushback. Anticipate that. The task force should discuss what possible responses their peers and colleagues might have, and they should practice how they would answer questions from confused or hostile individuals. These discussions are great opportunities to go over the roles of allies and of LGBTQ+ individuals. It is important for allies to know that there will be times when their peers want them to step up and speak with them—but that the dynamic should never be allies speaking *for* the LGBTQ+ community. This kind of discursive cooperation between allies and the LGBTQ+ community can and should be practiced in both peaceful discussions and more tense or oppositional situations.

Just because there is likely to be some negative reaction doesn't mean that changes shouldn't be made. It is too easy to say, "Now isn't the right time" or "Let's wait until the hubbub dies down." There is never a good time to make big changes; there will never be consensus on the treatment of a marginalized community.

At this particular moment in time, many schools are hesitating to change their policies and practices to be more gender-inclusive or are even taking affirming language out of their hallways and handbooks as

---

7　For instance, a sign that says "Girls' Restroom" can have additional language stating that "anyone who identifies as a girl or is most comfortable in a space for girls is welcome to use this restroom." While this sort of phrasing might seem like overkill, the first part of that addition clarifies that trans girls are welcome—"anyone who identifies as a girl"—and the second part leaves some space for non-binary or trans students who don't identify as girls, yet feel uncomfortable in spaces designed for boys.

8　If the steps outlined here feel like too much, can you put signage on the single-user restrooms in the building, adding a transgender symbol? Admittedly, this is nothing but window dressing, but visibility is so crucial. An all-gender restroom with a "trans" sign says so much more about an establishment's dedication to inclusion than "family restroom," and takes minimal resources to purchase and install.

they face backlash from political groups. But the recent legislation to suppress transgender students' rights, like the examples cited in previous chapters, makes it all the more imperative that schools—especially private, independent schools[9]—do this work in whatever ways they can. And, to return to an earlier point, conservative movements often criticize jargony, acronym-filled pieces of policy[10] that address small issues particular to transgender and GNC students. It is easier for the opposition to deride gender-inclusive policies as unnecessary or somehow insidious when they are framed as ancillary. This is another reason why it is so important to pin the work of gender inclusion squarely in the heart of a school's mission. While aspects of this work might seem like satellites of a school's main mission, as opposed to part of the mothership, the gravitational pull of the work should come from school's values—which are a harder thing for conservatives to attack. Moreover, this approach builds consensus among school constituencies about the goal, even if there's disagreement about the steps toward the goal.

For instance, with the example of the Genderbread mascot sign above, the task force found that some signs were taken down. Others were defaced. Most stayed up and sometimes gathered a few curious students around them, pointing and talking (and, yes, occasionally using offensive language). The most common negative response, though, was from teachers and administrators, many of whom said, "My students are asking me about these signs, and I don't know how to explain them." The task force realized that, though they had tried to anticipate this ignorance and offer informational sessions, the teachers who had attended those sessions had been the ones who had been interested. Many faculty who weren't had chosen not to attend.

With inclusion work, many faculty will make excuses along the lines

---

9 Sadly, a trend I have noticed in the past year is for parents who cannot, for work or financial or family reasons, relocate from a state that has enacted laws hostile to transgender youth to instead seek to place their child in a boarding school that supports transgender students. Boarding schools, which often enjoy a degree of curricular and programmatic freedom and often possess more resources, should use these privileges to help marginalized communities, including transgender students.

10 This isn't to disparage jargon and acronyms. This is to suggest that to move the policies ahead, it is more effective to adopt familiar language and deploy it. Cutting-edge ideas will gain more traction if they are framed and phrased in a familiar way. This is one of the few places where I'll advocate for a sort of "assimilation."

of, "That's not my area of expertise. I teach math, not gender." But every teacher and administrator knows that what we are really teaching goes far beyond our discrete content area. We are teaching students how to think and speak and write and reason, how to treat each other, how to work with a partner, how to organize ideas and manage time—and on and on. Inclusivity and empathy are part of what we teach—no matter what academic department we are in. It is incumbent on schools to provide and require training opportunities so that faculty can be ready to work with any student who enters their classroom.[11]

The scope of training and professional development will depend on the budget and schedule of the school—but it is important to remember that with work around inclusivity and equity, once is never enough. Schools often like to hire an expert, bring them in for a speech, and then check that item off the to-do list. But creating an inclusive space means training staff to be empathetic, to oppose discrimination and injustice across all fronts of identity, to be ready to use appropriate language and to be able to respond to challenging questions and remarks . . . and all that takes time, practice, and community. Part of the task force's work is to develop a lot of small-scale chances for faculty to engage with ideas around gender inclusion. Show a clip from a movie, share a news article, have a book discussion group. Keep the topic current; make it unavoidable.

All of this is preliminary work, laying the foundation. What about the first actual *changes* to be made? To reiterate: the task force has prioritized and organized the work that needs to be done. Using the guiding principles of what is pressing and what is practical, they have organized their work on a timeline. As the group begins to make changes—the major areas of which are covered in the following chapters—they should work in the short term while laying the foundation for the long term. The long term won't happen without steady pres-

---

11 The director of diversity, equity, and inclusion at Exeter has a wonderful way of enacting this. In the past, when some "diversity issue" (I use that expression with an eye roll) came up in a classroom, many teachers would quickly hand it off to the dean of multicultural affairs. Our director of DEI wanted to change this habit, and so she has inculcated the philosophy that all of us are directors of diversity, equity, and inclusion in our own classrooms. That space is our sphere of influence, and so we are responsible for the practices of equity and inclusion within the classroom: we can't pass it off to someone else.

sure and early attention. The long term isn't likely to happen if none of the short-term work gets underway, so it is crucial to address both.

ADDRESSING THE DRESS CODE

Every school will find a different starting point. But I usually suggest the dress code as a place to begin effecting concrete changes, for several reasons: Clothes are such an essential and highly visible aspect of gender; students are usually really invested in what they can and can't wear; faculty and administration are often frustrated by dress code enforcement; dress code affects every student, not just transgender and GNC students; and for students who are curious about and questioning their gender identity, clothing provides an easy way to experiment with gender expression—if the dress code has language that allows them to do so. All of these factors make this policy a great place to teach broadly about gender and identity and to examine how school policy can influence inclusivity.

I also like to use the dress code to teach about examining implicit patriarchy and classism in school policy. In recent years, many schools have moved to "gender-neutral"[12] dress codes—that is, policies that are devoid of any references to gender and instead describe attire permitted and prohibited for the student body in general. But even if your school has made this move, it is worth looking closely at the wording and framing of the topic. You might consider the language that is used to describe clothing and how that language can be classist or sexist. Words like "appropriate" or "decent" or "professional" often appear in school handbooks. These words are freighted with judgment and assumptions, which are usually steeped in an upper-class, White, Christian, patriarchal viewpoint. There is nothing objective about them.

As with other aspects of this process, starting conversations about these terms can be difficult but fruitful. A faculty conversation group might tackle just the idea that students should dress "professionally," as if they were going to work. That can seem like such an innocent idea. But what, exactly, are you assuming about workplaces? Have you

---

12 I find this language, like "co-education," to be a bit dated and inaccurate. "Gender-inclusive" or "all-gender" tend to be more pertinent terms.

thought that some professionals wear rubber overalls while working on a lobster boat, or utility wear as custodians, or scrubs at the hospital, or uniforms in a restaurant? What value judgments are you putting on such clothes that they are not deemed professional, compared to a Western-style business suit? And how do those judgments carry over into what students are expected to wear and, ultimately, be?

You can have similar conversations about terms that are problematic because of gender-based assumptions (and misogyny), words like "appropriate," "decent," "respectful," and so on. Appropriate for whom? Respectful of what? You might also consider the areas of the school where dress is governed in practice but not covered explicitly by the dress code. For instance, at graduation, prom, concerts (for musicians who are performing), and sports events, arbitrary rules around dress are often enforced in the absence of any clear policy for these scenarios.

Beyond the particulars of language and assumptions about dress, considering and discussing the rules can highlight a point I made earlier: Culture eats strategy for lunch. What's the culture around the dress code? Often when I visit a school to give a talk, I witness students entering an auditorium. Faculty are positioned at the doors or in the aisles, and their interactions with the students often goes as follows: "Take off your hat." "Tuck in your shirt." "Cover up your shoulders." This is the student-faculty culture that a dress code can establish: is it the dynamic you want at your school? How can you set up a dress code that isn't about enforcing a hierarchy and having a dozen snippy engagements with students, but that opens up conversations about self, community, and belonging?

For other schools, opening up the handbook to the dress code will reveal two columns. One lists what boys can and cannot wear. The other lists what girls can and cannot wear. So many messages are sent through these lists. First, that boys and girls should not wear the same sort of clothes—that it is wrong, for instance, for a boy to wear a skirt. Other messages come across more implicitly. Girls are usually permitted to wear all the clothes a boy can wear, but not vice versa. What does that suggest about girls' clothing? About boys who want to wear girls' clothing? And, of course, where does it leave students who identify as neither a girl nor a boy?

Often, the policy is more than just a descriptive list. Instead of saying: "Girls may wear jeans, blouses, sweaters, and skirts, and they may not wear tank tops, mini-skirts or shorts," many dress codes apply adjectives in a problematic way: "Girls may not wear revealing tops and must wear skirts of an appropriate length." Or descriptions are made in terms of bodies: "Shorts must reach at least mid-thigh; no shoulders or chest can be revealed."

I personally attended a high school and have worked for high schools that require boys to wear a shirt and tie (sometimes with coat)[13] to class while girls are allowed to wear much more casual clothing. When pressed about why boys should wear ties to class, the common reply is "To prepare them for the real world, for their jobs, for what comes next in life." (Never mind that the "next" chapter for some will be four years of college spent largely in sweatpants.) In terms of inclusion and diversity, this justification reveals a belief in a narrow line that students must walk in order to "make it"—not just in terms of dress, but also in terms of eventual profession—not to mention a gender-based hierarchy of whose future careers matter most.

After all, what about the girls? Does the lack of a "workplace-like" dress code for girls mean that the school doesn't think these students will hold "serious" jobs? These rules are clearly couched in historically patriarchal ways of thinking about gender: boys will go on to work for a financial or law firm; girls will be wives or otherwise separate from "serious" public sectors.

It's also troubling to look at the ways that dress codes can police bodies as much as they police clothing. Language about "revealing" or "appropriate" puts judgments on what parts of our bodies are shameful or, perhaps, "distracting." It's also extremely subjective and hard to enforce. The very sense that a girl's chest might be distracting (this is often implicitly why tight clothing or clothing with a low neckline is forbidden) assumes a heterosexual gaze and extends the long and problematic narrative of women/girls being "temptresses" and men/boys being helpless to restrain themselves. For centuries, society has hyper-

---

13 Don't get me wrong: When I transitioned, I *loved* this—gender euphoria—but that's beside the point.

sexualized women and girls, but the problem is not with women; the problem is with the view and the viewer. Dress codes should not be yet another place where men tell women and girls that it's their fault if someone else inappropriately desires, looks at, or touches their bodies—especially considering that, in this context, the students being scrutinized and sexualized are minors.

One school I worked with staged a great intervention as part of their work to change the dress code. The student council asked for time in a faculty meeting and organized five girls of different shapes and sizes each to wear the same shirt (in different sizes). The girls stood before the faculty—identically dressed—and asked which of them were in dress code and which were not. Answer? Three of them were and two were not. The two who were not were larger-chested and full-figured. What was being policed there? Not the shirt. At the root of the whole exercise, the "problem" was the girls' bodies, whether they were deemed to be "in code" or not. That's not fair. That's not right. And, yes, in the absence of a critical lens, that is how gender works. Also, notice that nothing in this example is about transgender or GNC identity in particular.

So, what's the solution? Like many cases this book will explore, there is no one-size-fits-all (sorry for the pun!) answer. Each school will have to weigh its values, its culture, and its needs in order to come up with the best resolution. Different schools I have worked with have arrived at a number of different solutions.

For some, the dress code can be simply and clearly restated using "all-gender" language. This might read as follows: *Students may wear jeans, khakis, skirts, dresses, blouses, and collared shirts. All shorts, skirts, and dresses must be knee-length or longer. Students may not wear ripped or torn clothing, T-shirts, athletic shorts, leggings, sweatpants, or sweatshirts.* Does this solve all dress code problems? Of course not. It is entirely Western-centric, for instance; it leaves open endless arguments over what constitutes a blouse or whether the collared shirt has to be buttoned, and so on. But it *does* make it clear that all students can (and cannot) wear all these clothes, whatever their gender identity.

Other schools don't want to sweat the small stuff, so they adopt a broadly inclusive dress code philosophy instead of a delineated list.

This type of policy might state that students should be able to express their individuality through their clothing as long as they respect the educational mission of the school. The goal with these philosophical statements is to invite students into a conversation about what it means to be in an academic environment (as opposed to at home on the couch or on the playing field)—since students are the ones to whom the code applies, what is their version of school-appropriate dress? Schools that are more student-centered or that want to decrease hierarchical interactions between faculty and students might opt for such a philosophy rather than a strict code. This is just another instance where it's crucial to consider your school culture before adopting a strategy.

Whatever statement a school finalizes, you must also look at cases that fall outside the standard fare; as mentioned earlier, these might include prom, graduation, or musical performances. Some of these situations can be tackled in a similar fashion as the main code. An orchestra, for instance, might simply state that students may wear black pants or black skirts paired with white shirts or white blouses. Other situations will require greater consideration and advance notice.

Let's take the case of graduation, a high-significance school event. It is important to give constituencies a chance to weigh in well before graduation (or prom) season, as well as a chance to absorb and respond to whatever changes are ultimately made. This is especially true for schools working in the wake of their first (or one of their first) transgender students coming out. As discussed earlier, in this context it is vital to stem the impression that all changes toward gender inclusivity are happening because of the transgender student. And, whether or not an out transgender or GNC student will be graduating, ample notice is key. If, in October, the school begins to openly discuss changing the gender-coded robes at graduation, the community will likely come up with a solution that, by the time May rolls around, is accepted by most of the class. Strategically launching this conversation in a school year when there are no out transgender or GNC students graduating might smooth this change even more.

Again, the solution will look different for every school. If your starting point is white robes for girls and green robes for boys, you can start with offering a range of possibilities: everybody wears a robe that is both white and green; white and green robes are assigned randomly; and so on. Know that there will be pushback to any proposed change—but if time is allotted to engage in conversation, important lessons can be learned. I would fully expect, for instance, that a boy at our example school might refuse the idea of wearing a white robe on the grounds that "white is for girls." This is a great moment to talk about how utterly random some gender designations are—and to affirm that tradition does not dictate reality. I always like to remind folks that high heels were designed for the men in King Louis XIV's court (in order to show off their calf muscles) [d] and that, until the 1940s, pink was considered a masculine color in the United States.[14]

Schools should run through these conversations first with faculty to make sure that all the teachers are prepared to dig into the misogyny and transphobia that are likely to bubble up in these conversations. If a wide swath of faculty members are given some practice with these conversations and are then expected to facilitate discussion in a home-room, advisory, dorm, or club space, gender is given space as a topic and issue within the fabric of the school. When I talk about shifting culture rather than just changing policy, these are the sorts of actions I mean. Indeed, faculty and administrators (as well as families and students) often avoid talking about gender because of the discomfort these conversations can cause. When I lead discussion groups, even the most well-intentioned folks will express concern that if they start talking about gender (or race, or any other potentially contentious topic), they will say something "wrong" or someone else will say something wrong or offensive. In doing work around inclusion and social justice, it is important to acknowledge: yes, this will happen. Someone will say something out of ignorance and offend someone else. And someone will say something out of overt bias and offend someone else.

But the fact that this will happen doesn't mean we shouldn't have these conversations. It does mean that we must prepare for and set up the conversations. They can't happen in a vacuum. They can't happen

---

14 A June 1918 article from the children's clothing trade publication *Earnshaw's Infants' Department* said, "The generally accepted rule is pink for the boys, and blue for the girls. The reason is that pink, being a more decided and stronger color, is more suitable for the boy, while blue, which is more delicate and dainty, is prettier for the girl." (See note *e*.)

without trained facilitators. They can't happen without some thought for who is in the conversation space. What's the history between these people? What's the hierarchical relationship? What are the demographics? They can't happen without other support systems being in place: affinity groups, feedback forms, anonymous reporting, and a general sense of communal identity and buy-in.

There has to be a balance between providing the chance for education and training and policing misogyny and transphobia. Schools need to have a sense of a social contract and clear guidelines when it comes to setting up conversations. When faculty sit down to consider, for instance, changes to long-held but problematic customs at the prom (like dress expectations, having a king and queen, or public "asks"), the conversation should start with setting clear guidelines. Establish that you will assume good intentions. Establish that, even so, good intentions do not erase hurt. Talk through how someone ought to respond to a hurtful comment and how the person who delivered that comment should respond to criticism. The facilitator might share some examples of coded language that sounds acceptable but is actually transphobic or misogynistic.

The above practices will, no doubt, elicit eye-rolling from some faculty members and commentary along the lines of, "Can't we just have the conversation? We're all adults." It is crucial to notice and name this tendency. Who are the people who feel comfortable in these conversations? Who are the people who feel that they don't need to say anything? Or that they can say whatever they want? Facilitators might start the conversation (after setting guidelines) by asking participants, "When was the last time someone commented on the appropriateness of what you were wearing?" Or, if that's too personal, the facilitator can share some case studies of ways that dress code has been handled in the past at the school. The point is to help the faculty members see themselves as stakeholders in this conversation.

OTHER STARTING PLACES

For some schools, dress code will not be the best place to start making real change. Other beginning steps might be in forming affinity spaces around gender identity and sexual orientation. For schools that don't have many affinity groups, discussing why these are important for marginalized individuals can be a great exercise in understanding how inclusion and privilege work. Or a school might work on making information about transgender and GNC identity more visible through posters and signage. Whether these posters contain educational information about terminology, or advertise resources and upcoming community events, the school might commit to making sure that positive language and images about transgender and GNC individuals are present in hallways and classrooms and common spaces throughout the school. And for schools that find themselves so restricted by legislation that they cannot act, a starting point might be to form discussion groups about recent legislative moves to familiarize more people with the rhetoric and talking points around transgender students' rights. Every school will have to figure out what feels right as a starting place.

There are many opportunities for change that might be meaningfully accomplished within an academic year. It can take a great deal of persistence and patience to continue to push forward—and also a great deal of organization to work robustly on the short-term goals and simultaneously make headway on the mid- and longer-term work. If the early phases of work create opportunities for education, conversation, and training, the later phases will be much easier. These first moves lay the groundwork for the larger and more controversial changes required for an institution to be gender inclusive.

NEXT STEPS

REFLECT

1. Make a list of the most common "problem spots" around gender—
what is causing transgender and GNC students the most discomfort and
difficulty. List the phrases you hear from faculty, administrators, or students' families about why the work of gender inclusion "can't be done"
(or can't be done now). Spend some time writing and thinking about
these problems, and see if you can develop some solutions.

RESEARCH

1. Reach out to peer schools and see what they have done. Spend some
time touring facilities or talking to colleagues at those schools to hear what
they've tried and how it has gone.

ACT

1. Form a task force.

2. Use the findings of the gender audit to create a timeline or to-do list.

3. Build in ample time for training, education, information sessions, and
focus groups. Try to generate interest, understanding, and enthusiasm for
your project.

4. Start small. Pick some sort of outreach or endeavor that can be done
in a short timeframe, with little or no budget, and that won't require any
effort from other constituencies.

5. Plan medium. Look at what your next step will be and start to scaffold.
Who needs to be brought onto the task force to do this work? What are
the budgetary implications? Who is likely to resist the change? When does
the work need to be done by?

6. Remember that there is concrete work (changing signs) and abstract
work (changing minds) and that both need to happen in concert with
each other. Even when the signs can't change—because of money or state
law or an administrative obstruction—the minds can change. Continue
the educational work.

NOTES

a. Jonah DeChants et al., "Homelessness and Housing Instability Among LGBTQ Youth," *The Trevor Project*, November 23, 2021, https://www.thetrevorproject.org/wp-content/uploads/2022/02/Trevor-Project-Homelessness-Report.pdf.

b. Brian Klosterboer, "Texas' Attempt to Tear Parents and Trans Youth Apart, One Year Later," *ACLU*, February 23, 2023, https://www.aclu.org/news/lgbtq-rights/texas-attempt-to-tear-parents-and-trans-youth-apart-one-year-later.

c. Sam Killermann, "Edugraphics," *It's Pronounced Metrosexual*, accessed March 5, 2024, https://www.itspronouncedmetrosexual.com/edugraphics/.

d. Matthew Wills, "Doctors Have Always Been Against High-Heeled Shoes," *ITHAKA*, May 11, 2020, https://daily.jstor.org/doctors-have-always-been-against-high-heeled-shoes/.

e. Cydney Grannan, "Has Pink Always Been a 'Girly' Color?," *Encyclopedia Britannica*, August 30, 2016, https://www.britannica.com/story/has-pink-always-been-a-girly-color.

CHAPTER FIVE:

GENDER IN THE CLASSROOM

The first day of class provokes anxieties for many students and teachers. *What sort of first impression will I make? Will the kid who's teased me since first grade be in my history class this year? How do I pronounce this unfamiliar name on my roster?* For the transgender or gender non-conforming (GNC) student, this moment can be additionally stressful if they are unsure what information about them has been shared with the teacher, what name and other information might appear on the roster. The transgender or GNC student might also wonder whether the teacher is equipped to respond adequately if a peer misgenders them by using the wrong name or pronoun. These moments are so fraught and uniquely liable to come up at the beginning of the school year. It is important to take steps to set things up so that the teacher has the information they need to support their students. Only then can transgender and GNC students feel secure entering the classroom, knowing that their teacher is prepared to welcome them as they are.

When a student comes out as transgender or GNC at school, the school should be ready with a gender support plan. For years, when transgender and GNC students transitioned, schools would respond to their needs on a case-by-case basis instead of a holistic one. As a result, many students who have just come out will tolerate being misgendered because they worry that a teacher will get angry if the student corrects them. Or a GNC student might feel like they are imposing on an administrator if they ask for a single-user restroom to be relabeled from "girls" to "all gender."

Part of the problem is the hierarchy: the students are talking to or correcting adults who grade and discipline them. The other part is the constriction of imagination. For instance, a tenth-grade student who has just come out as a transgender girl is unlikely to think it is possible to move into a girls' dorm if she is the first transgender student to come out at a school. Students are not often the agents of change at schools, so asking them to imagine what could be changed for them is an unusual experience. Instead of being in the position of asking those questions, the school needs to put itself in the position of providing answers. This is not to suggest that the school has a one-size-fits-all response, but rather a menu of options, suggestions of actions that are definitely available and that might be helpful, which the student can opt to pursue or not. I call this menu a gender support plan, and I've worked with several schools to develop variations of it.

To me, the crucial features of the plan are that it anticipates common problems at the school in question and that it brings teachers into the conversation (if the student wants that) to help create a wider net of support. The support plan should also acknowledge and articulate the legal limits of support, if any, and provide resources for students and families to navigate systems of support beyond the school. Schools who face such legal constraints should be able to explain those constraints clearly to students and parents. It is supportive to demonstrate that you understand the current situation and that you are fully aware of the legal limits and of what can be offered within them. Connecting the student to outside resources, even if those resources are out of state, though not the ideal solution, can absolutely reduce harm.

Whether the gender support plan is developed by the task force, an administrator, or multiple parties, it should ultimately have a home in an administrative office. Often, this is the dean of students' or the assistant principal's office. Since transgender and GNC identities are not illnesses, the gender support plan should not reside with the health department or with a therapist or counselor. Nor should it be the responsibility of an LGBTQ+ faculty member unless that faculty member holds an administrative position. If a school can think of a gender support plan as being similar to an Individualized Education Plan (IEP), that might be a helpful model. In any case, it is important to continue to reconsider the plan as it is utilized. Survey the students and talk to them about the plan. Is it helpful? Is anything missing? Does the process feel comfortable?

When a student comes out, they might tell peers or an advisor. They might share with a favorite teacher or coach. Hopefully these individuals will be able to offer support in the moment;[1] likely for some of them, this student will be the first transgender or GNC person they've known closely. When the student comes out, the friend or advisor hopefully will say that they care about the student, that they want to support them, and so on. But they may have no idea what to do next—and that's where the gender support plan comes in. It is crucial that all constituents at a school know that the plan exists and are able to help the transgender or GNC student decide if and how they want to utilize that resource.

Before diving into the details of the gender support plan, let me pause here to add a reminder about the many students in elementary, middle, and high school who will experiment with gender, question their gender, and explore different ways of expressing their gender but who will neither want to come out nor want to transition. Such behavior is to be expected: Experimenting and testing limits (in a variety of ways) is part of growing up. A boy who likes to wear dresses shouldn't be pushed to come out; a girl who asks a trusted adult what it would be like to take testosterone shouldn't be assumed to want to transition. These sorts of explorations and experiments are likely only to increase in the coming generations if current trends continue, and they are indicative of the younger generations' less rigid, more flexible views on gender itself. While anti-trans legislation and rhetoric target transgender and GNC people first and foremost, they also promote a cultural environment that censures this kind of exploration for people of all identities.

I have written a lot about helping students who do want to come out and who do want to transition. But many students don't. Many students happily and healthily occupy a space of gender-fluidity and

---

1 When I run training sessions for schools, I like to model different ways to respond to a student coming out. It is often quite surprising to hear what teachers think would be an affirming and supportive response and quite effective to then go through and really unpack what support looks like. For instance, when a student comes out, a teacher might say, "Thanks for telling me you're gay, but it doesn't make a difference to me." The teacher means that in an affirming way: *It won't change how I treat you*. But the statement lacks the kind of affirmation that many students are looking for in these moments. Many students want to be seen, noted, felt, real. Being gay *does* make "a difference" to them.

gender-expansiveness, and the presence of a gender support plan shouldn't be used to push them to change how they express or identify themselves at all.

A MENU OF OPTIONS

At a couple of schools I've worked with, the support plan has been compiled into a neat pamphlet that is then disseminated throughout the school. This makes it a little more visible and accessible. A student who is questioning might pick up a copy from a bulletin board in history class and be able to get a sense of the support available without having to put themself in a vulnerable position before they are ready to do so.

So, what should such a plan offer? I like to begin with a clear statement of the rights a student has. Ideally,[2] the support plan might articulate rights including the following:

- The right to be called by the name and pronouns of their choice[3]
- The right to confidentiality (within the bounds of state reporting laws)
- The right to medical and mental health services that respect gender identity and expression
- The right to use the facilities that they feel accord with their gender identity or that present the most comfortable option
- The right to feel safe, comfortable, and included in school spaces and activities

---

2 The restrictions that transphobic legislation may impose on the viability of gender support plans will be discussed later on.

3 This can, unfortunately, be a tricky spot to navigate, even in the absence of legislation controlling name and pronoun choices. Detractors will claim that this expectation impedes free speech. But many schools have policies regarding harassment and bullying that restrict speech. Deliberately misgendering a person—using a "deadname" (the name a transgender or GNC person was born with and/or used prior to transitioning) or the wrong pronoun— should be considered bullying or harassment. However, students and teachers might inadvertently use the wrong pronoun or the student's deadname, and this should not be considered harassment. The slip-up should be corrected in the moment, but honest mistakes will occur.

These rights are fairly clear and, with some small exceptions, apply to many students in many different circumstances; I don't think they accord any special rights or privileges or extend rights only to transgender or GNC students.

After letting students know their rights, a gender support plan can then enumerate the options that are available to students. Here's where the menu idea comes in, and here's where a student might need time to consider and digest the possibilities. When I work with students who are transitioning or who want more support in a certain situation (on a sports team or in a classroom), it is important to explain the full range of options and then to give them time to consider, acknowledging that a student might want to move gradually or might want to change their mind at any point. Here are some options that the plan might include:

- Students can use a name other than their legal name at school. Students can opt to use that name (and pronouns) in all spaces at school or in only certain spaces where they want to be out.

- Students can choose which pronouns and names should be used in teacher comments and other emails, reports, etc. that go home to parents/guardians.

- Students can ask for faculty or administrative support to set up a meeting that includes the student (or not, as the student prefers) so that the student can come out to their teachers, coaches, college counselor, etc.

- Students have a variety of housing options available to them and, as availability of rooms allows, may request a shift in dormitories at any time during the year.

- Students have a variety of sports options available to them, and depending on tryouts and league rules, the school will

- work with coaches and the athletic director to ensure that facilities, uniforms, and team culture are supportive.

- Students can have an updated photograph, along with any name change, posted in school directories and/or placed on their school identification card.

- Student email addresses can also be changed to reflect any change in name.

There are many other options that a school might want to make available. At some boarding schools, for instance, students might have school-provided health insurance. Options for medical transition might be available through this insurance; if so, they should be made known. Non-boarding schools might want to make clear the rooming options available for students who travel off-campus on a school trip. And for some schools, the second bullet, concerning communication with parents and guardians, might be a sticking point and an area for further discussion.

Lastly, the gender support plan should lay out the support that is available for the student, regardless of which options they choose. These are all absolutely optional to the student:

- Affinity groups or social support groups available at the school and/or in the community

- College counselors who can help students handle gender identity in the college application process, including athletic recruiting

- Mental health therapists and counselors, trained in supporting transgender and GNC students, available on campus and/or in the community

- Administrators and faculty who can respond to any bullying, harassment, or disrespectful behavior from fellow students, faculty, staff, or visitors to the school, and a clear

- reporting structure for when such behavior occurs

- Administrators and faculty who can extend support if a student is kicked out of their house or has difficulty coming out to their family, utilizing professional resources such as counselors and mediators who are trained to work with LGBTQ+ youth

Of course, if a school is going to articulate these principles and offer these options, it needs to be ready to enact them. That means that facilities need to have proper signage and accommodations for privacy. That means that rosters and other forms that use names and gender markers need to be updatable. And, most importantly, it means that schools need to have educated, trained, and prepared their community of faculty, staff, students, and families to understand gender identity and expression.

As noted, recent legislation at the state and local level has introduced a variety of limitations to the above rights, supports, and options. Several states have enacted bans on transgender student athletes participating in sports. Others have made laws regarding bathroom usage, and some school boards have made explicit rulings about schools' ability to use pronouns and names for a student other than what is printed on their birth certificate. For instance, pending Louisiana H.B. 81 would require "school employees to use certain names and pronouns for students unless parents have provided written permission to do otherwise" and would "provide that a school employee shall not be required to refer to any person by certain pronouns if contrary to the employee's religious or moral convictions [. . .]."[a] The vagueness of the language here ("certain") does not obscure the bill's true aim.[4]

It is crucial, of course, that schools follow the laws that govern them. It is also crucial that schools help students and families and teachers understand and navigate these rulings. A gender support plan is going to look very different in a state where transgender youth are banned from

---

4 Rulings such as these are disrespectful and invalidating on their face. When put into the context of sociological findings regarding correct name and pronoun usage's effects on the mental health of transgender and non-binary youth, they become all the more sinister: The 2021 National Survey on LGBTQ+ Youth Mental Health found that youth whose pronouns were respected by all members of their household were 11% less likely to attempt suicide than youth whose pronouns were not respected by anyone in their household. Similarly, youth who were able to change their legal documents to align with the gender identities were 14% less likely to attempt suicide than youth who were not legally able to do so. (See note *b*.) These findings put into hard numbers what should be obvious: that respecting a person's self-determined gender identity is an essential protective factor of that person's mental health and sense of belonging and that laws that make this impossible in schools are dehumanizing and injurious to the well-being of queer youth, and to educational communities as a whole.

getting affirming medical care, can't be called by the name they prefer, are restricted in their bathroom use, and can't join sports teams. The best support a school can offer in this sort of situation is to explain in plain terms: "Here is the legal landscape, here's the reality that we face." Acknowledge the limitations of what the school can do and point the student to resources in the community or online beyond the school.

Sadly, the best support the school can offer at these moments is to make sure the student has an adult that they trust at school who can monitor them and make sure they are managing the anxiety, depression, and dysphoria that are all too likely to be the result of these restrictive rulings.

BEING A HOSPITABLE TEACHER

As mentioned above—and throughout this book—being able to provide such robust support depends upon having trained and prepared faculty and administrators. Good intentions and the desire to help students are not sufficient to adequately support transgender and GNC students. Going back to my earlier dinner party metaphor for inclusion, this is where the questions of "Are you ready?" and "Have you provided food that will nourish them?" come up. Is the food prepared and on the table? Are the supports already in place? Have you anticipated what they will need and made sure that your school is ready?

The gender support plan is designed to help transgender and GNC students, but it can also be a good tool to help teachers.

When I work with transgender and GNC student groups, the difficulty of self-identifying as transgender or GNC to teachers is a common theme. Students often find these exchanges to be really hard, really uncomfortable. I try to get them to see this as a necessary discomfort, one they are probably going to have to live with for the rest of their lives (you don't just come out once as a queer person; you have these conversations again and again and again). Self-advocacy is a great skill for any adolescent to work on, and that's especially true for LGBTQ+ students. I sometimes work with students on elevator pitches for coming out—how clearly and concisely they can communicate their story. We role-play various conversations where their identity might come up, giving them a chance to practice saying their answers to common questions about their sexual orientation or gender identity.

Still, even with such help, students are often reluctant to tell a teacher face-to-face, or even in an email, about a new name or new pronouns. If a conversation can't happen, how else can a teacher find out? Indeed, when I run faculty workshops, one of the most common questions I get is "How should I ask about pronouns?"

It is still standard practice to, on the first day of school, go around the room and have students introduce themselves by name. Teachers often expand these introductions to include salient information besides names or an icebreaker question—so why not ask for pronouns? I am not fully opposed to this technique. I've been to colleges, high schools, and middle schools (not to mention conferences and workplaces) where this practice works very smoothly. But I do suggest that educators consider the environment where they work carefully and not just assume that it will work in one place as well as it would in another.

For instance, if you only have one GNC student, who has recently come out, in a class of twenty peers and a school of a thousand students, that child is going to be the only person to deviate from the "expected" set of pronouns. And you're asking them to do so aloud, with twenty-one sets of eyes on them, on the first day of school. That's a lot. Students put in these situations often tell me that they "chickened out" and didn't share their names and pronouns; that they ended up misgendering themselves in class because their best friend from childhood was there, and they hadn't come out to them yet; and so on. It takes substantial courage to proclaim your marginalized identity publicly, especially when you haven't yet built trust with the group of people you're coming out to.

In other cases, you might be teaching in a school where there aren't any transgender or GNC students who are out yet, and this may seem to be a perfect opportunity to teach cisgender students how to share pronouns. This is a laudable goal. But be sure to consider a couple of points.

First, there are, quite possibly, transgender and GNC students in your classroom or school: they just aren't out yet. They are there, questioning (or knowing), and looking around for any clue about how they will be received if they do come out. If you want to introduce the practice of sharing pronouns, you should do so in a way that doesn't seem patronizing to GNC and transgender students and that doesn't make it seem like you are speaking for them.

It is better to couch the pronouns practice in the general goal of inclusion—and better to introduce a variety of possible pronouns— than it is to drop a stand-alone lesson about transgender and non-binary gender identity. This is especially true if you do not have deep, personal knowledge about these identities. Your queer students are looking for hints that you are ready for them and are comfortable around people like them, not hints that you see them as exotic or fragile.

Second, the first time you introduce this practice of sharing pronouns at the beginning of the school year, you are likely to get some strange responses. In the best-case scenario, when a student simply doesn't know what a pronoun is, it's an opportunity to teach grammar. In the worst-case scenario, students will be hostile or transphobic. I've heard students, possibly intending to be funny, respond, "What pronouns do I use? The normal ones." Or protest, "Why do I have to answer? I'm not gay." Teachers have to be ready to handle any such responses.[5] If you let these comments go because of your own discomfort, you are showing your students that you aren't ready to be an ally, an advocate, or an inclusive educator.

Most teachers do want to address students with the correct names and pronouns, but beyond the approach described above, it usually isn't clear how they are supposed to get that information in the first place.

The gender support plan puts that decision in students' hands while providing them with guidance and offering structure for dialogue with their teachers. Ultimately, I think the best way for a teacher to find out about their students' names and pronouns is for students to share that information with the teacher directly. This can be in a casual conversation, a more formal meeting, or an email exchange; it could also come in the form of the administration printing the name and pronouns submitted by the student on the teacher's class roster, regardless of whether they match the student's official documentation (as opposed to the standard practice of including biological sex on the

---

5 If a school is working on a larger strategic goal of inclusion, it might be possible to come up with a best practice for pronouns within a whole department. This type of collaboration is discussed more at the end of the chapter.

roster, discussed in Chapter Three).

In cases where teachers do not receive this information directly from students before or at the start of the school year, what are the best practices for gender-inclusive introductions in the classroom? At the start of the year, I like to give students an opportunity to share pronouns silently. How I approach this will depend on the age of the students I'm working with as well as the broader school environment. Sometimes, I have students make little name tents out of index cards, and I ask them to write out the name they want to be called in class (making it clear that they don't have to use their legal name but can write down a nickname, etc.) and then, next to or beneath their name, to write down the pronouns they use as well. This practice might still bring up commentary or spotlight the one kid who uses "they, them, theirs," but it can be easier to write and display than to say aloud.

Another option I often use is to have students write me a letter during their first day in class or record a short video of introduction that they send to me as part of their homework. I have a standard set of questions I ask them to answer as well as a list of optional topics they might want to cover. I ask about name and pronouns; I ask them whether their names and pronouns are what I should use in class or just in private conversations; I invite them to share with me their concerns about participation in class, and how they view themselves as a learner, reader, writer; and so on. It's a broad introduction to their academic selves, and name and pronouns are the start of that.

In this age of virtual teaching and online course management, I have expanded my practices around pronouns, making sure that wherever my name is displayed—in the little square on my Zoom screen or at the top of my discussion board post—that my pronouns are included beside it. It takes a little extra time to figure out how to do this; every program is a little different, and sometimes you have to find a workaround. But I think this provides good passive modeling for students and colleagues. In the first class, I also tell students, "If your name and pronouns aren't displaying how you want, let me know, and I'll help you get set up." Again, no pressure to share publicly at that moment—but an invitation to do so if they want and a little nudge to bring this into people's focus.

I also work with students in the opening classes to set some norms for our community and discussions. We talk about interruptions, hand-raising, debates, coming in late, etc. If the students don't organically bring up the subject, I will prod a bit and ask what they would do if they didn't know how to pronounce someone's name or if they aren't sure which pronouns someone uses. Again, the exact language I use will vary depending on the age and situation, but the goal remains the same: I want to create an inclusive classroom space, and the students need to be taught that they have a huge role in this process.

No matter what approach a teacher takes on that first day, the follow-up matters just as much. A student might come out as transgender or GNC a week later, or mid-term. How are you going to find out? I like to provide regular check-in opportunities for my students, taking ten or fifteen minutes of a class every so often to have them write me a short note about how things are going. Again, I always ask about names and pronouns. I always ask about comfort levels in the class, whether students feel able to participate. Beyond that, I vary the questions depending on what I want to know: "How long is the homework taking, does the group project seem fair?" and so on.

It may be helpful to provide students a similar chance, on the school level, to update their information. Sometimes, the only time a student's name and gender are registered is when they are admitted to a school—and that might have happened a decade ago, or it might have been a parent or guardian filling the information out rather than the student.

Once a teacher has been briefed on a student's name and pronouns, it is incumbent on that teacher to use the correct name and pronouns. Honest mistakes absolutely happen. Correct yourself quickly and move on. Don't make a huge scene of apology. If another teacher or classmate misgenders the student, you need to correct them. Again, don't make a huge scene but do say something. A typical exchange in a class discussion:

GNC student: "The green light symbolizes Gatsby's desire for money."

Other student: "What she said makes sense, but—"

Teacher: "What *they* said. Continue, please. . . ."

That's it—no need to explain. No need to make the student apologize. Make the correction and right back to class. If I can, I like to follow up with both students separately. For the GNC student, I want to make sure that the other student isn't consistently misgendering them (or otherwise causing problems). For the other student, I want to make sure they understand the error they made but also reassure them that slipups happen and that I don't automatically think that they are being mean or bigoted.

Policies like Florida's H.B. 1557, the notorious "Don't Say Gay" law from 2022, are still quite new and are often subject to dispute. It isn't clear how much they will ultimately affect how schools' use of names and pronouns for students in the long term. Regardless, the presence of such bills is causing a lot of anxiety—for teachers who don't want to break the rules and face disciplinary consequences and for students who wonder whether they will be able to use the name and pronouns they identify with while they spend time in what is likely their main social arena, their school.

As murky as these waters are, I think the most important thing for schools to affirm is that, whatever the school board or state government determines about gender identities deemed to not "match" the information on students' birth certificates, bullying and harassment are against the rules. Teachers, students, and caregivers should be able to ask schools to establish clear rules and parameters around what constitutes harassment, bullying, or other problematic behavior. Any language used to taunt or belittle, whether that is a student's name or an ethnic slur, should be recognized as problematic and responded to by the school.

Similarly, students and teachers can ask for training in how to both recognize and respond to offensive behavior. If administrators and teachers share a common understanding of what is threatening or harassing and what is appropriate intervention in an area, then adults in a community will be more confident about disrupting the behavior and saying something. In many schools, this takes the form of "upstander" (as opposed to bystander) training and can be undergone by students and teachers together as part of building community understandings around behavior.[6]

Any word can be weaponized, unfortunately. If a student must go by their legal name, the teacher can figure out ways to minimize the use of that name in class. Teachers should also note people who mean-spiritedly or pointedly refer to the student with their legally required names and pronouns and report the harassment. Sadly, legal names are often used as taunts against trans and GNC people, and the new rulings around their use make transgender students easy targets for harassment, something schools should be aware of and care about.

Even when students' chosen pronouns are permitted, some adjustments may still be necessary. For instance, as mentioned in Chapter One, many people find the singular pronoun "they" tough. I still hear English teachers and self-appointed grammar mavens claiming that using "they" to refer to a single person is grammatically incorrect, even though the MLA and many other usage guides and dictionaries have indicated that a singular "they" is absolutely correct. For those historically and grammatically minded people, I point to the use of "they" as a singular pronoun in Shakespearean times . . . and also point to the fact that language, by nature, changes. We aren't still using "thee" and "thou," even though those pronouns were at one point grammatically correct.

In truth, I think the grammatical argument is a poor mask for cisgender and binary discomfort. The pronouns "she" and "he," even if used to refer to a transgender person, reinforce and abide by binary rules. "They" disrupts the rules. Resistance to "they" fits in with the pattern of resistance to GNC and non-binary people in general. I have had colleagues say to me of a GNC student: "When is that kid going to decide?" My usual reply: "I think they already have."

If you are reluctant to use "they," it is worth spending some time asking yourself why. Work through the assumptions you make about where a person will or should "end up" with gender identity. Are they

---

6 For more on this type of training, see the website of the Center for Anti-Violence Education.

informed by a covert desire to make transgender people less visible or discernable? You can have these beliefs with good intentions—you can be a supporter of trans rights—and still be unconsciously biased against GNC people. The binary is a deeply held belief for many cisgender people and one they may never have questioned.

And that questioning takes practice. Any change in name or pronoun takes practice. When someone you know changes their name or pronoun, you need to do your best to use that new name and pronoun all the time. No one gets to say, "But I've known you since you were a baby! I'll always call you—" Nope. Doesn't matter. If your coworker got a divorce and returns to her maiden name, you don't get to say, "I think of you as Stephanie Harris, and that's just the way it is!" Of course not. You respect your coworker's decision. That means that even when the person isn't in the room with you, you use the right name. You correct others who do not use the correct name if it's appropriate to do so.[7] Again, practice if you need to, for example by using the method described in Chapter Three (i.e., referring to your dog or cat or even your houseplant as "they" for a month or so).

Here are some final thoughts on names and pronouns in the classroom. In an ideal world, as noted earlier, a teacher's roster could be updated to convey students' preferred names and pronouns. In an ideal world, then, the roster plays a positive role in supporting gender inclusion.

The case is the opposite, however, at schools where rosters are generated the traditional way, that is, by automatically pulling students' legal names and the sexes assigned to them at birth. If a teacher is in the habit of reading their (traditional) roster to call roll, that teacher is eventually going to out a student, or further closet a student, or set up a student to be misgendered in that class. It takes a lot of courage for a student to correct the very first thing a teacher says, and few students will be able to muster that type of courage, particularly in our current political environment. It is the teacher's responsibility—and

---

7 Of course, you also want to be sure you know how out the person is. Usually, when a student shares a new name or pronoun with me, I ask them a couple of questions: "Do you want me to correct other people when they misgender you?" and "Who else knows?" Sometimes students will say, "Please don't say anything to anyone else." And it's important to respect that.

the administrator's responsibility—to think of students' safety in their classrooms and schools and do everything they can to prevent situations such as this.

Fortunately, databases can be reworked. If you are at a school with an IT department that can support you, it is often possible to coordinate with database vendors or with your school's staff to supply rosters with current, student-provided information.[8] The important thing is for the gender task force to flag rosters as a potential problem spot early on. Even though various issues may arise from the default encoding of this data, there are many ways to ameliorate these issues, such as training teachers not to call roll from the rosters, manually correcting names for certain students, and changing database codes.

BUILDING INCLUSIVE CURRICULA

Of course, there's more to building a safe classroom environment than accepting preferred names and pronouns. Whether it's the books on the shelves, the posters on the wall, or the content of the course, the material in a classroom needs to both reflect the identities of the students in the class and provide an entryway into other identities as well.

I'm an English teacher, so I consider the texts that I teach and the topics that I have my students write on. As we go through the literature, I bring in relevant historical context and terminology and we discuss race, religion, gender, sexuality, and so on. I have students write about their own identities and put themselves in relationship to other identities as well. It is pretty common for me to find that students who are cisgender, straight, and White haven't done much consideration of their race, sexuality, and gender; they consider themselves to be "blank" in these categories. In these cases, a lot of the work is getting students to realize that they do in fact have identities and to think about how those identities have been shaped.

Notice that in an English classroom, it isn't just about reading

---

8 Some databases make use of a nickname field that, if it is populated, can take the place of a legal name. Other databases will only list the nickname beside the legal name. In this case, it is sometimes possible to create a preferred/chosen name field that can override the legal name field if it is populated.

"diverse books." It is about making sure that students are equipped and required to discuss the topics brought up in those books. As amazing as it seems, I have absolutely witnessed English classes on *Othello* where no one talks about race at all—the students are just *so interested* in Iago's motives. Actually, they are *so afraid* to talk about race, and usually the teacher is, too. We as educators have to educate and prepare ourselves to have these conversations. We need to select books that will speak to the identities of our students and the ways that they move through the world; we need to make sure that our students learn to think and talk about gender, race, class, and religion.[9]

Inclusion is going to look different depending on the content area and course structure. One shared factor should be bringing students into conversations about the purpose of the class and the atmosphere of the class. Be open about expectations, not just of schoolwork but of behavior. This shouldn't be "top down"—the teacher telling the students what to do or not to do—but rather an affirmation of shared values and an understanding of how breaches of those values will be responded to.

Many times, English and history teachers are the ones who bear a heavier load of teaching about social justice topics. Since English is often the only class that students are required to take every term throughout high school, English departments can be viewed as having more content flexibility than other academic areas. But I think that every course has some space to bring gender (and other vectors of identity) into the conversation. Again, this can and should be passive (the art on the walls), but it should also be active. Even when teachers are restricted in how they may address topics of gender and sexuality in the classroom, harm-reductive approaches to building curricula are still possible.

In math classes, this could look like something as minor as writing word problems that include the use of "they" as a singular pronoun. Or

9 Sadly, there are schools where teachers are not able to select any of the texts that they teach due to district or state-mandated curricular guidelines. I have talked to teachers in such situations and admire that despite their frustrations, they have found ways to get alternate and additional texts into their students' hands. Some of these teachers are able to sponsor book clubs; others have displays of books in their classrooms that students are able to borrow. I even spoke with one teacher who made creative use of her supply closet to store books out of sight of administrators and students' families who might criticize her selection. She encourages students to select something "out of the closet." (Yes, English teachers love puns.)

in statistics, using case studies that involve real-life information about the transgender community. Biology classes should teach about anatomy and reproduction in a way that doesn't presume that students in the class are straight or cisgender; that doesn't present one way of behaving or one type of body as normal and all others as peculiar or strange. Whenever possible, the scientists whose material is studied and the case studies that the class considers should present a richly diverse array of identities. As we'll see in a later chapter on libraries, representation really does matter, and it's possible to pursue it throughout the disciplines.

Similarly, for those schools with a health education curriculum, every effort should be made to teach the class as if there were LGBTQ+ students present; again, don't presume folks are cisgender and straight. Too often, health education courses spend one day on LGBTQ+ "issues" and then move on, rather than integrating the perspectives of LGBTQ+ people into the general material being presented on safer sex, healthy relationships, and mental health. In presenting these topics to the class, the teacher should weave in material on LGBTQ+ identities in the same way they would any other topic—not draw special attention to the fact that they are doing so.

Often, when including work by or information on marginalized communities, teachers expect accolades (in the form of appreciation by members of those communities who are their colleagues or students) or presume to speak on behalf of communities to which they do not belong. Being well intentioned or having friends who are LGBTQ+ does not mean you can speak on behalf of that identity or know what that lived experience is like. But it does mean you can gain expertise and comfort with concepts and terminology and information and help others to do the same. Educators should consider these factors as they prepare their course materials and lessons.

All of these suggestions will require work on the part of the instructor: research, reading, retooling. A typical pattern for me as a teacher is to do a little self-assessment (sometimes with survey input[10] from my stu-

---

10 I typically ask students to tell me whether they completed the homework for the class, whether they found the work rewarding, if there was a text that particularly spoke to them, and so on. I like to assess their degree of engagement and then try to figure out why some students might feel more or less engaged than others.

dents) in the spring term of an academic year and let that guide me in what I want and need to work on doing better in the coming year. Then I put together a plan—often a reading list plus a goal of coming up with writing assignments and contextualizing material—and find a friend or two who will do the work with me. We can then meet over the summer and have discussions, share resources, run essay topics past each other, and try out writing exercises. If we come across great video clips that might help frame class readings, we can send them to each other. When the school year comes around, we can stop by each other's classrooms and share how something went—good or bad. Collaborating with other teachers helps ensure that I'm continually working toward my goals, and it makes things more fun in the meantime.

It absolutely has more impact if a whole department undertakes this work and commits to doing a better job of teaching about gender or race. This can be really helpful in creating a sense of solidarity and not making inclusion the work of a few teachers (who often themselves have marginalized identities). I have seen this work well with department policies on teaching texts with the n-word, for instance, and in departments that have developed best practices on providing trigger warnings for texts that include passages about sexual trauma. Helping to develop such policies can be part of the educational process for colleagues who are hesitant or ignorant about the topics at hand. Faculty meetings and training sessions are also great opportunities for teachers to practice using "they" pronouns, sharing their own pronouns, and expressing gender inclusivity in other ways. As I always say in diversity/inclusion work: Don't do it alone! And if you find something that works, see if it can be an educational opportunity to share with your colleagues about what you've learned.

But it is also all too likely that a whole department won't feel similarly inclined when it comes to gender inclusivity. In these cases, teacher will have to develop their own best practices. But I have found that it is a better expense of my energy to work with the willing and the interested. We feed each other and become more energized together. When I work with a coalition of the willing, when we have committed to this work and experienced growth through collaborating, then we are in a place where we can bring more reluctant colleagues along.

NEXT STEPS

REFLECT

1. Take stock of your own practices. If you are a teacher, write and reflect on the texts and topics you use in your classroom. If you are a caregiver or administrator, think about the LGBTQ+ supportive resources you are familiar with—what do you know about the support systems available in your area? What don't you know but think you should?

RESEARCH

1. Compile a list of community and online resources to point students and supportive families to, in cases where the school is prohibited from otherwise expressing gender-affirming support.

2. Operating within relevant state and local laws, investigate options for updating your school's database options when it comes to student names and gender designations.

ACT

1. Design a gender support plan, getting input and feedback from trans-gender and GNC students and alumni whenever possible, that enumer-ates a menu of options.

2. Train faculty, staff, and administrators on the gender support plan.

3. Make sure students and faculty know that the support plan exists—dis-play it prominently online and in hard copy.

4. Help teachers to audit their own classrooms, curricula, and practices. Offer trainings and discussion sessions to go over how to share pronouns, how to practice using the singular "they," what to do if a student is mis-gendered, and so on.

NOTES

a. The Given Name Act, H.R. 81, LA State Leg. (2023).

b. The Trevor Project, "National Survey on LGBTQ Youth Mental Health,"
https://www.thetrevorproject.org/survey-2021.

CHAPTER SIX:

THE BATHROOM (AND LOCKER ROOM) CONUNDRUM

For a high school English teacher, I know an awful lot about plumbing code and toilets. Mind you, I can't fix a leaking pipe, but I can tell you the rules governing commodes per occupant by gender in the state of New Hampshire. Perhaps this doesn't come as a surprise, given how much restrooms have dominated news stories around transgender people in recent years.

Between 2016 and this book's printing, a dozen states introduced legislation restricting transgender usage of public restrooms. Some of these initiatives failed or were repealed, but others have been reintroduced, such as Kansas's S.B. 180, enacted in July 2023 after the state government overturned the veto of Governor Laura Kelly.

"Are you all going to check the genitals of every trans child who walks into the restroom, or maybe just children in general, so you can figure out who's a male and who's a female biologically?" Democratic State Representative Heather Meyer asked Republican lawmakers, critically echoing points made earlier in this book about the limitations of segregating spaces according to cissexist standards.[a] Again, the question of what we're excluding/including based on—gender identity? gender expression? genitalia? chromosomes?—arises. Moreover, as Meyer brings up, who's checking at the door of the restroom? And what about non-binary individuals? How could two binary options ever accommodate them?

These so-called "bathroom bills"[1] have turned restrooms into a battle-

---

1 Not the best term because it minimizes what is really at stake. Yes, this is about bathrooms, but only in the same sense that Rosa Parks was about bus seats. It's really about civil rights.

ground and made the work of gender inclusion even more controversial. Many efforts at such legislation have been abandoned before being put to a vote, voted down, or overturned—sometimes because of economic pressure, such as the NBA refusing to hold its annual All-Star Game in North Carolina until the partial repeal of that state's restrictive bathroom law, 2016's H.B. 2.[2] But other efforts have succeeded. It is worth considering this broader context as we discuss how to make restrooms and locker rooms more gender inclusive. Even if your state has never had a bathroom bill introduced, the arguments used to advance these measures are likely to surface with any proposed changes to school restrooms.

Ah. School restrooms. The site of much dawdling, cigarette smoking, emoting, graffiti, bullying, gossip, vaping . . . and necessary bodily functions. Restrooms, along with locker rooms, are also often one of the most visible places of gender segregation in a school, and therefore are a fiercely guarded domain. Yet there are a number of problems with trying to maintain single-gender restrooms.

When proponents of "bathroom bills" talk about why it is necessary to keep transgender people from using the "wrong" bathroom, their main talking point is often safety. These arguments are usually couched in patriarchal terms: that is, if we let transgender women use a women's restroom, the women and girls in that room will not be safe. This sort of argument simultaneously suggests that transgender women a.) are not women and b.) are sexual predators (a position familiar from the years when gay men weren't trusted as coaches, teachers, etc.; that is, different equals dangerous).

Another related yet distinct argument might posit: If we let transgender women use the women's restroom, then what's to stop a cis man from barging in and saying that he has the right to use the restroom because he's "now a woman"? The idea that cis men inclined to sexually assault random women in public would be abetted by inclusive policies is illogical—if someone is harboring such designs, why would he care about what's "allowed"? Wouldn't he just act, regardless of state or institutional guidelines about who's legally permitted to use which bathroom?

And, more to our point here: In any such cases of reproachable

2 The ban lasted from 2016 to 2019. (See note *b*.)

violence, how would the extension of basic trans civil rights be more to blame than the persistent legacies of rape culture and misogyny?

Indeed, violence in public restrooms in general is quite rare (more on this in the next paragraph). This fear of cis men flitting willy-nilly in and out of women's bathrooms expresses the prejudice that many supporters of bathroom bills hold: that transgender identity itself is whimsical at best and cloaking sinister motives at worst. To disguise this bigotry, a smoke screen is being raised in the name of (cis) "womenfolk"'s safety. As Beatriz Pagliarini Bagagli, Tyara Veriato Chaves, and Mónica G. Zoppi Fontana point out in their study of the legal discourse surrounding gender-segregated public spaces, "The fact that we cannot guarantee with absolute unmistakability who may or may not be a potential 'sexual predator' seems to have a burden only for transgender women."[c] The real purpose of the bathroom bills and their attendant rhetoric is to exclude trans women and to scapegoat them for a culture of sexual violence in which cis men are more common perpetrators by far (see footnote 4).

The sociological data backs up what I'm saying. A landmark 2018 study by the Williams Institute at the UCLA School of Law was the first to specifically investigate the correlation, if any, between trans-inclusive policies for gender-segregated public spaces (including restrooms, locker rooms, and retail changing rooms) and violent crime in such spaces. The study looked at Massachusetts towns that had passed gender-inclusive bathroom policies and compared each of them to a nearby town (with a history of comparable crime trends) that had not passed such a policy. The analysis of the subsequent crime trends demonstrated that the passage of trans-inclusive policies failed to affect the number of criminal incidents in restrooms, locker rooms, and the like—and, indeed, that reports of privacy and safety violations in such spaces were "exceedingly rare and much lower than statewide rates of reporting violent crimes more generally."[d]

Stepping back from the claims that are made about the harm that transgender people, particularly transgender women, might perpetrate in public restrooms, the actual victims and potential victims in these situations are much more likely to be transgender women than anyone else. There have been a number of assaults on transgender women in women's restrooms—

cisgender women attacking them for no reason except their trans identity.[3] A 2015 study by the National Center for Transgender Equality found that 12% of the 27,715 respondents had been verbally harassed or sexually or physically assaulted while using a public restroom in the past year. Trans women of color were especially vulnerable to sexual assault.[e]

When it comes to school restrooms and locker rooms specifically, a 2019 *Pediatrics* study found that the prevalence of sexual assault of trans and GNC students in these spaces was 25.9% during a twelve-month period, according to its survey of over 3,600 US transgender students in grades eight through twelve—meaning that a quarter of these students had experienced coercive sexual contact in gender-segregated school spaces in the past year. This number is significant on its own and further contextualized by comparison to the national rates of sexual assault experienced by cisgender youth in school settings: that is, 15% of cisgender high school girls and 4% of cisgender high school boys. Among trans and GNC youth whose bathroom and locker room access was restricted by trans-exclusionary policies, trans girls and non-binary youth assigned female at birth were the most at risk for sexual assault while using the locker room or bathroom at school.[f]

So, even if we, for the sake of argument, allow for the possibility that trans-inclusive policies might inspire a small number of cis men to enact sexual violence that they would not have enacted otherwise (and, again, I believe this to be incredibly unlikely), does this hypothetical possibility outweigh the real harm that trans women and girls too often face when they simply try to use the facilities? I believe that the widespread introduction of inclusive policies combined with a shift in the way this issue is understood and talked about would bring the most peace to the most people.

Meanwhile, relatively few arguments are made against transgender men who want to use the men's room. Transgender men aren't considered a threat to the cisgender men and boys they might encounter in a men's restroom, so their presence isn't as controversial. Yet transgender men are the ones who are at risk when they use the men's room.

---

3 To be clear, as of this writing, no large-scale study analyzes the gender identities of those who physically attack trans women in the women's restroom or similar gender-segregated spaces. But anecdotal evidence combined with basic logic suggests that most such assailants are cisgender women.

According to the *Pediatrics* study, trans boys as a sub-group experienced the second-highest rate of sexual assault in gender-segregated school spaces, at 26.5% of the trans boys surveyed.[g] If the transgender man or boy doesn't pass, he is even more likely to be harassed or assaulted in a men's room by cisgender men.

And there's no reason to think that a trans woman would be able to use the men's room without harassment, either. Indeed, for all that women's safety is championed in these debates, the fact is that, even post-#MeToo, much of the sexual violence that cisgender men perpetrate against women and girls—cisgender and transgender—is either not reported, not taken seriously, or not properly investigated.[4] In other words, the safety of women and girls only becomes a prioritized issue when transgender people are involved, revealing just how much a confluence of transphobia and misogyny drive the agenda behind bathroom bills. Continued debate around and enactment of these bills enflames violence, overcomplicates the issue at hand, and obfuscates the actual question of safety in gender-segregated public spaces.

While every school's ultimate approach to this matter will vary, each should consider what acts of violence (and other problematic behavior) have actually occurred in their bathrooms and locker rooms. Schools can then develop policies that are based on reality rather than on hypothetical situations fueled by transphobic imaginations. It is very clear who the vulnerable parties really are in these situations, and it is incumbent upon schools to protect those who are most likely to be harassed: the transgender and gender non-conforming (GNC) students.

REEXAMINING SAFETY

When I ask teaching faculty to name the places in schools where they feel least comfortable, student restrooms and student locker rooms always are at the top of the list. Many faculty will even say that they

---

4 A 2016/2017 report from the Center for Disease Control stated that 94% of female respondents "reported having only male rape perpetrators in their lifetime," and The Rape, Abuse & Incest National Network (RAINN) has found that more than two out of three sexual assaults in general go unreported. Of the cases that are, only a small fraction culminate in arrest or prosecution. (See notes *h* and *i*.)

would never enter a locker room, often for good reasons around privacy and concern for liability.

That means that these spaces are largely ungoverned and without supervision. This opens the door for problems around the use of illicit substances and other social issues, including bullying and harassment, which often targets LGBTQ+ students' as well as straight, cisgender students whose bodies have developed at a different rate or in a different manner than most of their peers.[5] Bullying based on body size and shape is often informed by cisnormative and heterosexist assumptions, even when the target is not LGBTQ+. And even when there is no specific target present, the language and atmosphere in locker rooms and restrooms can be derogatory, misogynistic, and disrespectful in general.

Another question I like to ask when I visit schools: Are there students who are supposed to change for sports practice or PE class in the locker room but don't? The answer is always yes. Sometimes they change in a bathroom stall; sometimes they change in their car; sometimes they wear their gym clothes under their school clothes. There are always students who avoid the locker room (and the bathroom), and they are not just LGBTQ+ kids. They might be kids who are bullied, kids who are struggling with body image, kids who are slower to physically mature than others, and so on. Why don't they use these spaces? Because they don't feel comfortable, or they don't feel safe.

Put all these pieces together and we find ourselves at a productive starting point and understanding: Safety doesn't exist in locker rooms and restrooms, even if they are divided by gender. This is where I like to begin when I work with schools on inclusive locker rooms and restrooms, with the understanding that, contrary to standard assumptions, these spaces aren't working currently for many students and faculty. If we can agree on that point, then we can start to reimagine things more broadly.

It is important to start with the bigger picture here because, as we have seen, many schools have tried to manage transgender student needs through isolation or with a case-by-case approach. When

---

5 A 2019 report conducted by the US Department of Education surveyed over 24 million students ages twelve through eighteen about their experiences with bullying. Surveyed students reported the reasons they believed they were bullied by peers; across data sets, physical appearance was a leading reason. (See note *k*.)

it comes to restrooms, I often see schools tell a transgender or GNC student: "Instead of using the boys' room (or girls' room), why don't you use the staff restroom? Or the single-user bathroom in the nurse's office?" They will often, sadly, appeal to the transgender student's own concerns around safety and bullying by suggesting that the single-user restroom would offer the student more privacy and less risk.

This approach has several problems, including logistical ones. For instance, there may be a large school building with only two single-user restrooms. If the non-binary student has an algebra class on the east wing of the second floor and the single-user restroom is near the principal's office on the south side of the first floor, they are never going to get to class on time. Or they are going to have some serious bladder trouble. Or they are going to dehydrate themselves so they don't have to use the bathroom that frequently. None of this sounds like safety!

A more cultural problem is the simple isolation and segregation—because, although I'm critiquing the way that locker and restrooms tend to be set up, there's no denying their role in peer bonding and social development, especially for adolescents. After all, bathrooms and locker rooms are places where meaningful social gatherings take place. Sports teams have crucial conversations about tactics and plays in locker rooms; classmates share jokes and gossip when they use the restroom. To be told that a transgender student can only use a solo facility is to cut them out of this social aspect. Each time the non-binary student goes to a different bathroom than their peers, they are reminded that they are alone, that they are separate, that they are not like others and don't belong. Such stigmatization might even keep a student from coming out.

Indeed, the single-bathroom policy can only pertain to students who have come out or are known to be transgender and GNC. For every student who is out, there are several more in a school who are questioning, experimenting, and wondering about their gender. When a school only responds to out and open students, the needs of a larger group of students are being ignored.

Commonly proposed locker room solutions follow similar patterns. Well-intentioned schools will sometimes create a third space for transgender and GNC students in addition to the preexisting areas for cis girls and boys; I've seen some creatively re-purposed supply closets in my time. But, like the single-user restrooms, these spaces often are isolating and separate from the positive cultural experience of the locker room. Even more isolating, some schools have simply suggested that transgender and GNC students can be dismissed from physical education requirements, or the requirement to change into gym clothes, altogether.

Other schools have curtained off a corner of the locker room and suggested that the transgender student can go in there to change. Yes, that's possible, and they could (as many of their cisgender peers likely do) use a bathroom stall to change. But this is a bandage at best, a minor treatment that doesn't adequately address the harmful and uncomfortable atmosphere of the locker room, a problem that will exist for other students even if you remove the transgender or GNC student from the space.

Most schools don't intend to be cruel in consigning transgender and GNC students to a limited number of restrooms or a specialized changing area. They arrive at this solution because it seems non-controversial and easy: Nothing changes for most students. No facilities need to be modified. It can be a private, off-the-books arrangement for this one student. I always suspect that schools present this as a short-term solution, promising themselves that they will do better for the next transgender student . . . but simultaneously hoping that they won't *have* another transgender student. That's no way to approach inclusivity.

Again, advocates for transgender students won't make much headway if they ask for large-scale change to be done for the benefit of a very small minority of students only. Thinking about adjustments to locker rooms and bathrooms space in terms of *all* students also can help to re-center the conversation at this moment when transgender students are under attack. A school might hesitate to even address the topic of transgender students in locker rooms for fear of backlash and optics. However, they might have much more appetite to address policies around bullying, harassment, or privacy in locker rooms. To make the change appealing, it has to provide a greater measure of safety and comfort for most students and most faculty—or, at least, it has to not be an inconvenience to the majority. That's why I suggest approaching locker rooms and restrooms through the lens of all students and making the (usually) very accurate claim that in fact many students don't feel comfortable (or use) these spaces.

So, what's keeping students from feeling comfortable? What's keeping faculty from feeling as though they can enter these spaces? Nudity and privacy. And here, we ought to pause. Having just gone through an extensive discussion of dress codes and examined the many ways in which we require students (especially girls) to cover up, why is it that we allow, expect, and even require students to be naked in front of each other?

Once again, the answer to this question is found in patriarchy and the traditional origins of many schools. The gymnasium comes to us from ancient Greece; the very root of the word, *gymnos*, means naked. These spaces were all-male; they were places for athletic training and competition and also places for philosophical and political debate. Women were strictly forbidden. Gymnasia were the original "old boys' clubs." This concept was translated out of ancient Greece and into Europe and subsequently over to the United States.

Accordingly, masculinity and nudity are at the core of the gym and locker room experience. When I work with formerly all-male schools, older alumni will often wax eloquent on how they used to swim laps and walk around the gym hallways in the nude back in the institution's single-sex glory days. And if you weren't as well developed as the other fellows and were embarrassed by your physique? Well, maybe that would inspire you to work out a little more! Character-building. A bonding experience. These are the phrases I hear, alongside the suggestion that the school—in becoming co-ed and in restricting nudity—has given up on making "real" men with strong characters.

The fact that locker rooms are a vestige of this masculine culture only breeds further tolerance of misbehavior along the lines of "boys will be boys." When you have students from different races, different religions, different sizes, different abilities, and different cultural backgrounds all sharing a locker room, you have to wonder whose body is considered normal or standard and whose will be exotic or even weird. Those who say that being comfortable with being naked around others shows that one is well-adjusted are demonstrating the values of a very specific cultural heritage—but schools should not be dominated by the values of just one culture. The traditionality of a given view does not make it correct or optimal. If your school is committed to being inclusive—to welcoming a broad array of students and making sure they are all comfortable—they cannot continue to run programs and use facilities that were built for and by straight, cisgender, able-bodied, White, Christian men.

I don't doubt that some such men had a wonderful experience in these gymnasia of yore. But I strongly doubt that every student had a wonderful experience. And I know for certain that schools back then were not as diverse as they are now. Somewhere between 1965 and 1985 (give or take a few years), most schools in America made a commitment to diversity, to searching out and accepting a wide array of students. In recent years, more and more schools have admitted that diversity isn't enough. But even as many schools nod their metaphorical heads and say, "yes, yes, we need to be inclusive," they haven't yet come to terms with the fact that to be inclusive will require them to change: change their practices, change their policies, and change their facilities.

Inclusion requires looking at what your school is, understanding what put it there in the first place (usually patriarchy and White supremacy), and then committing to dismantling influences, however deeply rooted, that do not align with your institution's mission or values.

FROM ASKING "WHO?" TO ASKING "HOW?"

Most human beings, particularly adolescents, would like to avoid prolonged (or any) public nudity. Most human beings value some degree of privacy. Providing privacy and preventing nudity in schools does not limit anyone's freedom in a meaningful way. For a transgender boy who runs on the boys' track team in seventh grade, the ability to go into the locker room with his team after practice, to share in the banter and complaining about the tough workout, is meaningful. That he can then step behind a curtain or stall door and trade his sweaty clothes for a dry T-shirt and shorts, all while still laughing and talking with his peers, who are doing the same thing in their own cubicles, promotes collegiality, bonding, and allows for privacy. It doesn't have to be expensive to make effective change.

Let's consider a locker room first. Say one goal is to be able to have a coach walk into the locker room at any time and sit down with her team to talk over strategy for the next game—this is reasonable. Coaches are teachers, and the locker room could be considered part of their classroom space. It needs to be assumed, then, that the coach will not walk in while her students are changing. Regardless of identity, an adult school employee should not be seeing naked or partially naked students. Currently, if a coach wants to enter a locker room space, they typically will yell from the doorway, "Is everyone decent? I'm coming in!" This sort of dynamic tends to reaffirm the sense that the locker room is an ungoverned terrain. Meanwhile, in terms of infrastructure or policy, nothing is in place to protect students' physical privacy, whether from coaches or peers.

Indeed, another goal in revising the locker room space should be to minimize the likelihood that any student, regardless of their gender identity or expression, feels obliged to expose their body to their peers or else be marginalized for their unwillingness to do so. There is a balance to be found between creating a space that is safe and comfortable for peer and team bonding—which often happens best without constant adult presence—and a space that is able to be supervised by adults. Ideally, locker rooms should be spaces where adults can enter to check on things but where students can also feel like they have some privacy—similar to how dorms work at residential schools.

With all that in mind, the first step is to set a new community expectation for how locker rooms are run—namely, that there will be no nudity in public areas of the space. To make this feasible, a school will need to set up individual changing areas. New signage can help denote curtained-off spaces denoted as changing areas. Schools might make good use of shower rooms for this purpose—even at relatively small schools, it is typical to have three showers in a locker room, yet most athletic directors and coaches I talk to say that no students actually use the showers on a regular basis. So, preserve one shower, which can likely still be used to change in, and subdivide the rest of the area into individual changing areas. Bathroom stalls can also be used. In some cases, schools will find that they need to modify bathroom stalls to provide more privacy: lowering/raising the height of stall walls and doors and providing piano hinges (hinges designed to cover the space between the stall door and the stall wall) to close the gaps.[6] It is true that asking students to step behind curtains or into a stall might take a little more time, but intentional usage of the space ensures that the difference will be minimal once students adjust to the new protocols.

Those are infrastructural steps that can be taken with relatively minimal to-do. To shift the *culture*, the school may need to post a coach or teacher in the locker room for the first few weeks after the new rule is introduced.[7] The teacher or coach can direct students to the changing areas, making sure the public area of the space is reserved for chatting and other clothed activities. Students who already change in the bathroom stalls will no longer be marginalized for doing so. If students know that an adult is likely to be in the locker room, there's a greater chance they will use the changing areas. The adult's very presence changes the norms of the space even as student privacy is protected.

At one school where this approach was attempted in the girls' locker room, we asked for feedback after the first two weeks of the new expectation. There were some complaints about inconvenience. One student felt it took away from camaraderie to go into separate stalls to change. But there was also a team captain who said that it allowed her to talk to her team in the locker room and get them to listen, because people were more present and less anxious. Transgender students said they felt less spotlit when they went behind a curtain to change now that everyone else did the same. A Muslim student said it was the first time she'd ever felt that the school shared her values in terms of modesty. In short, those who said the new policy had a positive benefit were not just the transgender or GNC students. The change improved many students' experiences and those who were less enthusiastic about the change were not harmed.

There's still the question of who gets to use which locker room or

---

6   Additionally, for facilities that have urinals installed and where, for reasons of plumbing code, they must remain in use, schools should consider installing privacy barriers between the urinals.

7   Also, as mentioned in a previous chapter, this change shouldn't be made without ample discussion, input, education, and advance warning. No one should be surprised by this. Even better would be to get a group of coaches and team captains together to help plan where the changing spaces will be, to get advice on how to phrase the new expectation, and so on.

restroom. Again, this goes back to the question of what these sorting policies are based on. If a student arrives at your school in fourth grade as a boy and in sixth grade transitions to be a girl, there is likely to be some conversation (if not kerfuffle) over which restroom and locker room she should use. Why? Because everyone knows her biological sex. (Well, not really, but they are going to presume they do.) However, if a transgender girl who transitioned when she was in fourth grade joins your school in sixth grade—and she passes as a girl, choosing not to disclose that she is transgender—there isn't likely to be conversation or kerfuffle over her using the girls' restroom or locker room.

In short, we care about biological sex but judge based on gender expression. Yet neither of these is the category that matters. Who should use a girls' restroom? Anyone who is a girl, or anyone for whom it is the most comfortable option.[8] Who decides who's a girl? That person. An individual's identity is for that person to decide and for the community to support. If that sounds like a radical statement, then this is a good place to pause and do some thinking about why (as an individual or as a task force or focus group).

Truthfully, most of us are trained to accept individual identities being dictated by the state, a process known as interpellation. There is a lengthy and problematic history of governments across the globe imposing identities on groups of people and then deploying those identities for social control, genocide, and the consolidation of power among a small, elite group (whose identity is also closely controlled). So many of these disputed identities—whether based on race, religion, nationality, or ethnicity—are socially constructed. Who is White, for instance? That depends on where and when you are asking. There was a time in American history when neither Irish nor Italian individuals were thought to be White. So, who gets to determine who is White? Only the people who are within that privileged group, whose Whiteness and power are backed up by the state in turn.

---

8   This is less than ideal on several counts but does at least accommodate GNC students. I would say a better answer is: "Anyone who uses that space appropriately." In an ideal world, there would be an all-gender option (or none of the bathrooms would be gendered), to decenter the gender binary altogether. But I recognize that these stances are a little too radical for most schools to adopt.

When we don't allow the individual to determine their identity, then we're handing that power over to the group that already has the most power, the group that has a vested interest in preserving the boundaries of identity in a way that insulates their privilege.[9] In writing bathroom bills, the lawmakers (usually straight, White, cisgender, Christian men) are defining gender in a way that essentially writes transgender people out of existence. By linking gender to birth sex, cisgender lawmakers are denying that transgender women are women; they are legally defining them as men and further suggesting that their desire to use women's bathrooms makes them predators.

As we've seen, this binary thinking, while focused on oppressing trans people, also extends to harm those who are not trans or GNC by re-entrenching rigid, reductive understandings of both gender and sex. For instance, Kansas's bathroom bill, described in its body text as "the women's bill of rights," stipulates that a female "is an individual whose biological reproductive system is developed to produce ova."[1] This language at once confuses and conflates gender identity (woman) with sex (female); implies that trans men should use women's restrooms even though this makes no social sense; and defines biological sex in a way that excludes both trans women and cis women whose reproductive systems do not produce ova.

Defining gender in this way serves the interests of those in power. It supports the patriarchal structure by keeping cis men in the dominant position of protector (though also, ironically, men are simultaneously cast as the dangerous predator) and women in the subservient posi-

---

9 This is a much larger topic than is relevant to discuss fully in this chapter or, indeed, in this book. But it is a topic that schools interested in inclusion, individuality, and self-determination should explore. It also quickly leads to a question that I frequently field while working with schools on transgender identity: Almost inevitably, someone will ask me to explain why someone can be transgender but not transracial. That is, why can someone raised as a boy understand themself to be a girl and then transition and live in that gender authentically, but someone who is raised as White and understands themself to be Black not transition and live in that race authentically?

This is a complex topic—lots has been written on it—and digging into it is a great way to explore the differences between the social construction of race and the social constructions of gender. For the purposes of this book, my short(ish) answer is that race is 100% a social construction, as is gender expression. But gender identity is not. Gender identity has a biological (psychological, innate) basis. That makes the two situations here very different. But I do think that race and gender are comparable in the sense that we should not put schools (or other institutions) in the position of telling people who they are.

tion of potential victim, weak and in need of (manly) protection. The defining characteristic of the "victim," then, becomes the ability to bear children—even though that ability is not guaranteed for any woman, and certainly doesn't define womanhood for many. Further, the ability to become pregnant is not synonymous with the ability to be sexually assaulted, which, as discussed, is what many of these bills claim to prevent by dividing spaces by biological sex rather than by gender identity.

If your school is worried about sexual predation in your restrooms, with good reason and not because of imagined situations, then you have much more fundamental work in front of you than gender inclusion. But for most schools, this is not the actual concern. The actual concern is "who gets to use the girls' restroom?" and, behind that, "who gets to say who is a girl?" Schools should not be the arbiter of "who" anyone is—that is a matter for the individual to determine. Instead, schools should position themselves (as they have long been comfortable doing) as arbiters of behavior: "how" instead of "who."

The real issue isn't *who* uses a given restroom; the real issue is *how* they use it.[10] Schools should not be in the business of policing identity. A person shouldn't be "wrong" or not belong because of who they are—but they very well can be "wrong" because of how they behave.

I've worked with several schools that have developed a code of conduct or a set of behavior-based guidelines around bathroom and locker room usage. Establishing such guidelines has helped these schools not only move toward gender inclusivity but also to establish anti-bullying expectations.[11] At one school, I got the chance to work with the student council and a group of sports team captains to talk about bathroom and locker room culture. They were quick to articulate some clear and basic expectations: Clean up after yourself. Don't use your phone in the bathroom or locker room.[12] Avoid using violent, vulgar, and rude lan-

---

10 Of course, schools can consider rules for bathroom use that are not applicable to students. For instance, if there is an adult in a school building (perhaps an outside contractor), there could reasonably be rules about which restroom he can use since he is not a school employee, and so on.

11 Articulating expected conduct works especially well, I've seen, when combined with upstander training, which helps students (and faculty) learn when and how to speak up to prevent bullying, discrimination, and other harmful behaviors.

12 This guideline brought about interesting comments. Some students said they liked to text (etc.) while using the facilities. But many students felt that phones could so easily be used to take photos or record audio and video in a way that could be threatening or invasive and

guage. Respect others' privacy. These seemed to cover the basics, and the students agreed that as campus leaders they could enforce this sort of behavior. The school put together signs that could be posted inside each restroom and locker room stating these expectations clearly.

Why is it worth belaboring this point? Don't we all know how we should and should not behave in bathrooms and locker rooms? The point of putting this framework into place was to lay the foundation for a conversation about transgender and GNC people using those facilities. And to make sure that we were talking not about *who* should be in these spaces but about *how* anyone ought to behave in a shared space. By making the behavior, the how, the focus of the conversation, it once again centers this work on everyone in the school and on its core values. Reworking locker rooms and restrooms becomes not about accommodating one or two people, but about a reaffirmation of what good citizenship and community looks like at a school.

Once the group had established an agreed-upon set of behavior guidelines, we walked through a few potential situations:

A transgender boy, who has recently transitioned, goes into a boys' restroom and uses a stall. When he comes out to use the sink, another boy tells the transgender student that *she* should be in the girls' room and if *she* doesn't leave, *she'll* regret it.

A GNC student goes into the girls' locker room to change for swim practice. They use a stall to change, and when they come out in their swimsuit, two girls have their phones up, recording the GNC student. The two girls tell the student that they want proof to show their families what's going on in the girls' locker room.

Confrontations like these are all too common. They happen with students and adults. Often, bystanders can feel paralyzed, unsure of what they should say and how they should handle the situation because of

that the convenience of checking social media feeds wasn't worth that risk. These are crucial discussions to have with students so that they can start to examine and interrogate their own (and their peers') behavior and form collective agreements.

their own uncertainty around gender identity and belonging. A student might not be absolutely certain that a transgender boy does belong in the boys' restroom. Or that student might worry about being marginalized themselves if they stand up for a transgender kid. The student may not know what to say—how readily does "a transgender student has just as much right to use this facility because their gender identity is self-determined" come to mind?

If schools can make it clear through signage, training, and conversation that what's at issue is *behavior* and not identity, it is much easier for students to handle situations like these. In the above scenarios, the problem is the rude language and the threat and the use of a phone to record another student without their permission. These behaviors would be wrongly directed at any student, and focusing the conversation about facilities on such behavior allows the space to be inclusive and community-oriented and keeps the school from policing identity.

Of course, this does mean policing *behavior*, and schools should be in the position of doing this already. In the course of reviewing responses to gender-based harassment and bullying, schools can also review how they tend to respond to other types of inappropriate behavior. Many schools hand out consequences: detention, suspension, probation, and so on. Wherever possible, I encourage schools to think about discipline in a more full-system, holistic sense, to focus on students' social and personal development as opposed to a punitive system of cause and effect. Simply meting out a punishment is unlikely to help a student reexamine their actions and the prejudices behind them; education is the first step toward creating sustainable change (whether we're talking about individual behavior or institutional policy).

When gender-based harassment occurs, don't let the efforts at education stop. Just as students need training on how to intervene to prevent bullying, students need a justice process that holds that accountable for their own actions, one that teaches them *why* what they did was wrong and gives them a chance to reflect and grow. There are a wide variety of options that have been adopted by schools, many of them following a model of transformative justice, meaning that the perpetrator is not separated from the school community so much as taught how to live in community.[13]

Transformative justice offers a process where both students—the aggressor and the transgressed party—can feel supported and less alienated. One method of manifesting transformative justice when resolving conflict is the use of restorative practices. According to the International Institute for Restorative Practices, restorative practices are designed to "proactively [improve] climate and culture" and to "[provide] responses to wrongdoing that focus on repairing harm" as opposed to punishment."' Such processes, which can include circles as well as one-on-one conversations, help repair or, more likely, establish a sense of trust both between students and between students and their school's faculty, administration, and general culture. They are relationally based and consider the well-being of the entire community as opposed to only the individuals directly involved.

When justice and trust-building are at the center of a school's response to behavioral issues, two things happen: a.) both parties in the conflict at hand are less likely to feel alienated, and b.) that interpersonal repair can radiate out to the institutional and systemic structures surrounding the individual students. Transformative justice practices and the work of gender inclusion, along with other forms of identity-based social justice, are natural complements.[14]

BEYOND SINGLE-GENDER FACILITIES

Thus far, I've been presenting solutions for single-gender designated spaces. These are modest modifications to existing boys' and girls' restrooms or locker rooms: clear signage on the outside that establishes what the space is and the inside that spells out how the space is to be

13 As with several other topics that I've touched on, the full treatment of such a transformative justice system is beyond the scope of this book. That said, it doesn't make much sense to build a model of gender inclusion and then have a discipline system that isn't modeled on inclusion. Response to inappropriate behavior needs to be as much a part of the conversation as what constitutes inappropriate behavior. Schools shouldn't think of transformative justice as "light" or going easy on those who have broken the rules. Transformative justice is a lot more work, but it is an educational model and not just a punitive response.

14 More information can be found at the websites of the Just Schools Project, the Transformative Justice in Education Center at UC Davis, and the International Institute for Restorative Practices.

used—and what to do if there is a problem with the usage of that space.[15] Given that this is a book meant to guide schools on being gender-inclusive, one would be right to wonder why all the advice in this chapter has taken for granted that single-gender restrooms are indeed the way to go.

I'll be blunt in answering that challenge: single-gender restrooms are not the ideal. They are, however, the current reality. If there is a school out there where money is no object and there is ample time and legal license to fully renovate facilities, then much better options come into play. I'll indulge for a little while on what these all-gender, fully inclusive options would look like, recognizing that for many schools, these ideas are out of reach. That doesn't mean they aren't worth imagining and reaching for, though.

There are some schools that have simply removed gender designation from restrooms and instead hung signs that say "All Genders Welcome." Schools can do this if the state plumbing code permits it.[16] It can be done if the school culture will tolerate the shift. For some, this would be a radical move that would take a lot of education and conversation to persuade faculty, students, and parents/guardians. Further, most states don't have codes that would permit this—most schools have boys' restrooms with urinals (which presents a problem with making them all-gender, because most urinals don't have adequate privacy barriers). For these reasons, removing gender designation isn't a strategy I would recommend for most schools, though in some utopian version of the world, it would work just fine.

Likewise, I have mentioned in the preceding sections the limitations and hazards of providing separate, single-user restrooms. In some schools, however, this is the best and only alternative for transgender and GNC students. In this current political moment, the step of offering an alternative to the single-gender restrooms can feel like a bold

15 Signage might say: "Girls' Locker Room. For use by any student who identifies as a girl or who is most comfortable using a space designated for girls. Anyone using this locker room must refrain from harassing or threatening language or behavior, should not use a video or audio recording device, and must clean up after themselves." There should be numbers to call to report problematic behavior as well as indications of what other facilities are available: boys' locker room or an all-gender locker room or private changing space.

16 In some states, the code requires a certain number of commodes per gender (based on occupancy levels) before any "gender neutral" commodes can be installed. A town zoning inspector can help you to learn what your town or state requires.

move for some schools—even by just offering the use of the nurse's or office toilet. I'm disheartened to find that, only a few years after writing the first edition of this handbook, I have found myself giving this advice to schools: let your transgender student have a private restroom. Lately, the publicity and backlash that come with trying to make changes have proven to be overwhelming for transgender students and their families in some areas. Making the larger, bolder move to gender-inclusive restrooms isn't just difficult, it is dangerous.

That said, for schools that can entertain major renovations and shifts in space usage, better models can be found in some gymnasiums in Europe and in some restaurant restrooms. For bathrooms, an all-gender space looks like doing away with a room that is gender designated. Instead, within that same space there's a hallway, and on one side of the hall is a series of toilet stalls with full-length walls and doors (i.e., water closets). These are single occupancy and can be used by anyone. On the other side of the hall, a row of sinks. This model provides everyone with privacy in the toilet stall but removes the need to create a separate space for girls and another for boys. Everyone uses the same facility. Some newly renovated high occupancy restaurants have adopted this model. In addition to the gender innovation, it is a much more efficient way to use space and move people through the restroom facilities.

A similar model works for locker rooms. On one side of a hallway, there are cabana-style shower stalls. A user would step inside, lock the door behind them, disrobe, shower, and then dress. The lockers would be arrayed on the other side of the hall. Instead of having communal changing spaces, there are cabana-style changing stalls, or the shower stalls could also be used to change in. Teams can gather in team rooms, which don't have to be located anywhere near the lockers or the showers, to discuss strategy, learn new plays, and so on. Team rooms could be designed to be much more like classrooms—with the expectation that everyone is fully clothed—while also providing a space for team-bonding and camaraderie.

These are substantial changes that would make a profound shift toward gender inclusion by denying the gender binary a role in the way the space is set up. Right now, when athletes enter a gym, they are quickly funneled into separate spaces—boys in one and girls in another. By getting rid of locker rooms, there are more public and shared spaces for conversation and interaction, which suggests and encourages interaction and parity between all athletes.[17] These renovations are also very expensive and time-consuming and therefore unrealistic for many schools. But I still encourage schools to look at these models, to go online and study some of the photos, blueprints, and plans that describe restrooms and locker rooms like these more fully. The changes to these spaces wouldn't just promote gender inclusion; they would affect how students share space, how athletes interact with their teammates and coaches, and generally provide more safety and comfort for a wide range of students and faculty.

So perhaps this caliber of modification isn't possible for your school . . . right now. But keep it on the long-term list. Ask when the gymnasium and locker rooms are going to be renovated or when the dressing rooms of the auditorium are due for an upgrade. Make sure that any time there's work being done to change facilities, the architect and planners are aware that gender inclusion is a priority. If they don't know what's possible or desirable, they will continue to build the same single-gender facilities that have been present in schools for generations.

In the meantime, schools must make use of the restrooms and locker rooms that they have. They have to work within the confines of their state's plumbing code. They need to be patient and work to change school culture and educate faculty, parents, guardians, and students so that any adjustment to signage and policy goes smoothly and doesn't create so much backlash that the movement toward gender inclusion is shut down entirely. Again, part of making these spaces safer and more functional has nothing to do with gender-related signage and policy. It has to do with educating the students, particularly student leaders, about how to combat bullying and harassment and hold peers accountable to the agreed-upon guidelines for the space.

---

17 Though not the central concern here, it is worth mentioning that at many schools, the locker room (and other athletic facilities) are not "separate but equal." Usually, the girls' locker room is viewed as smaller, worse equipped, more inconvenient, etc. (This is often a function of schools designed for a single gender and renovated to accommodate a second.) Here, with all athletes sharing more of the same facilities, equality is more likely.

Start small. Even minor adjustments can make a difference. I worked with one public high school where a GNC student had come out and been told that they could use only the restrooms that were beside the principal's office. They were two single-occupancy restrooms intended to be used by families and guests and not on a hallway frequented by students. When I met with the student, they told me how difficult it was to have to literally run from their class to this one restroom and then back to class. It was out of the way, made them late, and separated them from their friends. We worked together along with a small group of parents/guardians and teachers to consider all the options and compiled a wish list—a set of ranked options for changing signage and usage policy that the student then showed to the principal.

None of them were approved. So, we accepted that this student would use only these two restrooms by the principal's office and made one last request—expecting it, too, would be shot down. Could the sign outside only these restrooms be changed? Again, we gave a ranked list of options. First, would they put the transgender symbol on the sign? Second, would they say, "All Gender"? If not, could they say, "Gender Inclusive"?

The principal agreed to none of these options but instead proposed a sign that would read: "All genders are welcome to use this restroom." On the one hand, this saga could be understood as a substantial defeat: the student was still being marginalized and inconvenienced; the administration was less than willing to make changes. I preferred to see some small victory. Somewhere, in at least one place in that school, there was a sign that suggested, ever so slightly, that there were more genders out there than just two.

NEXT STEPS

REFLECT

1.Spend some time remembering your own middle and high school times in locker rooms and bathrooms. Really go back and dig into those memories, jotting down recollections. Were you ever uncomfortable? Why? Did you perceive anyone else's discomfort? How did those spaces feel to you and your friend group? Could you perceive that there were other groups that experienced them differently?

RESEARCH

1.Familiarize yourself with your local plumbing code and any relevant local- or state-level legislation pertaining to restrooms and similar facilities.

ACT

1. Tour bathrooms at school—take stock of where they are and what number/type of commodes they have. Take a look at the locker rooms, too.

2. Hold focus groups for students, faculty, and coaches to hear how they feel about using bathrooms and locker rooms. An anonymous feedback form might be helpful as well. Try to get a sense of what is actually happening in these spaces, how safe and comfortable people feel, and what people would ideally like to happen in these spaces.

3. If there are openly transgender and GNC students or alumni at your school, invite their input on what facilities usage feels like and what options they would like to see.

4. Modify signage and train community about these modifications.

5. Propose changes to rules around nudity in locker rooms and educate the community about these standards.

NOTES

a. Sophie Perry, "Kansas' new anti-trans bill is so extreme some cis women could be banned from toilets," *PinkNews*, April 28, 2023, https://www.thepinknews.com/2023/04/28/kansas-trans-lgbtq-bathroom-bill-ban/.

b. Kevin Draper, "Finally, the N.B.A. Comes to Charlotte," *The New York Times*, February 15, 2019, https://www.nytimes.com/2019/02/15/sports/nba-charlotte-bathroom-bill.html.

c. Beatriz Pagliarini Bagagli, Tyara Veriato Chaves, and Mónica G. Zoppi Fontana, "Trans Women and Public Restrooms: The Legal Discourse and Its Violence," *Frontiers in Sociology* 6 (March 31, 2021), https://www.ncbi.nlm.nih.gov/pmc/articles/PMC8022685/.

d. Amira Hasenbush, Andrew R. Flores, and Jody L. Herman, "Gender Identity Nondiscrimination Laws in Public Accommodations: a Review of Evidence Regarding Safety and Privacy in Public Restrooms, Locker Rooms, and Changing Rooms," *Sexuality Research and Social Policy* 16 (July 23, 2018): 70–83, https://doi.org/10.1007/s13178-018-0335-z.

e. Sandy E. James et al., *The Report of the 2015 U.S. Transgender Survey* (Washington, DC: National Center for Transgender Equality, December 2016), https://transequality.org/sites/default/ files/docs/usts/USTS-Full-Report-Dec17.pdf.

f. Murchison et al., "School Restroom and Locker Room Restrictions," https://doi.org/10.1542/peds.2018-2902.

g. Murchison et al., "School Restroom and Locker Room Restrictions," https://doi.org/10.1542/peds.2018-2902.

h. Kathleen C. Basile, Sharon G. Smith, Marcie-jo Kresnow, Srijana Khatiwada, and Ruth Leemis, *The National Intimate Partner and Sexual Violence Survey: 2016/2017 Report on Sexual Violence* (Atlanta: National Center for Injury Prevention and Control, Centers for Disease Control and Prevention, June 2022), https://www.cdc.gov/violenceprevention/pdf/nisvs/nisvsReportonSexualViolence.pdf.

i. "The Criminal Justice System: Statistics," *RAINN*, accessed February 6,

2024, https://www.rainn.org/statistics/criminal-justice-system.

j. The Trevor Project, "National Survey on LGBTQ Youth Mental Health," https://www.thetrevorproject.org/survey-2021/?section=Introduction.

k. Melissa Seldin and Christina Yanez, *Student Reports of Bullying: Results From the2017 School Crime Supplement to the National Crime Victimization Survey* (Washington, DC: NCES, Institute of Education Sciences, U.S. Department of Education, July 2019), https://nces.ed.gov/pubs2019/2019054.pdf.

l. Kansas Women's Bill of Rights, S.B. 180, Kan. State Leg. (2023).
m. "Restorative Practices in Schools," *International Institute for Restorative Practices*, accessed February 8, 2024, https://www.iirp.edu/resources/restorative-practices-in-schools-k-12-education.

CHAPTER SEVEN:

AND WHAT ABOUT SPORTS TEAMS?

When I was in high school, I was a three-season athlete: soccer, ice hockey, and lacrosse. I had played soccer in elementary and middle school but had never played the other two sports before going off to boarding school in ninth grade. I was a soccer goalie (mostly by default; I was the only player willing to take the position), and for that reason I was asked to step into the net for JV girls' ice hockey the winter of my ninth-grade year. I had grown up skating on frozen lakes and ponds in Maine and I utterly fell in love with ice hockey.

By the time the season was over, the girls on my team were wondering whether I would join them for lacrosse. This wasn't a sport that I was at all familiar with, but I borrowed a stick from a friend and tried a game of catch. I wasn't that bad. But then I found out that in girls' lacrosse, like field hockey, the players wear skirts—kilts, I suppose, is the technical term, but to me they were skirts. No way. I was in ninth grade and had barely come out to myself as a lesbian; I'd only shared that questioning with a couple of close friends. It would be a few more years before I would embrace the word transgender and acknowledge what I had known my whole life: I was a boy, not a girl. That spring, I felt something so deep, so visceral: I would not wear a skirt.

It's kind of silly, right? It's just a skirt and only for games. I played on girls' sports teams and lived in a girls' dorm and fully occupied my life as a girl at the time—so, why balk at a lacrosse skirt? I can't explain it, except to say that this decision was one of the few places where I felt I could say no to something girly, and so I did, showing up for track tryouts instead. My lacrosse-playing friends, who admired how far I could throw the ball with only a couple of days of practice, quickly regrouped and said that I could be the goalie—the goalie didn't wear a skirt. I signed up and soon learned to love the sport. That visceral feeling never changed, though. On game day, I'd pull on the old, gray polyester football pants that were my goalie uniform, my teammates would fix their kilts . . . and I would shudder, feeling that I had narrowly escaped that terrible fate.

When I came out as transgender to the dean of students the summer between my junior and senior year of high school, one of the questions he asked me was whether I still wanted to play on my girls' sports teams. I did, emphatically. Sports were a huge part of my social life—my teammates were among my closest friends—and how I stayed mentally and physically healthy at school. I also knew that if I tried out for the boys' ice hockey or lacrosse teams, even though I had been a strong girl and a varsity starter, I wouldn't stand a chance of making even the boys' JV back-up line. If by some miracle, or out of pity, they did take me on the team, I knew I wouldn't belong. On my girls' team, I had status and standing. I held a position of influence as a four-year player. They would listen when I told them I was a boy, that I wanted them to use he/him/his as pronouns. If anyone gave me a hard time, I knew that I had friends on the team who would serve as allies and advocates. So, I stayed on my girls' teams my senior year.

It proved to be a good decision, though not without its problems. I loved my coaches and teammates. We worked hard in practice. By dint of being the goalie, often the only goalie, on the teams, I had already been different than everyone else. I wore different uniforms and padding and did different drills. I stood alone at one end of the field or rink. I had a unique perspective on the game, and a job like no one else. In short, it was the perfect place to be a transgender person: I was already on the margin and already expected to be out of the norm.

In both hockey and lacrosse, I wore a helmet, which meant that opposing teams couldn't get a clear look at me during the game. But after the game had concluded, both teams would line up and shake hands (or slap gloves, more accurately) and say "thank you" and "good game" to each other. I would always take off my helmet (it seemed more polite, and I was sweaty). In about half the lacrosse and hockey games that season, I'd then hear one of the other team's players or the opposing coach say, "Hey, they've got a boy on their team. That's not fair." It was usually said louder if my team had won the game.

On a few occasions, the other coach even called the referee over to make inquiries. My hockey and lacrosse coaches had an early crash course in transgender identity. I always liked to hear them say the lines they had rehearsed with me: "Yes, our goalie is a boy. That's Alex. He played for us for three years as a girl and now he's a boy. He's transgender."

Usually, that was sufficient to give the other coach or referee the general idea of what was going on—recall that "transgender" was a pretty new term in 1995. Sometimes they pressed a bit harder, and my coach would struggle through a few more details: "No surgery. No hormones. You know." It wasn't perfect and their words were sometimes awkward, but they were trying. I knew they had my back.

My favorite moment that captures the effort they put in to support me came when, in the middle of lacrosse season, we had our team picture taken. My coach Kathy Nekton joined the faculty of Phillips Exeter right when the school had gone co-ed in the early 1970s. She had been a staunch advocate for girls' sports for many years. As we all lined up on the benches, Coach Nekton called out, "All right girls! Look pretty!" She paused and added, "Except for Alex. You look handsome!"

Everyone laughed, but I could have wept with appreciation for the effort she made to help me belong on a girls' team and still be recognized as a boy.

When it came time to decide about college, sports became a tougher topic. A few coaches reached out to me about playing hockey or lacrosse for their teams. I puzzled over this for quite a while. I was looking forward to college as a place to start anew, a place where I would be surrounded by people who hadn't known me as a girl, a place where I could try living as "just" a boy. I thought that if I joined a girls' team, I would in some way be admitting that I wasn't "really" a boy—or, at the very least, I would be very out as transgender. So, I decided not to play varsity sports in college. Instead, I joined a "co-ed"[1] ice hockey club team. I lifted weights and ran on my own. I participated in tae kwon

---

1 This was the term at the time. It's not an inclusive term, as it implies a gender binary.

do classes. I missed sports tremendously.[2]

It wasn't until I started taking testosterone in my mid-twenties that I could fully engage in sports again. After a year or so on testosterone, I started running competitively and doing triathlons. I raced against cisgender men and often placed or won my age division. It was intensely satisfying to be competitive again and additionally satisfying, I admit, to be faster than biological males. I had gone from being, at age seventeen, a very strong, fit, athletic young woman to being—in an instant—a short, small, weak boy. Athletics had been a major part of my identity as a kid and adolescent. I was so grateful that testosterone had given me the chance to reconnect with that part of who I was (though I still wouldn't be making any men's ice hockey teams).

Since then, I've had the chance to coach middle and high school cross-country teams as well as high school ice hockey teams. All of this is to say that I truly value sports and understand the importance of athletics in the school experience. I believe it is crucial to get as many students as possible involved in physical activity, and if that physical activity includes membership in a team, all the better. At the same time, I recognize that sports, particularly at the high school and college level, are often very gendered spaces.

This has both benefits and drawbacks. I came of age through girls' sports programs, and I fully believe that girls need athletic spaces where they compete against each other. The physical and biological reality is that if all spaces on all sports teams went to the strongest and fastest (etc.) players, there would be far fewer girls on high school teams. Yet in the same breath, I would claim that there is room on girls' teams for transgender and gender non-conforming (GNC) athletes, and that there is room in a high school sports program for all-gender teams.

It isn't an easy puzzle to solve. Just a few years ago, court cases

2 As it happened, around Thanksgiving of my senior year, both goalies on the women's varsity ice hockey team went out with significant injuries. The coach asked if I would step in and practice with the team, and I did. They gave me a private space to change in, and from Thanksgiving through New Year's, I was on the team. It was amazing; I hadn't realized how much I missed that team dynamic. But it also made me realize I had made the right decision. The team—as is true of many single-gender spaces and particularly true of women's sports teams, where many women sadly feel they need to push against the "jock" stereotype by being hyper-feminine or even homophobic (adamantly denying that they are lesbians)—was a tough place to be a transgender person. A lot of the language and behavior was emphatically feminine, and I felt very much on the outside.

started popping up and the governing bodies of sports began trying to fairly arbitrate who could compete on which teams.[3] More recently, blanket bans—entire states forbidding any transgender girl from competing on any girls' sports team—have been passed in many states, including Arkansas (S.B. 354) and Texas (S.B. 15), and in some cases defeated, as with New Hampshire's H.B. 1251 (discussed later in this chapter).[4] The Biden administration has weighed in, elevating the topic to the national level, and more court cases and legislative rulings can be expected to follow. The rhetoric surrounding such pushes often imagines an epidemic of trans girls and women in particular rushing girls' and women's sports leagues so that they can secure unearned personal glory, not unlike the phantom would-be trans attackers waiting for the government's permission to enter the women's restroom.

For public schools in many states, and in athletic leagues where public and private schools compete, the reality is that it is now impossible for schools to allow transgender girls to compete on their teams. I do believe that this moment shall pass and encourage schools to look for ways to support transgender and GNC athletes in their schools, even when intramural sports aren't an option. This chapter will try to provide suggestions for ways to work in the atmosphere of these bans, as well as for solutions in places where there isn't a ban.

PREVAILING ATTITUDES TOWARD GENDER IN SPORTS

As is the case with restrooms and locker rooms, including transgender students on sports teams tends to provoke a knee-jerk response, one that tends to be directed at transgender girls specifically. While, as noted, many of the trans youth sports ban bills specifically restrict the rights of trans girls and young women, very few transgender boys or young men

---

3 See the 2021 *New Yorker* article by Masha Gessen for a very good summary of the situation. (See note *a*.) Laws that exclude trans girls from participation in sports programs are currently being considered in a number of state legislatures; there is no doubt that this area of law and practice will change considerably in the next few years.

4 The landscape of this kind of legislation is, as noted, ever changing. Organizations such as the Movement Advancement Project (MAP) make it easy to stay up to date on various laws impacting LGBTQ+ equality by state. (See note *b*.)

have been prevented from trying out or playing for male teams.[5] Mack Beggs is one notable exception—the transgender boy who wrestled in Texas and was not allowed to compete in the boys' tournament.[6] In fact, there is a reasonably long-standing practice of allowing cisgender girls to play on some boys' teams.[7] In many states, under Title IX rulings, girls can join football and baseball teams because those sports are not offered for girls. The reverse, however, is not true: boys cannot join field hockey or softball teams.

There's a lot going on in these rulings. Again, some of it is based in the very reasonable desire to preserve a terrain for girls and young women to compete on. Pioneers in women's sports had to fight very hard to win the right to have teams at all, and many women athletes and coaches are fiercely protective of what they have gained. The typical argument against allowing a transgender girl, or a GNC student whose biological sex is male, to join a girls' team is that they will have an unfair competitive edge. For instance, the Biden administration's proposed addendum to Title IX, while prohibiting any blanket bans against trans student-athletes, still allows for more discrete restrictions around gender-based participation if those restrictions are argued to serve "fairness of competition."[f] If a male body has gone through puberty, or even only part of puberty, that body is likely to have anatomical advantages in musculature over female bodies. Concerns are raised that if, for instance, a transgender girl were allowed to join a girls' basketball team, she'd be more likely to injure other players due to her strength advantage over her peers.

A similar line of argument is that transgender girls who join girls' sports teams are more likely to be starting players, they are likely to win races, or they will dominate the field. In short, the fear is they will be better athletes and take spaces that have been designated for "real"

5 See *Sports Illustrated*'s 2022 story about the specific implications of these laws for transmasculine people and how the logic for the bans is simultaneously disingenuous, sexist, and transmisogynistic (note *c*).

6 Mack Beggs' case was covered extensively. A good summary of Beggs' situation can be found in the 2018 *Washington Post* article by Cindy Boren (note *d*).

7 Examples abound, often with national media coverage. Leilani Armenta made headlines in 2023, for example, right as transgender students as were being banned from "opposite" gender teams. (See note *e*.)

girls—an argument founded on the highly problematic premise that transgender girls *aren't* "real" girls. Finally, people will argue that if a boy is allowed to transition and join a girls' team, then lots of boys—frustrated, perhaps, at being cut from the varsity team—will simply join the girls' team, and quickly, girls' athletics will be overrun.

I hear this last argument quite often, and I've been hearing it for a long time. Perhaps its most famous historic instance comes with Renée Richards. Richards is a transgender woman who had sexual reassignment surgery in the 1970s, when she was in her forties. Richards had played tennis (among other sports) in high school and college (on men's teams) but had been working as an ophthalmologist for many years before she transitioned. However, after sexual reassignment surgery and years of hormone therapy, Richards took up tennis again, playing in women's tournaments and eventually playing professionally in the 1976 US Open. Richards' tennis career was contested every step of the way. The United States Tennis Association ultimately demanded that she submit to a test to determine her chromosomal makeup and a court battle ensued. In newspapers and sports magazines, pundits claimed that Richards' eventual victory in court spelled the end for women's tennis. Men, they said, would soon flock to compete in all the women's tennis tournaments.

Needless to say (in case you haven't been paying attention to women's professional tennis), that didn't happen. It didn't happen for several reasons. First, gender reassignment is not a decision that one makes lightly or quickly. Second, for a man to pretend to be a woman to compete in tennis would be to risk tremendous social stigma. Most men wouldn't want to "embarrass" themselves in such a way. This connects to the third point, the fact that there isn't sufficient incentive for men to want to enter women's sports. Compared to men's leagues, there sadly isn't that much money or prestige there. Tennis may be one of the few sports where there's even close to parity in compensation for women and men athletes.[8]

---

8 Grand Slam prizes are the same for men and women, but that's not to say that everything's equal all the time. Peter Bodo's September 2018 article for espn.com details how the pay gap in Grand Slam tennis changed. (See note *g*.) However, writing for NYU's student newspaper in September 2019, Danial Hashemi delineates how women in professional tennis are still paid less. (See note *h*.)

I think it is important to consider Renée Richards's case. Too often, transgender people can feel like an invention. When a transgender or GNC student comes out, schools and other institutions feel like they are suddenly confronting these ideas for the first time, with no sense of how things will or could go—when, in fact, there is a rich history of transgender people. Much can be learned from looking at the legal and medical treatment of these individuals.[9] As was discussed in Chapter One, people who make these types of exclusionary arguments conflate sex and gender and fail to understand the difference between identity and anatomy. They reserve the right to be the ones who determine identity or to determine what elements will be used to decide identity.[10] So, what's the solution to how to divest from such transphobic understandings of gender and athletics and include transgender students in sports?

The answer is, there are lots of them. I'll approach the solutions from the higher levels down, starting with the Olympics, then college, and then on to high school and below. I do this not because I think readers of this book will need to prepare for Olympic qualifiers but to give a full sense of the range of responses to transgender and GNC athletes, including among the global athletic elite. From there we can consider the fairness and practicality of these existing policies for educators at the high school or middle school level.[11]

---

9 All this said, Renée Richards has, in recent years, taken a stand against transgender women being allowed to play in professional women's sports (note *i*). The questions of competitive advantage have not been fully explored medically or socially. Though I am not in the business of predicting the future, I do think it is likely that the coming years will see some substantial shifts in sports' governing bodies around inclusion of transgender women. As with all change, I expect there to be both gains and retreats.

10 And, just as gender inclusion is beneficial for everyone, a culture of skepticism toward people's gender identities harms everyone, cisgender people included. In February 2024, Natalie Cline, a member of the Utah State Board of Education, was pressured to resign after she made a since-deleted Facebook post implying that a player on a Salt Lake City high school girls' basketball team was transgender. While this obviously shouldn't have been a problem regardless, the student in question was cisgender. Cline's post sparked a wave of cyberbullying toward the student. In the face of criticism, Cline merely replied that she'd removed the post once she'd been informed of the student's identity (information to which she was never entitled) and "defended her intent [by] saying that the girl 'does have a larger build, like her parents'"—essentially using size-based discrimination to prop up her attack on a minor's gender and claiming a thin or small build as a requisite of "real" girlhood. Again: cissexist standards of gender stand to harm and exclude people of all identities and bodies. (See note *j*.)

11 I don't think much needs to be stated about specific policy prior to middle school (or perhaps even high school). Until children have gone through puberty, there is no biological need to separate students during sports practices. There is a long-standing social practice of doing so, but male and female bodies prior to puberty have negligible differences when it

The International Olympic Committee (IOC) has recently made a number of rulings around women's sports and transgender athletes.[12] Transgender athletes weren't allowed to compete in the Olympics until 2004. The first set of guidelines stated that transgender women athletes had to have completed sexual reassignment surgery, have legally changed their gender, and have been taking hormones for at least two years. In 2015, the rules were adjusted to state that transgender women athletes must have been living in their reassigned gender for four years and have a blood testosterone level below a certain level. More recently, in 2021, the IOC released a new framework for gender inclusion, which moved away from a blanket testosterone-based standard.[l] This document leaves the setting of standards of fairness up to each individual sport. So, while the overarching principles are much improved with regard to a holistic understanding of gender and humane treatment of athletes, in practice individual sports are still policing based on testosterone levels. There are no official restrictions on transgender men who wish to compete in the Olympics on men's teams.

There's a lot to be learned just from the shift in these regulations. Between 2004 and 2015, when the guidelines were substantially revised, the Olympic committee realized that many countries don't allow for legal changes of gender, surgery is prohibitively expensive, many transgender people don't want or have access to surgery, and different bodies respond in different ways to hormone therapy. Even today, in many countries, medical transition is financially impossible for most people. Worse, in many countries, medical (or social) transition is completely illegal. However, the reality is that even though the guidelines don't explicitly require surgery, many athletes will meet the hormone levels only if they undergo medical castration.

comes to athletic ability. (See note *k*.)

12   The IOC has also made rulings around intersex athletes and "female athletes with differences in sex development." The most prominent of these cases is that of Caster Semenya, a runner from South Africa who is hyperandrogynous, meaning she has naturally high levels of testosterone. (See note *m*.) The treatment of individuals with what are called Differences of Sexual Development (DSD), in sports and beyond, needs to be discussed. Semenya doesn't personally identify as intersex, but many others with DSD do. Like gay, lesbian, and bisexual students, intersex students face many of the same challenges that transgender and GNC students face, and many of the measures described in this book would be helpful in creating policies and facilities that would also be inclusive of intersex students. But the focus here is on transgender and GNC students.

On the collegiate level, the National Collegiate Athletic Association (NCAA) for many years had a policy that determined which athletes could compete on which teams based on sex assigned at birth and hormone levels. It worked differently for transgender men and transgender women: A transgender man, assigned female at birth and not taking testosterone, could compete on the women's team. That same transgender man could also choose to participate on the men's team. If that athlete begins taking testosterone, however, he was no longer eligible to compete on the women's team. A transgender woman was automatically eligible to play on a men's team. If she started hormone therapy (testosterone suppression), she was eligible for women's teams after a year of treatment, or she could continue to play on men's teams indefinitely. If she was not undergoing hormone therapy, then she could not play on a women's team.

Recently, however, the NCAA issued guidelines that closely mirror the IOC's new gender inclusion framework, which means things are shifting but aren't necessarily becoming more inclusive. As with the Olympics, it is unclear what individual sports at the collegiate level will determine to be the rules for fair play. However, historically, the NCAA has clearly been interested in testosterone usage/levels as a determiner for belonging. Essentially, they have designed a policy where the intent is for women's teams are being populated by those with low testosterone levels whereas men's teams can have any level of testosterone.

As with the Olympic guidelines, the NCAA's requirements for eligibility would be unreasonable for most high school age transgender girls. Additionally, the requirements for transgender boys are problematic in another way. Most transgender boys are smaller in stature than cisgender boys—not just in terms of height but in terms of shoulder width and so on. It is unlikely that transgender boys would qualify to compete on most men's teams.[13] It *is* likely that many transgender boys would look at the NCAA rules and, if they wished to continue competing in college, decide not to start taking testosterone so that they could continue to qualify for the women's team.

The decision to undergo hormone therapy is a deeply personal one

13 There are notable exceptions to this in collegiate, Olympic, and professional sports, particularly with individual sports and those with categories determined by weight class, such as wrestling and boxing.

and should entail a lot of thought, research, and discussion (with a medical professional as well as others). There are many good reasons and many bad reasons to begin or delay hormone therapy. It strikes me as problematic to have to weigh continued athletic competition (which may come with scholarship opportunities among other things) against medical reassignment. Many transgender and GNC individuals who choose to undergo hormone therapy report decreases in anxiety, depression, substance abuse, and self-loathing. It is hard to council a high school student to delay such life-changing treatment to continue to be able to play soccer—yet policies like the NCAA's stand to encourage just that.

Finally, when it comes to the high school level, policies and guidelines vary widely. On one end, there are states that require athletes to compete according to their sex assigned at birth.[14] On the other end are states (or leagues) that allow students to play on the team that best fits their identity. In the middle are those states that have specific policies around hormone therapy—these rules apply almost exclusively to transgender girls, providing a sort of "waiting period" (usually around one year) after starting hormone therapy before they can play for girls' teams.

The conversation has recently shifted to the national level with the House of Representatives approving a bill that would completely bar transgender women and girls from competing in sports designated for girls and women,[n] which the Biden administration's proposal, mentioned earlier, is meant to counter. Though this bill, H.R. 734, isn't likely to become law under the Biden administration, it is important for educators and students and families to take stock of how this argument is being shaped on the national political stage. In taking on the question of sports and gender, the conservative movement is centering the argument of biological essentialism: that the sex we are assigned at birth is what determines our identity and shapes the role we are to play in society. The dangers of this approach are significant and crucial to grapple with—and not just for transgender individuals.

Again, while the IOC's guidelines could not possibly be translated

---

14 Some of these states, such as Arkansas, make allowances for 1) any student who has sexual reassignment surgery and changes their birth certificate legally (highly unachievable even for those high school students who would want to do so), and 2) girls to join boys' sports when that sport is not available for their own gender (e.g., football and baseball).

directly to school settings, I still think there's analytical value in considering what they, as the gold standard of gender policy in global athletics, might mean for trans and GNC student athletes. As a school works on gender inclusion in athletics, many parents/guardians and administrators will suggest "just following what other organizations do," and coaches, league officials, and other state- or district-level actors might reasonably look to the IOC for reference while developing their local policies.

The current IOC guidelines are much more enlightened than the original guidelines, but they are still problematic. Unequivocally prioritizing biology over identity is problematic, and so is requiring medical transition. If these guidelines are very difficult for Olympic athletes to meet, they would be even more so for athletes at the high school and middle school level, who have less agency over their medical affairs and ability to be out and self-advocate than adult, professional athletes.

If you imagine applying the IOC's standards to high school athletics, it is fair to say that almost no transgender girls would be allowed to compete. Few transgender students in general can start taking hormones in high school. Assuming gender-affirming care for minors is even legal in the student's state, a prescription for hormones requires parental or guardian approval, a doctor's supervision, and, though not nearly as expensive as surgery, money. For a person born male to lower their blood testosterone level to a point where they'd be permitted to compete on a girls' team, they would need to have been taking estrogen for at least six months and up to two years before they aim to compete. That would mean the athlete would have had to have begun taking hormones in ninth grade to be eligible to play by their junior year, and it is unlikely for that to be possible (not to mention, few high school leagues have the means to check blood testosterone levels).[15] Certainly, only students with financial means and very supportive parents/guardians would stand a chance of meeting these guidelines.

MAKING THE MOST POSSIBLE CHANGE

15 It is more likely that students with supportive parents/guardians and doctors will be urged to go on puberty blockers; these drugs are useful in several ways, but they will not lower blood testosterone levels sufficiently for current Olympic standards, should those be what high schools apply.

To work on gender inclusion in athletics at your school, the first step is to figure out what your state's guidelines are and to determine who the governing bodies are for the sports your school competes in. Schools may compete in leagues that have different rules than those set by the school's state. This is particularly true of private schools, which generally have greater leeway as they aren't beholden to state rules in many aspects of their governance. In some states, municipal areas have set their own rules for transgender athletes—in California, for instance, there is a state policy as well as a separate Los Angeles School District set of guidelines. Each situation is unique. Start here and see what guidelines already exist at state level that your school should catch up to (in the event that the state you are in has inclusive practices)—or assess the work that you'll need to do with your state's or league's governing bodies.

In public schools, work to change policies concerning transgender athletes often involves the school board, the state legislature, or appeals to the justice system. The fight for inclusion is ongoing and fraught. For example, in Connecticut, the state laws are very clear and supportive of transgender athletes. They include a "safe schools" statement about name and pronoun usage and locker room access, as well as a commitment to allow transgender students to compete on teams that most align with their gender identity. But these laws have been challenged in court. The most recent set of lawsuits was spurred by the success of two transgender girls who ran for their high school track teams. Running for the girls' teams, these athletes won a number of races at the district and state level. A cisgender girl's family sued, claiming unfair athletic advantage for the transgender girls, and the case is, as of this moment, still being adjudicated.[o]

To give an example of just one transgender student's fight to be included in athletics, I offer the story of Sarah Huckman.[16] I choose her as an example because both of us are from New Hampshire and I have followed her story closely. In fact, I've had the chance to be on panels with her, testify in front of the legislature with her, and so on. Sharing Sarah's story gives one a thorough perspective on how hard this fight

---

16 Sarah recounted her and her family's activism in her speech at GLAD's 2018 Spirit of Justice Award Dinner (note *p*).

can be even with a very supportive family and even in a state that is a mix of liberal and conservative.[17]

Sarah came out and began living as a girl in middle school. At that time, she fought for the right to use the girls' restroom. With family support, she made her case to her school administration, the school board, and the superintendent and got a one-time (meaning one-student) exemption.[18] In middle school, Sarah wanted to run track and, under New Hampshire public school district policy, a superintendent has the right to permit athletic team participation by any student. Sarah was permitted to run on the girls' team with no further ado.

Things changed when Sarah entered high school. In New Hampshire, high school athletics are governed by the N.H. Interscholastic Athletic Association (NHIAA), and, in 2015, the NHIAA required transgender high school students to have gender reassignment surgery before competing on the team of their gender.[19] The Huckman family appealed to the state athletic association but were unsuccessful. They then reached out to the GLBTQ Legal Advocates & Defenders (GLAD), an LGBTQ+ legal aid association.

In the wake of enlisting a GLAD attorney, the Huckmans learned that the NHIAA would now allow individual schools to make decisions about which teams a transgender athlete would play on. This decision ultimately opened a path for Sarah to compete, but it did nothing for gender inclusion more broadly—a larger-scale expression of the "special accommodations" response discussed earlier in this book, where issues of gender are handled as if they affect only individual students instead of as holistic concerns. This story illustrates that even when a student and their family have the time, energy, resources, allies, *and* desire to fight, victories can still be partial.[20]

---

17 New Hampshire is a state whose politics are best categorized as independent and mixed. There are liberal enclaves and conservative enclaves, and legislative control flips between the two parties almost every session. This has provided both opportunities and challenges to getting legal protections for transgender people.

18 This was both a good and a frustrating outcome: good for Sarah, and a good precedent, but the individual exemption meant the next transgender student who wanted to use the boys' or girls' room would have to fight the fight all over again.

19 This is a paraphrase of what the policy stated. It is evident that the language here completely ignores the existence of non-binary athletes.

20 The GLAD attorney also felt that even the revised NHIAA policy violated student

In the years since that decision, Sarah has continued to fight for transgender rights,[21] advocating for the passage of a 2018 state legislative bill (ultimately successful) that explicitly bans discrimination against transgender individuals and speaking against a 2020 bill (ultimately defeated) that would have banned transgender girls from competing on girls' athletic teams.[q r 22]

This is all to say: the fight for gender inclusion in athletics can be very challenging, particularly at public schools. But the path to inclusion is clear. Given that most high school students (to say nothing of those in lower grades) will face large barriers to beginning hormone therapy or sexual reassignment surgery, if not being barred from them outright, it is unrealistic and unfair to set these as conditions for participation in sports. Allowing students to pursue athletic opportunities that align with that student's identity is a superior policy.

Here I'll pause because it is crucial not to be too restrictive in these guidelines. A transgender boy might prefer to play on the girls' team. If they are not taking testosterone, there is no reason, in terms of competitive advantage, to deny that person access to the girls' team—or to mandate that they must join the boys' team. Likewise, policies that are tightly worded around identity as a condition for membership (i.e., language that says a student may play on the team that "matches" their gender identity) leave GNC students out of the picture entirely—how is a non-binary student supposed to have an identity that aligns with a boys' or girls' team?

So, what's best? The most inclusive language a school can offer would permit any student to try out for any team that feels most comfortable. The most inclusive athletics program would have teams that are designated girls' teams, boys' teams, and all-gender teams. Examples

---

privacy because of some requirements to share confidential medical information.

21 If you'd like to learn more about Sarah Rose Huckman, she has been profiled by *Teen Vogue* (note *q*) and featured in the 2021 Hulu original documentary *Changing the Game.*

22 The language of that latter, transphobic bill, H.B. 1251, is interesting to look at: "This bill prohibits public schools from permitting a male student to participate in a student sport designated for females [. . .] If disputed, a student may prove that she is of the female sex by presenting a signed physician's statement which shall indicate the student's sex is based solely upon: (a) The student's internal and external reproductive anatomy; (b) The student's naturally occurring level of testosterone; and (c) An analysis of the student's chromosomes" (note *s*). That degree of required "proof" exceeds even that of the Olympic level and bans any transgender or intersex person on its face—you cannot change your chromosomes.

of all-gender sports can include wrestling, fencing, bicycling, and ulti-mate frisbee.[23] Policies and programs like this allow students to have a high degree of self-determination. The transgender boy who has come out his junior year can stay on the girls' basketball team if he feels he belongs there. The GNC student can wrestle at one hundred and ten pounds without making any statement about their gender identity. And that's in line with how cisgender athletes are treated as well. The school isn't policing students—there's no inspection of birth certifi-cates, no doctor's notes, no blood tests.

Of course, it may be the case that a league won't allow transgender athletes to play in games. Schools should investigate whether transgen-der athletes are still allowed to practice with the team and suit up for games, even if they can't compete in official games or matches. And schools in such situations should work with the league's governors to review the policy and propose changes, as discussed earlier.

Beyond the rules, though, education is crucial. A school or league or metropolitan area may permit transgender girls to play on girls' teams, but that doesn't mean that the league is ready for them. Any school with openly transgender athletes wants to be in clear commu-nication with league officials, referees, and coaches on other teams to make sure that there will be no discriminatory action, no questioning of eligibility, and respect for names and pronouns. Too many trans-gender boys and girls have gotten on the field only to have the oppos-ing team, or their fans, taunt them for who they are. This cannot be accepted as part of the standard "banter" between athletes. Coaches, in concert with parents/guardians and the school's gender task force, should be prepared to advocate for their students on and off the field.

---

23 There is a difference between all-gender sports and co-ed sports. All-gender sports don't (or shouldn't) have reference to boys or girls at all. There are ultimate frisbee leagues where teams are co-ed rather than all-gender, meaning each team is required to have a certain number of boys and a certain number of girls on the field at one time. Additionally, if a sport is all-gender, it should be reflected not only in the language and treatment of players but also in the facilities and uniforms. (I have encountered schools, for instance, where cycling is an all-gender sport, but there are two different uniforms—one for boys and one for girls.) Because of financial constraints or numbers of students, some schools will find it impossible to support an all-gender team. These schools should consider ways they can allow the designated boys' and girls' teams to interact—cross-country and track are great examples of sports where it's often possible for everyone to practice and train together, which provides students who don't fit the binary the chance to interact with a wider range of genders.

I will here reiterate what I have said in earlier chapters: the policies don't matter nearly as much as the culture does. Any group of educators, students, or parents/guardians that wants to do the work of gender inclusion in athletics should focus on working with coaches, captains, and athletic directors first. Educate and inform this core group of influencers. Make sure they understand what gender is and how it is different from biological sex. Talk robustly about why schools have sports programs and the larger role of athletics and physical education in school culture and students' personal development. Discuss, frankly, the historic tendency for locker rooms and sports teams to be places where bullying and hazing take place.

Once again, these changes won't be successful if all they do is try to accommodate a small group of marginalized students. A girls' team can't be expected to abruptly know how to handle a GNC teammate. A coach may not yet have fully absorbed the sort of conversations he'll need to have with families when there is a transgender boy on his team. And so on. These changes will be better accepted if they come in a larger package of education around community and inclusion. Spending practice time talking about trust and honesty, about identity and belonging, can seem to some athletes and coaches like wasted time—better off running sprints. But the ability of a team to be successful depends upon these very values: the ability to be honest, to share and collaborate, to trust and respect. In thinking about the larger structure and program of a school, this is yet another place to revisit the idea of overall mission. How do athletics fit into the work, writ large, of the institution? How do teams uphold the same values as classes and clubs? Every space on campus needs to do the work of inclusion.[24]

It's a big job, and this work will do more than make sports programming an inclusive place for transgender athletes if done well. If you want your policies to stick—if you want them to actually be carried from paper to practice—you have to educate and shift the culture so that your school's athletic program is fully prepared to live by these values.

Recent legislation may have schools and leagues feeling that it is

24 This is true for gender and is also true for race and ethnicity and other marginalized identities. These can't be issues that addressed only on one day of the year or in one campus space. The school has to be committed to inclusion in every space.

impossible to work toward including transgender athletes. Indeed, the political climate in some states and school districts has made even having this conversation, let alone creating change, a dangerous endeavor. For schools that want to press forward with inclusion, I would encourage stepping outside the binary and looking at creating something new. Rather than trying to fit transgender and GNC students into a system designed for the binary, why not create a team that is, from its inception, all gender? I don't mean to suggest that we should give up the fight for the inclusion of transgender girls on girls' teams. But I do think that for some schools, an alternative approach is necessary.

NEXT STEPS

REFLECT

1. Do some writing and thinking about the larger ideas around sports. What is "fair" when it comes to competition? Why do we value sports in schools? Why do we have separate boys' and girls' teams? Spend time sorting through the assumptions you have.

RESEARCH

1. Research local league rules and guidelines around gender as well as any applicable state or local legislation.

2. Consider what all-gender sports options you can make available to students. This might be especially key for schools operating under restrictive state or local provisions.

ACT

1. Talk to any teams, coaches, or schools in your area who have out transgender athletes in their athletics program.

2. Work with coaches to make sure everyone has a good understanding around inclusion, bullying/harassment, and gender. Start this work well before you try to make any changes and try in the process of education to identify coaches who are interested in the topic and could be allies.

3. Draw up proposals that fit the current rules of your league for how transgender and GNC student-athletes can be incorporated into teams.

4. Draw up proposals that ask the league to change rules to be more inclusive, if necessary.

5. Ascertain how you can start to move that proposal through the system.

6. If new all-gender sports programs have been added, promote them.

NOTES

a. Masha Gessen, "The Movement to Exclude Trans Girls from Sports," *The New Yorker*, March 27, 2021, https://www.newyorker.com/news/ our-columnists/the-movement-to-exclude-trans-girls-from-sports.

b. "Bans on Transgender Youth Participation in Sports," *Movement Advance Project*, last modified January 24, 2024, https://www.lgbtmap.org/ equality maps/youth/ sports_participation_bans.

c. Julie Kliegman, "Lawmakers Say Trans Athlete Bans Are About Protecting Women's Sports . . .," *Sports Illustrated*, January 25, 2022, https://www.si.com/golf-archives/2022/01/25/ luc-esquivel-trans-sports-ban-boys-and-mens-teams-daily-cover.

d. Cindy Boren, "Transgender wrestler Mack Beggs wins second Texas state girls' championship," *The Washington Post*, February 25, 2018, https://www. washingtonpost.com/news/ early-lead/wp/2018/02/25/transgender-wrestler-mack-beggs-wins-second-texas-state-girls-championship/.

e. Justin Gamble, "Jackson State University debuts first NCAA Division I female kicker at an HBCU," *CNN*, October 16, 2023, https://www.cnn.com/2023/10/14/us/ leilani-armenta-jackson-state-university-reaj/index.html.

f. Collin Binkley, "Biden administration proposes rule to forbid bans on transgender athletes but allow limits," *PBS NewsHour*, April 6, 2023, https://www.pbs.org/newshour/politics/ biden-administration-proposes-rule-to-forbid-bans-on-transgender-athletes-but-allow-limits.

g. Peter Bodo, "Follow the money: How the pay gap in Grand Slam tennis finally closed," *ESPN*, September 6, 2018, https://www.espn.com/tennis/ story/_/id/24599816/ us-open-follow- money-how-pay-gap-grand-slam-tennis-closed.

h. Danial Hashemi, "Examining the Tennis Pay Gap," *Washington Square News*, September 16, 2019, https://nyunews.com/sports/2019/09/16/ tennis-pay-gap-problem/.

i. Joyce Wadler, "The Lady Regrets," *The New York Times*, February 1, 2007, https://www.nytimes.com/2007/02/01/garden/01renee.html.

j. Matt Lavietes, "Utah official faces calls to resign after falsely suggesting teen girl is transgender," *NBC News*, February 8, 2024, https://www.nbcnews.com/nbc-out/out-news/utah-official-faces-calls-resign-falsely-suggesting-teen-girl-transgen-rcna137903.

k. "Girls Are As Athletic As Boys, Study Says," *Huffington Post*, June 7, 2012, https://bit.ly/4azFrCG.

l. International Olympic Committee, *IOC Framework on Fairness, Inclusion and Non-Discrimination on the Basis of Gender Identity and Sex Variations* (Lausanne, 2021), https://stillmed.olympics.com/media/Documents/Beyond-the-Games/Human-Rights/IOC-Framework-Fairness-Inclusion-Non-discrimination-2021.pdf.

m. Bianna Golodryga, Ben Church and Henry Hullah, "Caster Semenya says she went through 'hell' due to testosterone limits imposed on female athletes," *CNN*, November 6, 2023, https://www.cnn.com/2023/11/06/sport/caster-semenya-totestosterone-limits-world-athletics-spt-intl/index.html.

n. Annie Karni, "House Passes Bill to Bar Transgender Athletes from Female Sports Teams," *The New York Times*, April 20, 2023, https://www.nytimes.com/2023/04/20/us/politics/ transgender-athlete-ban-bill.html.

o. Devan Cole, "Former Connecticut high school athletes urge appeals court to revive their challenge to state's trans-inclusive sports policy," *CNN*, March 23, 2023, https://www.cnn.com/ 2023/03/23/politics/connecticut-transgender-sports-lawsuit-appeal/index.html.

p. GLAD Law, "Sarah Huckman, featured speaker at GLAD's 2018 Spirit of Justice Award Dinner," *YouTube*, 8:44, video, October 16, 2018, https://www.youtube.com/watch?v=V57D3Hv8zvw.

q. Sydney Bauer, "A Day in the Life of Three Transgender Athletes: What it Takes to Be Elite," *Teen Vogue*, July 19, 2021, https://www.teenvogue.com/story/transgender-athletes-what-it-takes-to-be-elite.

r. Daymond Steer, "Kingswood athlete speaks out in support of bill," *The Conway Daily Sun*, June 13, 2018, https://bit.ly/4aWE4xw.

s. Sarah Rose Huckman, "Sarah Rose Huckman: As transgender athlete, I oppose HB 1251," *The Conway Daily Sun*, February 12, 2020, https://bit.ly/4aUp03t.

t. Relative to participation in school sports programs for female student-athletes, H.B. 1251, NH State Leg. (2020).

CHAPTER EIGHT:

LIVING TOGETHER: DORMITORIES, SCHOOL TRIPS & SHARING ROOMS

I have lived in dormitories for almost twenty years. When I used to tell people that I ran a residence hall of sixty teenage boys, I most often got expressions of sympathy, pity, or awe: *How can you stand it?* The truth is, I really enjoy living with teenagers and helping them to learn how to be independent, to connect with their peers, to create and sustain a community, and enjoy a life lived together. I often think that I did more teaching in the dormitory than I do in the classroom.

The dormitory I lived in for the longest stretch of my career was a large, rectangular brick structure with lots of small rooms spread along hallways, with a bathroom and shower room located in the middle of each floor. Whenever I walk around campus, I marvel at all the things that have changed so much in the last twenty or thirty years—the laboratories in the science building, the group workspace in the library—and then reflect on what hasn't changed at all: the dormitory I live in.

Okay, yes, the bathrooms and common room have been updated. But the sense of what this dormitory is—a place to house boys—hasn't changed at all since the building was constructed in the 1800s. Really wrapping one's head around this is a crucial part of starting to do the work of inclusion. The gender binary is as solidly reinforced, as dependable and relied upon, in the social structures of the school as the very bricks of the dormitory walls.

The building itself suggests a sense of containment and confinement—walling away a hazard—but also privilege and protection: within these walls, boys can be boys. I say this often—not just about gender, but also about race and religion: most of the schools in this country, including the school I work at, were founded by and for straight, White, Christian men. Everyone else who has come along after that has been added to the school as an awkward appendage. As it pertains to gender, there is nothing that makes this more apparent than dormitories.

For those readers who are doing inclusivity work at day schools, I urge you not to skip this chapter—true to form, I will couch the conversation of dormitories in the larger context of culture-shifting around gender. Thinking these issues through in every element of the educational environment deepens understanding of how all the parts work together. At the end of the chapter, I will talk about how to manage short-term rooming situations that many schools experience, such as on school field trips.

HOW THE GENDER BINARY IS INHOSPITABLE

When we house students at schools, the long-standing tradition is to put boys and girls in separate buildings and to establish a set of rules that governs when they can be alone in private spaces without adult supervision. Most parents, guardians, educators, and students take these sorts of rules and separation as givens. To begin the work of inclusion, as is so often the case, one needs to step back and ask: Why? What are we gaining by housing students this way? As with restrooms and locker rooms, the most common answer is safety. Let's dig into the idea of safety in the context of housing and be blunt about what we mean and expect by that.

Most boarding schools began as all-boy institutions. Apart from possibly requiring boys to be in their own rooms during study hours or after "lights out," there were no restrictions on who could be in someone else's room and no explicitly stated rules about sexual interaction with other students.[1] When schools began to consider going "co-ed," the conversation about whether or not girls should be added to the

---

1 This doesn't mean such behavior didn't occur—and it doesn't mean that, when discovered, such behavior wasn't punished. Boys caught in sexual interactions with other boys faced severe consequences. Being dismissed from school or forced into forms of conversion therapy were two common responses. What's important to note here is that none of this was written into the rules or policies—there was no on-the-record expectation or accommodation for homosexuality.

student population followed fairly predictable lines: Would they be distracting to the boys? Would they be capable of rigorous academic work? Would families want to send their daughters to live on a campus with boys? The school applied a lot of energy in policy and marketing to make it abundantly clear that girls would be "safe" on campus. They would be housed separately from boys and there would be strict rules about unsupervised visiting between boys and girls in residence halls (indeed, many schools forbid this entirely and still do).

The fear here—the safety that's being talked about—clearly has to do with sexual activity: sexual assault and consensual sexual activity that might lead to pregnancy. Schools were very afraid of the lawsuits and loss of reputation that might ensue if news of assault or pregnancy were to become public. To be blunt in a way few schools then and now are willing to be, the housing and the rules were very clearly set up to keep penises and vaginas away from each other.[2] What we know now, in 2024, is that separate buildings and strict rules do not prevent sexual assault, nor do they prevent consensual sexual activity. Anybody who believes that a ten-foot gap of sidewalk between a boys' dorm and a girls' dorm will prevent sexual congress has clearly not spent much time with teenagers.[3]

Even if these rules and dormitories did prevent sexual assault by separating boys from girls, they completely ignore gay, lesbian, and bisexual students. A gay boy housed in a boys' dormitory generally has no rules stating when he can be in other boys' rooms. The only guidelines rest on the entirely heteronormative assumption that sexual activity between students of the same gender is impossible or would never happen.

To be clear, I don't think the problem with this situation is that gay boys (and lesbian and bisexual students) need rules to keep them under control; that's not what rules usually do. Rather, I think that schools, which will inevitably have rules, need to stop pretending these students don't exist. Policies and rules are one way that schools show that they care about—that they have taken the time to consider—student behavior and experiences. By having written policy about same-

---

2 I put it in these blunt terms to make it clear that even though the language of dormitories is often "boys and girls" (which refer to gender identity), the reality is that biological sex is yet again the real concern.

3 What *can* prevent sexual assault? Education and a shift in school culture.

sex sexual activity, it names and makes visible these people and this behavior. Without this visibility, students are at risk. If, for instance, there's a non-consensual sexual encounter between two boy students, the presence of a policy—the plain language of it—might make it more possible for the victim to report what happened. Rules also makes it clear what the consequence will be; even though gay students were not mentioned in early rule books, boarding schools historically certainly didn't hesitate to expel any boy caught in a homosexual encounter or suspected of same-sex attraction, even if it wasn't acted upon.

At many schools that I've worked with, dormitory rules in handbooks apply only to heterosexual interaction, but instead of creating an "anything goes" atmosphere for LGB students, there's been a practice of "off the books" rules for these students. For instance, a dorm faculty member in a girls' dorm might become aware of a student in a lesbian relationship. The faculty member might observe the two girls cuddling on the couch in the common room. Maybe the student has trusted the faculty member and come out to them. Sadly, what often happens next is that the faculty member decides it is no longer "fair" or "safe" for the lesbian student to be allowed to have her girlfriend, or any girls, in her room. A special, impromptu rule is made for this one student, based solely on her sexual orientation.

Not only is this clearly discriminatory, but it also potentially outs the student to her peers or to other faculty. Any other queer student observing this occurrence would probably feel a strong incentive not to come out to any dorm faculty or be open about their relationships—otherwise, they would find themselves similarly restricted. Needless to say, this is a very poor outcome for student mental health and social development.

Rules should apply uniformly to all students, both in their letter and enforcement. Boys, girls, and non-binary students. Straight and queer, cis and trans students. Rules should be written in a way that makes it apparent a.) that the school knows it houses students with a range of gender and sexual identities and b.) that it has designed the rules (and the housing) for *all* of them.

Recently, I worked with a school that had their first transgender student come out. The school is a small one, with just two boys' dorms and two girls' dorms. Like many boarding schools, it is set in a remote location. The students therefore spend most of their time on campus and the dorms serve as the most important social nexus.

The transgender student, who had come to the school as a girl and transitioned in his ninth-grade year, was eager to move out of the girls' dorm and into the boys' dorm. The administration had some hesitancy about this move. I spent time with the students and with the faculty, touring facilities, teaching some workshops, getting to know the campus and the culture. When I sat down to discuss the reluctance many deans felt about letting the transgender boy move into the boys' dorm, I was surprised by how blunt they were.

"The boys can be pretty cruel," one said.

"There's a lot of teasing and horseplay," another added.

"I lived there for five years, and they get up to some stuff late at night," a third dean said.

The general impression I received was that they knew the culture in the boys' dorm was mildly violent and tended towards harassment, and they were accepting of that. Moreover, their comments implied to me that they didn't want to move the trans boy into that space because they knew they would get complaints if they asked the school's culture to shift at all towards being more accepting and kind.

I was taken aback. Why, if they knew that this went on, did they tolerate it? When I asked, I was greeted by shrugs.

"It's their home. It's the place where they can relax and be themselves," one dean finally said.

I absorbed that for a bit. It was sort of like looking at a messy swine yard that hasn't been mucked out for a while and then throwing up your hands—pigs like mud!—without wondering why the farmer has let things get so disgusting. I had worked with residential schools long enough to know what the deans were really saying: "You know, this is just how boys are, and we can't and shouldn't do anything to change it." All with a wry chuckle because—in truth—most of the deans had been those boys at one time. I also knew that if I talked to the boys in the dorm, most of them would express fondness for the current culture of their residential situation.

The way single-gender dorms work is sort of like the classic tree-houses of childhood. They're walled off and a sign hung out front: No girls (or boys) allowed. Then the rope ladder is dragged up, and the boys (or girls) inside feel that in the privacy and intimacy of a single-gender space, they can do away with certain rules of decorum. For the boys, who—by dint of personality, looks, abilities, or strength—land at or near the top of the heap, these spaces are wonderful. For the rest, well, it depends on that student's desire to conform and ability to withstand pressure. The smaller the school and the fewer the residential options, the more monolithic the gender expectation will be. One boys' dorm? One way to be a boy.

And that's the pressure that this transgender student was feeling. He had socially transitioned. He had good support from the girls in his dorm and from the faculty. Most people on campus were doing well with his name and pronouns. But he had heard that he was the butt of jokes in the boys' dorm, that they discussed him and misgendered him, and if faculty chided them, then they just waited until the faculty went to bed.

This transgender boy wanted desperately to prove that he belonged, that he was a boy. The standard of "boyness" on this campus was set in the boys' dorms. He knew that until he lived in that space, he wouldn't be considered a "real" boy. As I talked with him and talked with the administration, I felt a real sense of loss. The transgender student wasn't wrong; he wouldn't ever be a boy on that campus if he kept living in the girls' dorm, but living in the boys' dorm would likely be terrible for him—even he admitted that.

When the binary is insisted upon, when it's the only option available, self-expression becomes quite limited. In a more relaxed environment, a range of gender expression is available: through different styles of dress and behavior, through engagement in different activities. In a healthy school, there are many types of girls and boys as well as non-binary students. But in a school where gender is literally confined and defined by brick (or wood or concrete) boxes, there is little range for self-expression. If you want to fit in, you must limit yourself to that box.

I felt terrible for that transgender boy—who so wanted to belong, to just be one of the boys. But who also knew that, if it weren't for that dormitory culture, he would want to be a very different sort of boy. He liked theater and singing, but he gave that up and joined the wrestling team. Did he like wrestling? *Shrug*. It was what the "cool boys"—the leaders in the dorm—did. I think this transgender boy caught the attention and the sympathy of the faculty because his journey into boyhood at this school was quite visible. I would guess that dozens and dozens of cisgender boys had undergone the exact same process that this transgender boy had— only, no one had marked their journey as notable because the school expected it, called it "growing up" or "fitting in" or "figuring things out."

Here is one more instance where thinking about all students and gender as a universal feature of identity is crucial for a school to do this inclusion work well. As with locker rooms, so with single-gender dorms: these spaces create interior cultures that reflect and reinforce the cultural expectations of gender they have been conditioned to. The power and the privilege of normative gender expectations simply get magnified in these spaces, which is restrictive and stifling for cisgender students as well as transgender students.

The solution for this school was a difficult one, involving dismantling some monolithic cultures and structures.[4] The school was hesitant to move forward. Wouldn't it be easier just to make arrangements that would satisfy this one transgender boy—get him through the three years he had left at the school—and then carry on? Yes, that would be easier. But it would mean turning away from the culture that was degrading and harmful to many cisgender students as well as students who were transgender or gender non-conforming (GNC). I found myself telling this school—as I have insisted throughout this book—that if they did this work well, it would help *all* the students at their school feel at home.

REBUILDING DORM CULTURE

So, what does gender- (and sexuality-) inclusive housing policy look like?

---

4 I have focused, in sharing this anecdote, on the boys' dorm culture. In many ways the girls' dorm culture was just as problematic, but I wasn't as invested in studying that culture while I was at the school. However, I don't mean to suggest that only boys' dorm insist on a narrow and troubling definition of gender.

I've worked with dozens of schools to discuss and design all-gender housing, and no two conversations have gone the same way. Some schools have gone through months of planning only to decide it isn't right for their school. Others have had to put off introducing all-gender housing until they built or remodeled a dorm. Some have opened all-gender dormitories of more than twenty students, and others have started houses with just five or six residents. It all depends on what housing stock is available on a campus and what the school culture is. Just as was discussed in the chapter on restrooms and locker rooms, a larger change is going to come with community expectations that may or may not be met.

One school I worked with in developing all-gender living spaces wanted to have a test run of some of the new expectations and rules that were being proposed. (This is usually a really good step to build into the process, as it provides robust feedback before policies are finalized.) The idea was to see how students would adapt to an expectation of "no nudity in public places." A girls' dorm was selected for the pilot study, and we surveyed the students and asked about comfort in the bathroom and in other common spaces. This was a typical girls' dorm: The students weren't parading around naked all the time, but it was common for girls to walk down the hallway to the shower room without many clothes on or, on hot days, to be in the common room in sports bras, for instance. This was also a typical girls' dorm insofar as it had students in it who were out as queer, who were questioning and experimenting with gender, and students who were cisgender and straight.

The new expectation came with clear guidelines. As anyone who works with teenagers knows, the phrase "no nudity" isn't sufficiently clear if you want to prevent students from being scantily clad. The dorm head, together with the student dorm leaders, designed fluffy bathrobes (with the dorm name embroidered) for every student. The robes were debuted at a dorm meeting, where the student leaders explained to the other residents that the robe would be considered the least a student could wear around the dorm. The students generally liked the bathrobes and found them comfortable—it was a small gesture and a minor expense to make the new rule a bit clearer and a bit more palatable. Additionally, the bathrooms were modified on each floor, with an extra layer of curtain added a couple of feet in front of each shower stall. The dormitory was told that they needed to step inside the curtain before disrobing.

For the next month or so, the dorm went about its normal routines of pizza parties, homework sessions, and Sunday brunches. At the end of this time period, we sent around another survey and also met with a focus group of students to record reactions to the bathroom renovations and the new expectations. There were a few complaints about restrictions and how the new rule took away their freedom. Most students were neutral; they liked the robes, and the new rules weren't a huge inconvenience. And several students reported (mostly in the anonymous survey) how much they liked the changes to the bathroom.

One student wrote that before the changes, she never would have said that she felt uncomfortable in the bathroom, but she realized now how much more relaxed she felt with the new curtains. It didn't matter if someone else was in there brushing their teeth: She could change and dry off without wondering if they were looking at her in the mirror. Another resident said she appreciated being able to be confident while hanging out in the common room; she often felt self-conscious when she was the only one there wearing "lots" of clothes. But now she could spend time there without the sense that others were judging her on this basis.

The conversations that ended up coming out of this focus group were good ones to have in any dorm: body image, language in common spaces, privilege. That last point was a really salient one that the committee hadn't anticipated. But many of the girls who felt that their rights (to wear no more than a sports bra) had been taken away engaged in good discussions about how living in a community might require them to forgo something they wanted in order to create a better living situation for everyone. That's a tremendously important lesson for a teenager to learn.

This intervention helped the school to see that changing long-standing dorm practices was possible and that with some guidance, students could make profound shifts in their behavior as they learned how to live in a residential community. Many schools feel that a crucial component of opening an all-gender dorm is to have a residential curriculum and student leaders (as well as dorm faculty) who have been trained to teach and reinforce it. This curriculum can and should talk about gender and sexuality, about healthy relationships, and consent. But it should also talk about sharing space, being aware of others, sleep hygiene, cleanliness, and a host of other details that, together, make a residential community safe and mutually supportive.

I would further suggest that such a curriculum belongs in *all* dorms and can be a significant part of opening the conversation about living together responsibly in single-gender as well as all-gender spaces. The term "curriculum" can suggest something highly academic, but I've seen multiple iterations of residential curriculums at different schools and many of them are less scholarly and more interactive. Residential curriculums might be formed around group events: a dinner, a s'mores night at a fire pit, a trip to the beach, a Friday night movie-watching party. The point is, in part, to put away phones and to be with one another. Around a fire pit, you might do something as minor as circulate a set of conversation cards, allowing a student to draw one, read it out loud, and start a conversation. Or you might assign the residents of a dorm a podcast to listen to and then sit down in the common room with some pizza to discuss. The faculty and student leaders can decide what the dormitory needs to talk about: Race? Sexuality? Bathroom hygiene? And then figure out a relaxed and social way to bring the conversation to these places.

This might seem elementary, but so often dormitories are just viewed as places to house students. Put them in their rooms, keep them quiet during study hours, have them go to bed at lights out. There's often no thought given to teaching them what it means to live together. But, like so many life skills, this can be taught. At the start of the year, time and space needs to be given to forming some values and articulating goals: "We'll know we have a healthy dorm when . . ." Or, "I want to live in a dorm that . . ." This allows students to put into their own words to what a community looks and feels like.

From there, regular, supervised engagement are needed to make sure that everyone is equally involved and able to speak up about their living situation. Some dorms might take on "sustainability" as their residential mission. Another dorm might decide they want to focus on "mindfulness." And a third might want to talk about "gender and sexuality." How autonomous, how wide-ranging, and how mandated this curriculum is depends on the school culture.

The crucial move, though, is to acknowledge that dormitories aren't hotels—they are parts of a school and play a unique role in student education. Likewise, they are key sites for promoting cultural change in regard to gender.

Even if an all-gender dorm isn't in the cards for your school right away, single-sex dorms are still important places to introduce gender-inclusive practices and culture-building.

TESTING THE WATERS

On the facilities side of things, the best candidate for a new all-gender dorm is usually an existing dormitory with single rooms. To provide full privacy, the dorm's bathrooms should be able to be remodeled. These changes don't need to be major or expensive: They might involve adding a bolt-able stall door in front of a shower to add a changing area; they might involve modifying toilet stalls to have lower/higher walls and piano hinges on the door. Whatever the physical modifications needed, for most schools, opening an all-gender dorm feels like a big leap. In order to make it as successful as possible, the school should make it clear that living in the all-gender dorm would be a choice, that students would opt into rather than be required to live there. To that end, it can help tremendously to poll the student body to find out the level of interest before proceeding.

In order for the poll to be accurate and meaningful, the school should first hold some informational sessions (run an article in the school paper, etc.) about what an all-gender dorm is and how it might be managed on campus. This could also include a "test run" of the sorts of policies that would apply to the new dorm, as described above. The poll would then ask students about their interest in living in an all-gender dorm. It is best to rank this interest. The rankings might be:

1. "I need to live in an all-gender dorm."

2. "I'd prefer to live in an all-gender dorm."

3. "I am open to living in an all-gender dorm."

4. "I would not like to live in an all-gender dorm."

If your school has both residential and day students, it's most practical to distribute this poll to students who live on campus. It can additionally be helpful to ask what dorm the responding student currently lives in. The survey could then reveal that of the fifteen students who said they "need" to live in an all-gender dorm, eleven are currently occupying "girl beds" at the school. You might also want to have the student list their current grade—if most of the interest comes from students who are about to graduate, say, that matters for planning.

The language of the ranking is also important. The idea that a student might "need" an all-gender dorm is meant to open the door for LGBTQ+ students, who are among those who might feel most uncomfortable (or even unsafe) in a traditional boys' or girls' dorm. The range down from there will give the school a feeling for how much enthusiasm and how much openness there is toward this idea, while also reassuring the students that if they aren't interested, that is fine.

Once the school has the results of this survey, they can proceed to look at what housing options are available based on the numbers. Did only seven students say they *needed* this dorm space? What if you added in everyone who was very interested? These numbers should help schools come up with at least a couple of viable housing options.

Again, depending on what housing stock is available, the reality may not perfectly match the students' or committee's ideal. I've worked with schools who have used a "wing" of a dorm, or even a floor within a dorm, because smaller, standalone housing options weren't available. A self-contained housing unit is ideal, but this may not be possible for some schools, so flexibility is key. So long as the space has a sense of privacy and autonomy—their own common room/hang-out space, their own entrance—it is possible to make a variety of arrangements work.

ENGAGING PARENTS AND GUARDIANS

At this point, if not before, it becomes very important to engage with students' families and make sure they know what is going on. Parents and guardians don't necessarily need to be brought into the weeds of policy-making, but they should be informed and invited to the conversation about the new all-gender dorm. Many parents and guardians will have questions, and the school can learn a lot from answering them; consistently engaging parents and guardians builds support and trust over the process of developing this residential option.

Sending information out in a family newsletter or email while the school is in the planning process can be a low-key way to begin educating parents and guardians on the benefits and conditions of the new all-gender dorm. Likely, such a bulletin will get feedback. In most schools I've worked with, parents and guardians hear the phrase "all-gender dorm" and have some very inaccurate assumptions. Many schools hesitate to inform families fearing (or knowing) that they will hear from conservative and intolerant families who want to prevent the school from moving in this direction. But informing families doesn't mean that a school is empowering them to determine school policy. Rather, a school is inviting those parents and guardians to open their minds and engage in the conversation. Instead of fearing an oppositional response, schools should take all feedback and concerns as a chance to educate and inform their parent/guardian population as well as to clarify their own goals.

Like many other fears that surround the process of gender inclusion, the initial concerns are often unfounded, hypothetical, worst-case scenarios mostly having to do with sexual assault or consensual sexual activity. Still, the goal of dialoguing with families is not to change the parents' or guardians' minds; or get them "on board" with the project: it is to be open and forthright about the work that is being done—even in the face of adversity. This is a great chance to model respectful discourse for students and a great chance for schools to engage parents and guardians in the context of their institutional mission and values. These will be difficult conversations, to be sure, but they are also often galvanizing, reminding schools that there is a real need to be inclusive and welcoming in the face of intolerance and hostility.

One major question schools will need to address before any dorm is opened: Should parents and guardians get to approve or deny their child's request to live in an all-gender dormitory? The answer will depend thoroughly on school culture. Some schools engage families in many stages of their child's program: parents and guardians must sign off on course selection, must approve of trips off campus, and so on. Other schools encourage minimal parental involvement to foster student autonomy. As a general rule of thumb, I ask schools this: If a student wanted to switch dorms (from one girls' dorm to another, for instance), would the parents and guardians be brought into that conversation? If the answer is yes, then likely they should be not only consulted but required to approve their child's move to an all-gender dorm. If, however, parents and guardians usually are not involved in such a discussion, a school might consider informing them but not letting them deny the request. These are sensitive areas, and again, transparency between the school, families, and students is key.

In my version of a perfect world, parent/guardian approval for living in an all-gender dorm would not be required. Many transgender and GNC students find that school is where they can be out; school is where they have support; school is a place that allows them to be themselves. Many transgender and GNC students maintain two selves, especially early on in their coming out process. They get to live in their true gender at school and, when they go home, they revert to who they used to be, the gender their families understand them to be. Requiring a parent/guardian to sign off on moving to an all-gender dorm might mean that students who really do need this space would be denied the chance to live there.[5] I have certainly seen this happen.

Sometimes parents and guardians have an inkling that their child is in the process of coming out or transitioning, and they want to stop rather this support it. They might deny the move to an all-gender dorm, thinking that they can prevent their child from becoming transgender by keeping them in the single-gender environment, that this will somehow enforce the appropriate gender norms. This approach does real

5 This same logic is sadly very much at play with legislation that requires consent from students' parents/guardians before the student can be called by their chosen name and pronouns, for instance.

harm to the student who is questioning, exploring, or transitioning. For the good of both individual students and residential school communities, boarding schools should foster and support independent decision-making by students. Parents and guardians should be fully informed and involved in the conversation, but if the school culture can tolerate it, students should be able to make decisions about their day-to-day lives for themselves.

POPULATING THE ALL-GENDER DORM

Once the school has identified the housing options and settled on the approach to parent/guardian involvement, they can design the specifics of the selection process for residents of the dorm. Often, schools decide residential arrangements in the spring of the year, after admissions numbers are mostly settled. In the initial year or two of the all-gender dorm, the school might feel more comfortable having a slightly different process of applying to live in this dorm, perhaps involving a short interview or writing a paragraph or two about why a student wants to live in the dorm. An interview provides a moment for a dean or faculty member to review the community expectations and the rules of the all-gender dorm with students and to ask applicants a bit about how they would handle themselves in the new space, how they think it will be different from living in a single-gender dorm, etc.

This isn't meant to force students to come out but rather to assess need and sincere interest. As I've worked with schools to open all-gender dorms, I have found there is a consistent fear—sometimes from trustees, sometimes from students' caregivers, sometimes from faculty—that straight student couples will attempt to move into the all-gender dorm together. Adding the non-cumbersome step of a short essay or interview can be a good way to allay this concern.

On the other hand, the school can gain some truly important information from conducting these applications. One school I worked with asked for a short paragraph on why students wanted to move into the all-gender dorm and received many applications with full-length essays attached. These students were passionate and varied about their inter-

est. Some expressed the desire to live more openly as non-binary individuals, with people who wouldn't demand that they explain themselves. Others said they were tired of living in boys' dorms and hearing
derogatory talk about girls. Schools have a chance to gain some real
insight about the needs of their students and the deficiencies of their
residential programs from this process.[6]

In tandem with designing a selection process for residents, the task
force should also make sure that ample, accurate information about the
all-gender dorm is available. Whether this comes in the form of a presentation at student council, an article in the newspaper, or a series of informational sessions (with pizza as an incentive) depends on what will garner the
most attention. These outreaches should involve a little bit of marketing
and PR, a little bit of gender education, and a healthy dose of myth-quash-
ing. The goal is to help students make decisions about where they want
to live (and what they think about others' residential decisions) based on
accurate information—including emphasis on the fact that these dorms
are not just for transgender and GNC students. This messaging might also
describe how the culture and community experience in these dorms will
be different and possibly more positive than traditional options.

Once the applications or selections forms are in, the school should
assess the numbers and take a few other factors into consideration.
Ideally, the composition of an all-gender dorm is a mix of everything.
Students should be queer, straight, cisgender, transgender, and non-binary, as well as from a diverse background in terms of race, socioeco-
nomic status, ethnicity, and so on.

In fact, if you find from your early polling and focus groups that the
only students who want to live in your all-gender dorm are LGBTQ+
identified, then I would suggest stepping back and reconsidering.
Creating an all-LGBTQ+ dorm (or at least a dorm perceived to be so)
would risk further marginalizing those students. Yes, they would have
strong affinity and support within their dorm, but they would weaken
their support structure in the overall campus community. Moreover, if

---

6 Should applications and interviews turn up such results, the school would ideally take this
as a moment not just to start an all-gender dorm but also to reinvigorate the ways in which
they run their other dorms. Maybe all the dorms need a residential curriculum. Maybe certain
dorms need to have more robust training of their faculty and student leaders.

the perception is that "all the gay kids" are living in one dorm, the culture in the other dorms might skew to be more homophobic and less accepting. Rather than moderate language and behavior, the attitude might become: *If you don't like it, move to that other dorm.*

The goal is to create more safe, supportive, and comfortable spaces on campus, not fewer. Ideally, some transgender and GNC students would want to remain in single-gender dorms and some would want to move into all-gender dorms. If the trend seems to be that all, or almost all, of the transgender and GNC students want to move out of their single-gender dorms, this is a signal that a school needs to step back and work really hard on the current dorm culture before forming an all-gender dorm—similar to the test run study described in the Rebuilding Dorm Culture section above. A school in this situation might need to examine long-standing dorm traditions, gendered behaviors, and practices that are tolerated within all-boys or all-girls spaces, whether by students or faculty. Focus groups and conversations with alumni might inform this work, as would focus groups with students and faculty, especially if these groups can be run by someone not in the administration, in order to encourage honest feedback.

It is also important to recognize when the move toward gender inclusion is outpacing the ability of school culture to adapt. Premature changes may do more harm than good. Hopefully, though, the interest in the dorm is robust and varied, and the resulting community is as diverse as all the other dorms on campus.

REVISITING STUDENT VISITATION

During its first year, the all-gender dorm will likely be paid extra scrutiny—from families, from students, from trustees, from faculty, from alumni. Any discipline problems or violations of community standards around sexual behavior that arise in the all-gender dorm are especially likely to be magnified. As issues arise, and they will, it is important that schools keep things in perspective as they work with the other parties toward solutions. The administration should try to contextualize and remind folks that all dorms have similar issues that arise from time to time, especially around sexual activity.

Speaking of which: Whether or not a school is in a position to open an all-gender dorm, it should consider its policy around sexual activity from an angle of gender inclusion. I alluded to this problem when discussing gay, lesbian, and bisexual students in single-gender dormitories, how language governing sexual behavior often doesn't acknowledge these students' existence. Most schools have policies that are written for straight kids in single-gender housing. Some typical samples:

> "Boys may only visit the common rooms of girls' dormitories during evening visiting hours, 7–8 p.m. on school nights, and 7–10 p.m. on Friday and Saturday nights, when a dorm faculty member is on duty."

> "Girls may go to boys' dorms, or boys to girls' dorms, only from 7–8 p.m. Upon arriving in the dorm, the visitor must check in with the dorm faculty on duty before proceeding to the host's room. The door of the room must be propped entirely open, the overhead lights must be on, and students must be sitting upright for the duration of the visit."

Clearly these are gendered, heterosexist policies. They hyper-sexualize interactions between boys and girls. Everything about these rules is written in a way that suggests something dangerous will happen if schools don't carefully govern every movement when a boy and a girl are in a room together without an adult constantly present. Many schools view private dorm rooms as threatening, a liability risk.[7] And yet, boys and girls—straight and queer—interact with each other all the time in ways that are non-sexual. They go to class together. They run their cross-country workouts in the woods together. They meet in the library and study calculus together. They sit at dining hall tables and look at silly videos on their phones together. They can and do

---

7 This is not a book on sexual assault prevention or on adolescent sexual development, though this is certainly a topic that any school would want to carefully consider. Good resources on this abound, and schools should actively engage on professional development related to this topic.

interact with each other, without constant adult supervision, in ways that are completely respectful and platonic.

While it doesn't principally affect LGBTQ+ kids, this point is a tremendously important one when it comes to gender inclusion. Too often the rules of visitations make it utterly impossible for girls and boys to hang out in dorms without the implication of a sexual relation. This renders boy-girl friendships very difficult, which is a shame, given that friendships, connections, and bonds formed in high school can have lasting effects on students' college experiences, careers, and beyond.

As we can see, any revised visitation or parietal policy should be written to apply equally to all dorms. But this process will be particularly crucial if a school opens an all-gender dorm. Such dorms render traditional policies moot, since they are cast in terms of boys and girls having separate dorm spaces. So, what should replace these rules? I've facilitated conversations on visiting rules at several schools. Like the dress code, this is not typically an easy or popular topic. Usually I like to start by having the different constituencies state their idea of a good policy.

What you get is often a hilarious constellation: Students will say that they want to be able to visit any other student in any place on campus at pretty much any time without burdensome rules around supervision or limitations on privacy. Faculty or administration will say that any student interactions not in a public place should be supervised by adults. There's a pretty vast gulf between those points. The work to be done is to come to some points of mutual agreement, to prioritize inclusion, and to admit from the start that no one is guaranteed to think the outcome is perfect or, frankly, even good.

A baseline agreement needs to be that sexual activity between students cannot occur in campus spaces. Research done on sexual assault and adolescent development, as well as liability studies done by lawyers, clearly shows that schools cannot condone sexual activity amongst students. This doesn't mean that schools can assume it doesn't happen; schools need to robustly teach students about healthy relationships and safer sex. Schools need to have gender-inclusive rules about consent and sexual misconduct. Schools need to teach students what affirmative consent[8] means, what sort of behavior is coercive, and so on.[9] Students often are not happy to agree to a campus-wide ban on sexual activity, but it is a necessary starting position: The school is not going to provide spaces on campus for students to have sex regardless of the genders of the students involved in that sex.

Once that bridge is crossed, you're in the weeds. From an angle of inclusion, the end goal should be to couch school residential policies in the idiom of "students" instead of "boys and girls" and to not assume that all students are straight. What might ensue is a more process-oriented conversation about trust and privacy, about community and relationships. Just as schools are about more than just academics, visitation policies are about more than visits, or even sexuality.

These are fascinating conversations, ones that schools seldom feel they have time to engage in, and yet they are essential for building a true sense of community. When I facilitate these conversations, I ask faculty and students to be imaginative, to suspend judgment and try to think through a variety of scenarios. It is so important for faculty to hear what students value and for students to understand the position of responsibility (and liability) that faculty are in. There needs to be mutual respect. Unsurprisingly, the outcomes of this review process can vary widely. I'll outline some possibilities below and try to explain the benefits and pitfalls.

On the extreme side of being gender-inclusive but generally restrictive, a policy might read: "No student may be in any other student's room except when dorm faculty is on duty, the guest has checked in with dorm faculty, and the door to the host's room is open." A rule like this would even apply to residents of the same dorm and, for most school cultures, that is much too restrictive. Part of what makes dorm communities vibrant and supportive is the easy interchange amongst students, hanging out during free time and working together during study hours.

8　This refers to an understanding of sexual consent that is explicit and never simply assumed or implied. See SUNY's definition of the term: "Affirmative consent is a knowing, voluntary, and mutual decision among all participants to engage in sexual activity. Consent can be given by words or actions, as long as those words or actions create clear permission regarding willingness to engage in the sexual activity. Silence or lack of resistance, in and of itself, does not demonstrate consent. The definition of consent does not vary based upon a participant's sex, sexual orientation, gender identity, or gender expression" (note *a*).

9　This is a tricky balance to maintain; it can seem hypocritical to have a rulebook that states "no sex" and a health center that offers a bowl of free condoms.

However, a school could still argue that for reasons of supervision, room doors needed to be open if a student has any guests, regardless of gender.[10]

On the inclusive and permissive end of things, a school could permit students to visit any other student's room at any time before final dorm check-in, perhaps with a required sign-in to the dorm via an app and a policy that students living within the same dorm can visit each other with no oversight at any time.[11] Many schools would find that a policy such as this incurs too much liability for the school, however, since they wouldn't be providing any direct supervision. Some more permissive schools have a tiered approach, allowing older students more hours and more privacy (doors closed) when visiting each other.

In general, I think a school has to find a balance between letting students have spaces where they can easily hang out with friends and providing a reasonable expectation of supervision. A school might find that balance by saying a guest can visit a student's room at any time during the class day (that's likely an expansion on current visiting hours) *and* that the host's door has to be open whenever there's a guest in the room (that's likely a reduction of student privacy, since traditionally, students often can have same-gender, same-dorm visitors with doors closed). Pairing these two changes means that students "get" something even as they are "giving" something up.

Whatever shifts a school makes, it needs to be able to convey information about the changes to its students and faculty without laying the responsibility for those changes (which are likely to be unpopular) at the feet of the LGBTQ+ students. Yes, the push is for inclusivity. But the school should make these rule changes with multiple goals

---

10 This rule would be hard to enforce after hours, when the dorm faculty member goes to bed. However, most rules are hard to enforce during this time.

11 This latter point is an interesting one to unpack. Why should students within the same dorm get different rules than students in different dorms? What makes them more "trustworthy" with each other? The honest answer is that I think many schools have a policy like this in place simply because they always have and it is easiest to enforce. But, in trying to rationalize why this would be permissible, we return to the need for a residential curriculum and attention to dormitory culture. If the students living in a dorm have taken the time to establish "norms" and have formed bonds and trust through shared conversation and activity around what it means to live together, there are reasonable grounds to trust them more. I have heard students compare dorms to teams in terms of the intimacy—and even heard LGBTQ+ athletes and residents (as well as students living in all-gender dorms) talk about "dorm-cest," meaning that two people from the same dorm (or team) shouldn't be in a relationship together because they are family. That is certainly good advice for a number of reasons.

in mind: more open and welcoming dorm communities, for instance (if doors on the hallway are more likely to be open), or de-sexualizing interactions between girls and boys. At base, the policy should be designed—and spoken of—as a way to help a broad range of students and to support the campus community as a whole.

As schools consider putting a new policy in place, they should ask whether it will be read as a net loss of privileges. If it will be—even if the school feels that it is for a good reason—it is crucial not to push such a policy change out in tandem with opening an all-gender dorm. The dorm will be blamed. Sometimes, a reasonable solution is to pair the perceived loss of privilege (for instance, a new rule that restricts when first-year, sophomore, and junior students, regardless of gender, can visit another student's room) with a perceived gain of privilege (for instance, that seniors might be allowed expanded hours of visitation).

FIELD TRIPS, COMPETITIONS, AND MORE

So far, this chapter has discussed scenarios that are relevant to residential schools. Most schools aren't residential, but many do take their students off campus at some point, on field trips, for athletic or club competitions, and other special events. Some of the guidelines expressed above can pertain to these situations, but it is also worth considering in greater depth because non-residential schools will, in general, have a very different level of parent/guardian involvement than residential schools. Many of these parents and guardians are coming to campus on a daily basis rather than only occasionally. Thus, whereas residential schools can come up with a policy that works and is discussed primarily by students and faculty, in day schools, students' families are a major stakeholder and will need to be involved in the conversation to a greater extent.

When I ask schools about their rooming policies for field trips, I usually get a standard answer: "We book hotel rooms with two double beds and put four kids of the same gender, without thought to sexual orientation, into the room." When I ask why, I usually get an answer that cites convenience and cost. Dig a little deeper, and students and faculty will share that if four kids are put into a hotel room with two beds, quite often, only two of those students sleep in the beds and the other two camp out on the floor. Clearly, even a perceived sameness of gender does not guarantee students' comfort with sharing close quarters with classmates. If the school has a transgender student, usually they give that student a room on their own. Another common practice is to ask the transgender student who they are comfortable rooming with. Even a quick review of these practices shows that they are less than ideal—neither equitable nor inclusive.

One student per bed is a place to start. Schools can work with hotels to provide cots or rooms with space to set up an air mattress, if spreading students out into double rooms is cost prohibitive. On the other hand, shared rooms can also work on a gender-inclusive basis. Unless the school is taking hundreds of students at once off campus, it is usually manageable to ask students to list three or four other students they would like to share a room with (again, depending on numbers, this could be five or six or more if that makes the process more workable).[12] If schools ask students to list their desired roommates, gender doesn't have to be the primary determining factor.

In my experience, most students will, in fact, list students of the same gender to be their roommate. (Of course, you need to be alert to a couple—queer or straight—that wants to try to room together. Guidelines for the room selection process can clearly state that this isn't allowed.) If students are allowed to identify their preferred roommates, the transgender or GNC student will have a chance to clearly state who they feel comfortable with and then, hopefully, a match can be made with one other student. What takes primacy in this process is student comfort and pre-existing relationships—not gender.

Some schools find it is easier instead to have students identify classmates they would *not* want to room with. I do appreciate that this approach can simplify matters, and it can clearly keep kids from being placed with someone who has bullied or harassed them. My concern, though, is that it also would condone homophobia or transphobia. Suppose that there is one GNC student on your trip and you ask students who they would *not* want to room with, and the GNC student

---

12 The school should also provide the caveat that room assignments are subject to change. We all know that the unpredictable happens (sickness, emergencies, etc.) and things have to be shuffled.

is identified on most of those requests. Honoring those requests would promote exclusion, validating the idea that if a transgender person makes a cisgender person feel uncomfortable, it's the transgender person's fault. Ideally, a school could develop a system that lets students self-advocate and select those people they would *like* to be with.

Not singling out the transgender student for special treatment is another place to start; schools should have a process for assigning roommates/rooms that works for every student. The question of whether a transgender or GNC student is out, or the degree to which they are out, can also complicate these kinds of considerations. For instance, if a transgender boy has socially transitioned in fourth grade and joins your school in sixth grade, some of his peers might know, but parents and guardians might not. If he selects boys to room with or girls to room with on the field trip, a school should be ready to consider his choices the same as any other student. Too often, schools feel compelled to tell other students' families about the presence of a transgender student, which is a profound violation of privacy. Concerns about gender and sexuality should absolutely be discussed with parents and guardians and faculty before there is a specific individual case. In other words, policy should be formed and discussed proactively, not reactively.

Beyond the selection of roommates, there remains the much more fundamental topic of how students are expected to behave in their rooms. Too often, schools just toss the kids into these spaces and tell them to go to sleep. Placing kids in a residential situation, even just for one or two nights, is a moment that requires some teaching. Students should be involved in discussions on how to share space, on how to respect privacy, on how to resolve disputes. Adult presence can help, of course, but students should go into a rooming situation knowing what to expect—what is appropriate and what is not, regardless of who else is sharing the room.

For instance, a school might talk about changing clothes and nudity, asking that students change in the hotel room's bathroom rather than in front of each other. Having these conversations can empower students to ask for the privacy they need when they are alone in the room with a peer. Setting clear guidelines and expectations around nudity and similar behavior can also mitigate concerns that transgender or GNC students have about sharing a room and perhaps do the same for parents and guardians whose children might room with a transgender or GNC student.[13]

A third point to consider when revising a school's rooming policy is the question of family involvement. As I stated above regarding all-gender dorms, this component will depend greatly on school culture. One approach is to send out a permission form when the trip is announced. If the parent/guardian gives their student permission to go on the trip, they are agreeing to let the school select the student's roommate(s); the permission form should plainly outline the process that will be used to determine this.

If this approach fits with the general way that parent/guardian involvement is handled by the school, it can be very helpful for faculty and administrators to keep parent/guardian input to a minimum. Often with rooming, there are thinly veiled racist, classist, and homophobic parental disputes, often phrased as claims that someone "wouldn't be a good fit" or that the roommate pair just "wouldn't get along." However, other schools may want to more fully involve parents and guardians in the conversation, especially those with younger students, and develop formal guidelines for how families fit into the process, including policies around chaperones.[14]

In this section, as well as in the sections pertaining to changing names and pronouns and school records, I have highlighted the need to include parents and guardians in the process in some form. This is a point worth reiterating and highlighting in this current political climate. Conservative legislation targets parents and guardians from two angles. In those cases that involve criminalizing gender-affirming care, supportive parents and guardians are the target as well as trans youth. In those cases involving "parental rights" (I won't go into the irony of this label-

---

13 Again, it is worthwhile for a school to share these guidelines and to invite parents/guardians into a conversation about the trip well in advance of roommate pairs being assigned. Ideally, too, this won't be the only area that the school is gearing toward more gender inclusivity.

14 Many schools have the practice of using parents and guardians as chaperones for off-campus trips. It is really important that chaperones receive some training—being a parent or guardian is not the same as being a chaperone, and a parent's or guardian's values might not match those of the school. Particularly around gender and sexuality, all chaperones should receive some information and some clear guidelines for how to treat students and what the rules are regarding who can and cannot be in which rooms and places.

ing[15]), schools as well as trans youth are the targets when they allow students to go by names or pronouns that parents haven't approved.

As with pronouns and names, so too with dormitories and school trips, where parents and guardians are concerned: The school needs to understand the needs of its students and it has to communicate in advance to their families. Students' caregivers should know before the enrollment contract is signed, before the field trip permission is granted, before the dorm change is announced, that the school has a gender-inclusive policy in place. Get input rather than reactions. Yes, some parents and guardians will disagree and maybe even leave (or threaten to leave) a school over these policies. But others will feel welcomed and new families who need this kind of support will be attracted because of publicized practices.

THE WORLD OUT THERE . . .

A final note on rooming situations and off-campus trips: When taking students off-campus, schools need to be aware of laws regarding transgender individuals. This is particularly true if a school manages any overseas travel. In some countries, sadly, being LGBTQ+ is against the law. Even in countries (or states or localities) where it isn't overtly illegal, LGBTQ+ students who are used to being visible and out might find that they are shunned or harassed for their identity. Schools should be aware of the environment that they are bringing their students into and decide whether it is emotionally healthy to do so. Within the United States, there are many places that extend no legal protection to transgender individuals. Transgender and GNC people may be refused public accommodation in hotels, refused service at restaurants, and so on. It is incumbent on the school to look up the laws of the area to which they are taking students and carefully weigh the decision to travel to places where such discrimination is legal.

Recent legislative actions in a number of states have banned medical transition for transgender youth (and, in some cases, adults). At

---

15 Okay, I will just briefly—as mentioned in Chapter One, no parent has the "right" to dictate the person their child is or will become. I also find the framing of parents' rights as oppositional to children's or students' rights questionable on its face.

this moment, it doesn't appear to be the case that the student them-self would be penalized for receiving gender-affirming care, although some bills promote the punishment of parents and guardians and phy-sicians for connecting youth with such care; it is unclear whether a school acting in loco parentis during a school trip could likewise be censured. Nor does it seem in any state that a youth who is undergo-ing gender-affirming care would be taken into youth protective services while traveling through a state that prohibits such care. Nonetheless, as I've noted, these legal situations are fluid and evolving, and I would strongly encourage schools to know the laws of the states where they are traveling and, if the trip includes a transgender or GNC student, to establish contact with the local hospitals and clinics in advance of traveling. If that student broke a leg, got into a car accident, etc., would there be doctors and clinicians who would treat them? It is upsetting and saddening that schools and families must consider such realities.

NEXT STEPS

REFLECT

1. Think about your own experience in dorms (if any) or in chaperoning overnight trips (if any). Whether you were a student (or camper) or a teacher, counselor, chaperone, spend a little time reflecting on your experiences: How were rooms assigned? What felt comfortable and uncomfortable? Did you have peers who felt vulnerable or excluded? Could you perceive that some students felt comfortable and others did not?

RESEARCH

1. If opening an all-gender dorm, assess the level of interest in the student body and design an application.

2. For non-residential schools, review policies for rooming when students take off-campus trips.

3. Review parents'/guardians' role in approving roommate assignments per current policy and encourage student autonomy where possible.

4. Before going on a school trip, look into the legal situation of the destination when it comes to transgender rights, in order to best protect your trans and GNC students (and your school).

ACT

1. Tour your dormitories and look at the existing facilities.

2. Conduct focus groups or surveys of dormitory residents to get honest assessments of dorm culture.

3. Based on steps 1 & 2, evaluate the feasibility of opening an all-gender dorm.

4. Design residential curriculum to promote inclusion and community building. Train resident faculty and student leaders.

5. Rewrite any visitation policies to remove reference to gender and to avoid heteronormativity.

6. Discuss changes to policies and facilities early and often with all constituencies.

NOTES

a. "Definition of Affirmative Consent," *SUNY*, accessed February 20, 2024, https://system.suny.edu/sexual-violence-prevention-workgroup/policies/ affirmative-consent/.

CHAPTER NINE:

WHAT ABOUT SINGLE-GENDER INSTITUTIONS?

In 2014, women's colleges across the country found themselves in a swirling debate: Should they allow transgender men to graduate from their institutions? Should they admit transgender women? How much should they adjust their policies and facilities to accommodate transgender students? Could sisterhood be changed to siblinghood, or would something fundamental to the school be lost? 2014 was, for some reason, the year that many women's colleges reached a critical mass of transgender and gender non-conforming (GNC) students on their campuses. Articles were published in leading newspapers and magazines, explaining the situation and arguing about how best to proceed. In its exploration of the topic, *The New York Times* dangled the provocative phrase: "When women become men at Wellesley."[a]

There are thousands of single-gender institutions in the US: all-girls and all-boys schools from pre-K through graduate level, most of them private institutions. Summer camps for boys and summer camps for girls abound. Even within an all-gender institution, there are sometimes classes that are divided for boys and for girls, according to subject area (STEM classes for girls) or grade level (middle school being gender-segregated, for instance). The history and science behind single-gender education is fascinating, and even if your school is thoroughly all-gender, aspects of this chapter may well be worth considering in terms of fully informing your understanding of gender inclusion.

Women's colleges and girls' schools arose in the United States throughout the nineteenth century, a time when girls could not attend most institutions of higher education. The founders of many all-women colleges and all-girls schools sought to demonstrate that (White) women were capable of the same degree of academic rigor and achievement as (White) men. They wanted to show that they ought to be included—if not included in the schools, then included in the professions and life after schooling. Some of these were formed as "finishing schools," places where girls could learn domestic arts and prepare themselves for marriage and life in society. Others were formed as academic institutions providing rigorous studies in science, mathematics, and classics at a time when these fields were deemed by many men to be hazardous or inappropriate for girls.

Many of these schools also established themselves as a sort of sanctuary or oasis. To be an intellectually curious girl in nineteenth-century America was rarely easy. Because of their gender, these girls were denied opportunities or, if included, were often teased or ostracized. The all-girls schools and women's colleges were places where girls could be students and scholars, their gender no longer the most salient issue.[1]

Like all institutions, single-gender schools should acknowledge, understand, and grapple with the question of why they were formed, what the beliefs around gender were at that time, and how those understandings have shifted since. Today, all-girls schools continue to market themselves as providing a unique opportunity in terms of gender. For some schools, the selling point is the safety of an all-girl environment. Such institutions market themselves with subtle suggestions that an all-girls school is free of sexual predation and keeps girls focused on studies rather than dating. Others appeal to a sense of school spirit and leadership: at an all-girls school, the class president, the top scholar, the best athletes—all of them are girls. Girls will have a greater opportunity to learn to lead if they don't have to compete with boys.

Another common selling point is the all-girls school's unique ability to counteract sexist practices and beliefs in academia. By elementary school, many girls have already absorbed the sense that "girls aren't good

---

1 I am here focusing on the history of all-girls institutions and not all-boys; all-boys schools usually did not have such a deliberate purpose when they were founded. Because of the patriarchal structure of our society, all-boys schools were simply "schools." They became notable for their single-gendered-ness not at their founding, but in their continued existence as such past the point when many similar schools went "co-ed." Thus, their histories are not as relevant to this conversation. However, this chapter's ideas about working toward inclusion are just as pertinent to all-boys schools as to all-girls schools.

at math," or discovered that "only boys do robotics," such that by high school, fewer girls are enrolled in upper-level math and science classes. Many all-girls schools offer curricula and academic structures that seek to counteract these tendencies. For instance, some all-girls school thoroughly integrate the arts and sciences—learning about physics through dance and creating "maker spaces" that teach girls to use 3D printers or table saws to produce art. Other schools adopt a more experiential curriculum, taking students out into the field to study and learn about biology and chemistry. And yet others make it a point to have guest lecturers and visiting scholars who are women and who are advancing in technological and scientific careers.

It is also true that all-girls schools and all-women colleges are very gender-aware spaces. I will admit that when I first started reading about transgender students coming out at all-women colleges, my first thought was: Why would they want to stay there? In my own experience as a trans-guy, I certainly wouldn't have wanted to "out" myself every time I answered the common question of where I went to school. It wasn't until I had a former student attend an all-women college and then come out as transgender that I was really able to comprehend what makes all-girls schools and all-women colleges such supportive places for many transgender and GNC students.

Students who come out as transgender on these campuses often want to stay—or, already out, want to apply to join the school—because all-girls and -women's schools have a clear commitment to considering gender as part of education. There's usually active and ongoing conversation about patriarchy, feminism, and the way gender works in schools and the broader world. I get how that can be exciting, and also comforting, for a young transgender or GNC person. There's a much greater chance that they are going to be surrounded by people who already understand the basics concepts around gender identity and expression and who are deeply interested in considering the implications of these constructions. Which is all to say: Single-gender schools need to be prepared for the transgender and GNC students who are on their campuses or who would like to be on their campuses.

EXPANDING "SINGLE-GENDER"

There are two angles a single-gender school will want to consider when they talk about gender inclusion. The first is legal and the second is philosophical. Single-gender schools occupy an interesting legal position. In most states, they maintain the right to discriminate based on sex. Depending on the state, this is codified with different language, but the general idea is that, during the admissions process, they have legal right to say no to anybody whose birth certificate says "male" (in the case of an all-girls school). If a single-gender school wants to be gender inclusive but also maintain its position as an all-girls school, it should investigate the legal territory carefully. Schools have been able to negotiate a variety of positions, but the language needs to be handled carefully, in terms of talking about gender identity, legal sex, and so on. But, to me, this is a side note next to the more important question of philosophy: Where and how do transgender and non-binary students belong at a single-gender school?

Let me describe a situation that I've encountered at a number of all-girls schools. In ninth grade, a student joins the school—she loves it there, dives in, does well in class, makes the varsity basketball team, embraces the school's ethos of "others above self," takes poetry and coding classes, and, like many adolescents, wonders: *Who am I?* In the student's second year, she tells a few friends that she is thinking a lot about gender: *What is it really? Why does it matter so much? How many different ways are there to be a girl?* The friend group has late-night conversations in the dorm, deliberating about what it even means to be "gender non-conforming"—aren't many of the girls at the school "non-conforming" in some way?

The girl and her friends try new looks: short hair, dyed hair, a nose piercing, tight jeans, baggy flannel shirts, shirts and ties with skirts.

When junior year rolls around, the student tells some of her friends, "I think I might be transgender." In private, with friends, the student switches pronouns (to *he, him, his*) and begins using a new name. As the year continues, his friends encourage him to come out. He's doing well in classes, he's starting to get ready to apply for college, and he thinks his parents will be okay with this, so he comes out to his

183

advisor and dorm faculty.

This is the most common situation that I encounter with all-girls schools in terms of transgender students attending is just what I elaborated above: A student already attending, in good standing, who is often well known and well-liked transitions. Sometimes the student is a top scholar. Sometimes they are a team captain, or a student council president. Their picture is in the newspaper and the alumni bulletin for the awards that they win . . . and the student is a boy. On the surface, it doesn't look "right": It looks like there's a boy attending an all-girls school. When alumni and parents and guardians see the pictures—or when they visit campus and see the students in action—the optics of the situation can seem at odds with what they thought the school was. Yet, for many of the teachers and students attending the school, it feels absolutely "right" for the trans-boy to be there. Faculty will say they knew him when he was a girl, that the transition process felt natural, that he's part of the school.

I highlight this situation because, in addition to its prevalence, it also highlights the need to think about a variety of constituencies and a deeper philosophical approach to gender and belonging. Some single-gender schools just try to keep their transgender boys and GNC students "off the books"—not mentioning them in publications or website material—and hope in this way to side-step having to make more difficult and widespread decisions. To me, this sort of "resolution" actually only fixes a marketing problem and does nothing to address inclusion or the school's understanding of gender: It's a dodge, not a solution at all. Better to consider all the admissions and branding options available and weigh them against the school's mission, as discussed in Chapter Two.

Usually, all-girls schools can articulate a clear idea of who they wish to admit: female-bodied students who identify as girls.[2] With that as a starting point, it is a great thought exercise to consider the situation I described above. What do you do with that student who was "prop-

---

2 Again, when I work with these schools, I have to push them on this. They will say "girls," but they will mean "students who are female as well as girls." And, historically, this is who they admit—female-bodied, girl-identified individuals. But of course, they don't "check" on the genitalia; both sex and gender are taken on the word of the parent/guardian.

erly" admitted as a female-bodied, girl-identified student in ninth grade and who has now come out and started to live as a boy in his senior year? According to some single-gender school policies, the proper response would be to tell him, "You can no longer attend the school." The all-girls school can be polite and professional about it; they can help the student find a new school and write him good recommendations. But the bottom line for some schools is, "We are an all-girls school, and he is a boy and should not be a student here."

On the surface, this logic may seem like, if not necessarily inclusion, institutional recognition of the student's self-identification. But, by insisting that he is a boy, period, the school is in effect erasing the transgender student's past—the reason he was admitted to the school—and forcing him into a binary that isn't sufficient to explain his whole self. Yes, he is a boy. But he's not a cisgender boy. The school might want to simplify policies by insisting on gender in the binary only, but the very nature of transgender identity—and, I would argue, the very nature of gender—makes this impossible.

Another pitfall of this type of policy: What if the student, hearing of this policy and confronted with having to leave, says: "But I love this school. I'll pretend to be a girl for the rest of this year just so I can stay?" Would the school accept that reaction and let the student stay? Do they see any problems with this situation? Clearly, there's a conflict here. On the one hand, the school gets what it wants (a "girl" as a student)—but it is also inflicting some real harm on the student by incentivizing them to be closeted and to maintain an artificial identity. Effectively, the school is saying, "You can't be who you are if you want to stay here." Is that really in line with the school's educational mission?

Another way to reframe the situation is to ask, "What if the hypothetical student hadn't come out as a boy, but as GNC or non-binary? What if they used 'they' as a pronoun and, in gender expression, sometimes looked masculine and sometimes looked feminine and sometimes looked androgynous. . . ?" Would the school allow them to stay? Or would they say (accurately) that the student is not a girl anymore—and then ask them to leave the school?

In other words, what exactly is the school policing? Appearance?

Self-understanding? And what is the school hoping to teach and accomplish with its students?

Again, historically speaking, all-girls schools were founded in response to gender-based exclusion in education, which, in the nineteenth century, was understood solely as the marginalization of cisgender (as we'd say today) women. There's a very cogent argument to be made for updating that same, still relevant premise to encompass contemporary understandings of who is oppressed because of their gender identity, a group that includes transgender, gender non-conforming, and non-binary people along with cisgender women and girls. This re-envisioning of the all-girls school's original purpose is akin to what I've proposed about schools connecting the work of gender inclusivity to their institutions' established missions and values.

Any school that works with adolescents has to factor students' self-discovery into its educational goals. That is what adolescence is all about, and schools are in the business not just of delivering course content in the form of mathematics and literature, but also of providing ethical frameworks and preparing students to live full lives. To offer a curriculum that nurtures an understanding of self and the self's relationship to the world, and then to remove anyone who comes out as transgender or GNC, is hypocritical and harmful.

Thankfully, most single-gender schools that I've worked with don't require students to leave if they come out. Most single-gender schools that have transgender and GNC students come out want to make sure that they are supported at the school and feel comfortable staying there. When it comes to all-girls schools, they also want to figure out whether they can retain their single-gender designation and have transgender boys. I think the answer is both yes and no.

Even if a single-gender school took a very hardline approach and asked anyone who didn't identify as a girl to leave the school, they would still have transgender and GNC students (in the closet) at the school; they would still have alumni who came out as transgender or GNC after graduating. So, there will be men who have gone to that all-girls school—no matter what the admissions and matriculation policies may be (unless the school seeks to remove transgender alumni from the ranks, which strikes me as a difficult process).

Schools of whatever kind shouldn't be in the business of restricting or determining students' identities. In fact, schools should be in the opposite sort of business: encouraging exploration and understanding; encouraging students to engage intellectually with the questions of who they are, what good they can do, and how they want to move through the world. Schools might expect conformity to rules and guidelines around behavior, but schools shouldn't demand or indeed desire conformity when it comes to identity and self-understanding; this leads to very poor mental health outcomes for the students. (Not to mention: Demanding identity conformity is futile. You can attempt to police *behavior*, but written policy can't determine a person's essential qualities.) So, while an all-girls school might have explicit rules barring sexual intimacy, they shouldn't have a rule that says you can't be a lesbian. The same would extend to gender identity.

REVISING POLICIES

So, what does this ultimately mean for single-gender schools in terms of policy and practices? It means that the limitations on what genders can attend the school should apply at the time of admission, and only at the time of admission. Within the legal constraints permitted by the state the school is in, a school should have earnest discussions about who the school is for: All girls born female? Anyone who is female? (If so, by what definition? As discussed in Chapters One and Seven, biological sex isn't as cut and dry as it's often assumed to be.) Anyone who is a girl? Anyone of a marginalized gender identity? Schools will come up with different answers to this question and will face different constraints based on state law. Some all-girls schools now admit anyone who is born female who identifies as a girl or as neither a girl nor a boy; anyone who is born male and identifies as a girl; and anyone who is born neither male nor female (intersex)[3] who identifies as a girl. Other all-girls schools now admit anyone who identifies as a girl, period, and

---

3 As discussed in Chapter One, this is not actually a definition of "intersex," but I think this is the identity that schools intend to include with this type of language.

some have opted to admit only those who are born female.

It is also possible for a single-gender school to decide to no longer be single-gender. Some schools have done that in recent years—Deep Springs College, historically all men, in 2011; Pine Manor College, historically all women, in 2014—though often the movement away from being single-gender has more to do with finances or other outside pressures than it does with inclusion. Most single-gender schools are hesitant to make this change due to fear of losing their alumni base's support. But, if a single-gender school is engaging in a robust conversation about all possible changes, it could be beneficial to at least consider what it would look like not to be single-gender any longer.

These are significantly different outcomes that I outline here, with significantly different implications about the motives and cultures of these schools. I believe that some of these possible positions are more inclusive than others and are better set up to support transgender and GNC students. However, I also understand that each school will have its own sense of mission and vision and will need to make decisions within that framework. To me, the most important thing is for single-gender schools to have an open and honest discussion—ideally *before* they are handling the case of individual student—and to make a decision that has been shared and reviewed by students, faculty, and alumni.

Let's step back from single-gender schools for a moment and put this conversation in a larger context: Beyond schools, there are a lot of single-gender organizations, groups, and spaces. These include summer camps and scouting troops. Sports teams and affinity groups. Fraternities and sororities. The work that needs to be done is not the abolition of all single-gender spaces or institutions; the work that needs to be done is inclusion. Yet, we live, teach, learn, and work in a world that makes frequent use of exclusion—and sometimes with good cause. There are times when a group needs to say: this is a place for X and not Y. Affinity groups are a good example; Black students at a school for instance may need a space in which they can talk with other Black students and not have to defend or explain themselves to peers who do not share that identity.[4] I would not argue that every space needs to be open

---

4   The reaction, unfortunately, to such a group is sometimes for White students to say: "Fine,

to every person on the basis of race or gender. Rather, I would ask that schools and other institutions look at their reasons for being exclusive, to consider what status and privilege are being protected, and at what cost.

In the end, I find single-gender institutions to be not much different from sports teams and dormitories. There are compelling reasons to keep some teams and some dormitories designated as single gender, just as there are compelling reasons to make all-gender options available as well. In sports, a school or league may decide to run a girls' soccer team and allow transgender boys to play on that team. It is a team designed for girls, but (some) boys can play on that team. It is not an all-gender or non-gender team: It is a girls' team with boys on it. Inclusion comes not in the official gender designation, but in the way the team behaves. Do they design T-shirts and signs that say "Go Lady Raiders!"? Do they call out to their teammates by saying, "Come on, girls!"? Or do they modify their language to reflect that there are players on the team who don't fit the binary?

The same is true for single-gender schools. There are many philosophical and legal reasons to keep a school designated as all girls. But that school is very likely to have transgender boys and GNC students in attendance, whether they are out or not. Will those students feel that they have a place within the school? Will they see themselves as fully present members of the student body? That's where the real work of inclusion happens.

---

then we'll form a White affinity group." My typical sarcastic response to this is, "The rest of the school is your White affinity group." But, less cynically, a White affinity group could be very helpful in getting White students to understand and talk about their own racial identities, how structures within society (including their school) have given them privilege, and how to be allies in the work for racial justice.

NEXT STEPS

REFLECT

List and reflect on the reasons you value single-gender education models. What is powerful about being a single-gender institution? What would be lost if you were an all-gender institution? Be specific and reflect on the particulars. Then, reflect on what could be gained—or rather, how those possible losses could be transformed into inclusive wins for more students.

RESEARCH

1. Find out what peer single-gender schools are doing when it comes to gender inclusivity. Look at written policies where available. In cases of institutions without specific policy regarding transgender or GNC students, see if you can talk to faculty and find out about protocol that might be off the books.

2. Review the experience of current transgender and GNC students at your school as well as recent transgender and GNC graduates.

3. Assess the mission and history of single-gender education at your school and try to align the historical purpose with the current mission.

ACT

1. Form focus groups to talk about what being a single-gender institution means. Try to create groups that have a particular affinity (LGBTQ+, international students, students of color) and include alumni and parents and guardians as well.

2. Putting together the information from step 1 and the Research steps, come up with some possible changes to policies and practices. Consider the student experience from admission through graduation in examining what might change.

3. Bring a range of options (putting your school in the context of peer single-gender schools) for moves that could create more gender inclusion and present these to administration and the board (and legal counsel as well).

NOTES

a. Ruth Padawer, "When Women Become Men at Wellesley," *The New York Times*, October 15, 2014, https://www.nytimes.com/2014/10/19/magazine/when-women-become-men-at-wellesley-college.html.

CHAPTER TEN:

THE KIDS ARE ALL RIGHT (USUALLY)

In the past few years, I've seen interest in education on gender identity soar. When I first started speaking to schools, I got requests from gender studies departments at colleges and from Gay-Straight Alliances at the most liberal of high schools. These days, schools across the country arc interested in learning more about gender. Most often, though, when schools reach out to me, they ask me to come and talk to their students. My reply is always the same: I'm delighted to talk to the students, do a session with the whole school, follow up with affinity groups, classes, and clubs—but what I'm really interested in doing is meeting with the adults.

This is a harder sell. Schools are in the business, after all, of educating students; they are comfortable requiring kids to attend a workshop or go to a lecture. There are fewer mechanisms for requiring the adults in the community to be continually educated through ongoing professional development. But whenever possible, I like to run faculty seminars, workshops for administrators, and conversation sessions with parents and guardians.

When I get a chance to meet with this broad range of constituents, usually what I find is that the students have greater familiarity and comfort with language and concepts around gender, and adults are more polarized. That is, many students will say they know someone who is transgender or gender non-conforming (GNC), will demonstrate an ability to use "they" as a singular pronoun, and can explain the difference between gender identity and biological sex. In comparison, in a population of parents and guardians or faculty, I usually find a small group that's really well-versed in gender, another small group that resists any sort of conversation about transgender identity, and a majority of adults in the middle, kind of wondering what's going on.

While it is important to provide ongoing educational opportunities for students around gender identity, if a school wants to make lasting changes to promote inclusion, that school needs to do some serious, coordinated, and sustained work with the adults in the community. Too many schools set up something like a task force for inclusion, let that task force work in private, and then do a big "ta-da" reveal at the end, showcasing all the changes that need to be made. That is pretty much a recipe for disaster. As I've outlined in earlier chapters, to the greatest extent possible, schools need to work toward gender inclusion in a way that is transparent, that invites conversation, that anticipates those who will resist the changes and seeks to acknowledge that resistance.

As a general rule, I think that adults should be given the opportunity to engage in learning and conversation around gender in frequent, low-stakes settings. A half-hour coffee club in the mornings can watch a five-minute video on gender identity and then have a discussion. A book club can meet for an hour once a month and, in the span of an academic year, work through six books about gender identity. Newsletters or bulletins—whatever the vehicle that schools use to communicate to parents and guardians—should include a regular column or section that either teaches new terminology around gender or updates the community on what the gender inclusion task force is up to. There should also be regular presentations to the faculty during meetings, showing drafts of proposed restroom signage and so on.

All of this keeps the conversation sustained and normalizes the topic. If there's only one meeting that raises gender identity for discussion, everyone's feelings will be pent up—which makes them then liable to explode—or people will simply skip that one meeting and avoid the conversation altogether. Frequent, low-stakes conversations give people with a range of views and levels of understanding an opportunity to engage, to question, to doubt, and then to repeat and try it again.

Even so, you will undoubtedly find resistance when you do this work, and it is important to be prepared to work through and around those points of resistance. In particular, I want to address senior administrators and parents and guardians in this chapter and talk about ways to respond to resistance from these areas.

DECISION-MAKERS

When assembling a task force to do the work of gender inclusion, it is important to have influential people from all the school's constituencies. You want student leaders, you want vocal parents and guardians, you want devoted faculty and ranking administrators. You also need, early on, to have a practical understanding of governance. How is change made at your school? Who gets to decide? For some schools, this will be a board of trustees. For other schools, decisions come solely from the superintendent or the principal. And in other cases, a school board (often populated by parents and guardians) makes many decisions.

Take a look at the governance structure and try to anticipate where resistance will come from. It is often hardest at a school where just one person makes the big calls—but even in those scenarios, there is usually a council of senior staff or an advisory board who assists. Try to get someone from that group to join the task force. If that isn't possible, then set up a time for the task force to make a presentation to that group or to a subset of that group.

The latter is usually a very good strategy when approaching a board of trustees or a school board. These boards tend to be large and have varied interests; there are many demands on their members' time. Working with a subcommittee (or asking the board to form up a subcommittee on equity and inclusion) can give a task force the chance to meet with and educate a smaller group of influential individuals. Presenting to such groups provides an opportunity to build partnerships, increase support, and get feedback before working with larger groups down the line When the time comes for the whole board to vote on a proposal from the task force, the subcommittee members are already familiar and can help shepherd their colleagues through the process.

All that said, it is unfortunately quite possible to encounter major resistance from school boards and administration in general. There are many books, essays, and articles that chart the course of how families and allies have taken the fight for inclusion to the next level. Sadly, many of these stories end with the family of the transgender student heading for a new school. Sometimes, they end with a legal class wending its way through the courts, resolved only after the student has graduated. It can take a long time and a lot of energy to make substantial change.

Particularly at this moment, when the legal rights of transgender youth, medical practitioners who support gender-affirming care, and caregivers who want to help their children transition are all on the line, more and more families are simply departing from schools and communities and states that aren't supportive. This option is available only to those with the privilege of money and mobility (arguably, the ability to medically transition is something only available to those with the privilege of wealth and access, too). If a school can provide support and inclusion for gender diverse students amidst this stormy climate, that school will be a safe harbor that saves lives. It is well worth some controversy and difficult conversations.

WORKING WITH STUDENTS AND THEIR FAMILIES

Parents and guardians are another group that really need to be worked with for a fully transparent and effective process around building gender inclusivity. As you consider the changes and approaches outlined in this book, one area to consider carefully is student privacy and communication with parents and guardians. This can be a topic that creates a lot of resistance and needs to be handled with care.

At schools, whether a boarding school or a day school, students often maintain an identity that is different from the one they maintain at home. This can be as small as the boy whose parents have always called him "Stevie," but who in tenth grade starts going by "Steve" at school. This can be the girl who gets off the bus in eighth grade and goes straight to the bathroom to put on the eye makeup and lipstick that her parents don't want her to wear. Or it can be the White boy who has a Black girlfriend and knows his parents are bigoted and wouldn't approve. And it could be the student who has recently asked their teacher to use "they" and their first initial, J, instead of the name and pronouns they have been known by before.

In each of these circumstances, what would a school do? In which case would a teacher or administrator feel obligated to call the students' parents and guardians and inform them of what was going on at school? And why? How would the teacher or administrator justify their decision to violate the student's privacy in this way?

With most schools that I'm familiar with, few of these instances would be reported home except the last one. And that's a problem. All of the examples have to do with identity and expression, values and beliefs, but somehow, only the one involving a change in gender identity feels necessary to report. Of course, I don't think it is. I think that students have a right to privacy and should reasonably expect confidentiality unless they are engaging in behavior that makes them or others unsafe.[1] And if a student has not disclosed their gender identity to their family, they may well have reason to believe it would be uncomfortable or even unsafe for them to do so.

But I also recognize that keeping such behaviors private can put teachers and administrators in a difficult position. Imagine that you're J's advisor (from the example above) and are getting a phone call from J's parent or guardian: "I hear that my daughter is going by a new name at school. I don't want her to do that." How do you answer? You certainly don't want to lie to the parent or guardian. You don't want to out the student to the parent or guardian, either. And though the impulse might be to say, "That's something you should discuss with your child," you don't want to drop this very heavy burden on the student's shoulders.

Because I run and work with affinity groups for LGBTQ+ students, I am often amongst the first adults that a transgender or GNC student will come out to. After telling me that they are questioning or that they want to transition, often the next thing they say is: "Please don't tell my parents." That's a promise that I (unless I'm worried about their safety)

---

1 Of course, as discussed, some state and local laws void this very expectation of confidentiality by requiring consent from parents/guardians before a student can be called by a name or pronouns that differ from what's indicated by their birth certificate. In such circumstances, unfortunately, a call home is legally required.

make. I can and should be able to promise that I won't tell anyone unless the student expressly asks me to tell that person.

After that, when a student has come out, usually, I like to try and listen—I keep asking them to *tell me more*. What are they thinking? What are they feeling? I don't try to "fix" anything, and I don't try to "help" by making suggestions for what they can or ought to do. My goal when a student first comes out is for them to feel affirmed and heard, to know that there's an adult who supports them. I end by telling them that I'm glad they came out to me, honored that they trusted me, and that they can expect me to follow up and check in on them.

Admittedly, that last part is a little sensitive. We all know what it's like to be asked a question on a topic that we don't feel like discussing. I never want to force an LGBTQ+ student to talk about their identity if they don't want to. But I do want to make sure they have the chance to talk. So, I will usually email and ask them to find a time to stop by to chat—I'll initiate the contact but let them control the timing. In that second or third (depending on how things go) conversation, I will swing back to the student's initial request for confidentiality: How's the coming out going? Have they told others? What's the response been? How are things at home? I try to lead into questions about what they are concerned about in terms of their parents and guardians' response. Do they have reasons to believe their family will reject them? Are there other factors stressing their parents or guardians that make the student not want to bring this topic up?

If the student is part of an affinity group I have a role in, I will try and set "coming out to family" as a topic of conversation. In this group, we will not only share how things have gone, but also rehearse or role-play conversations that we want to have or imagine might happen with people who we intend to come out to. It can be really helpful and affirming to know that others share the same concerns but have been able to come out to siblings or parents and guardians, despite the anxiety and concerns about doing so.

In most cases when I work with students, after having these initial couple of conversations, I can sincerely tell them that things will be better if they come out to their parents or guardians (although there are some very clear and important exceptions to this, discussed below). From there, I try to work with them to get them to imagine what it would take for them to feel ready to do so. Sometimes the answer is just time. Sometimes it might help if they come out to a sibling or an aunt first. Other times, they just want to wait until after Thanksgiving. And sometimes, I can offer to talk to the parents or guardians—with or without the student present—if the student thinks that would be helpful.

Sadly, it is sometimes true that the student has very good reason to fear coming out to their parents or guardians. They may have had another relative who has come out and seen their parents or guardians treat that person cruelly or talk about them in a demeaning way. They may have parents or guardians who are abusive, emotionally, or physically, already, and coming out to them would only add another dimension to the trouble. Or their parents or guardians might belong to a political or religious group that has strong rhetoric against the LGBTQ+ community. In these cases, I encourage the student to think about a broader net of safety and support. I try to assess whether they are uncomfortable or unsafe at home. If they are unsafe—if they say they are being abused, for instance—I will immediately report that to the appropriate authorities. But if their parents or guardians take them to a church every Sunday where they hear that LGBTQ+ people are sinners and will suffer for those sins, that's certainly not a healthy or supportive environment, but it doesn't rise to the level of making the child unsafe.

Either way, these are difficult circumstances that can result in major changes in the student's home life. Sometimes, the student will have a sibling or cousin or aunt who is supportive—someone who might be able to provide them with a home if they were kicked out. Other times, that support just isn't present in the family, and I will work to identify a community organization that can help. There are often regional support groups for LGBTQ+ youth that can provide good housing resources. And if the student is at a boarding school, it is often possible to coordinate support from constituencies within the school—whether that comes from mental health counselors, day student families, or alumni resources. Ideally, it wouldn't come to that, but a student needs to know that if they are kicked out, they won't be on the street, and they won't have to go to a shelter where their identity isn't respected.

Back to that dreaded hypothetical phone call, when the parent or guardian of J has said: "Is my daughter using 'they' as a pronoun? What's going on?" Before I make any response, I want to know where the student is in their conversation with their parent or guardian—that's one of the goals of the strategy I outlined above. Only then do I want to engage the parent or guardian and find out where *they* are. So, my response to J's caregiver's inquiry is likely to be something like: "I've had a lot of great conversations with your child lately. We've talked about English class and soccer, and pronouns and debate club. I'm interested to hear what's on your mind and what you're concerned about."

Again: I don't want to lie, and I don't want to out the student, and I don't want to absolve myself of responsibility by suggesting that the parent or guardian just needs to talk to the child. I'm hoping to open a door to a conversation (admittedly probably a difficult one) with the parent or guardian about their fears, their concerns, their doubts. Quite often, the parent or guardian has a very good idea of what's going on with their child (though maybe not the right language for it), and if I can gently listen and help them be realistic about their fears, it can be a productive call. If all goes well, I can end by suggesting that they let their child come to them with this topic rather than making it a confrontation. That the parent or guardian be patient and try to signal openness and willingness to listen, but not force their child to talk to them about this topic.[2]

The above way of handling parents and guardians works if the teacher knows the student well and has a parent or guardian who is comfortable calling and talking, which is a very involved approach on both the school's and family's parts. To connect with a wider range of caregivers, and students, a school can also offer—or direct parents and

---

2 This is almost always the best approach. I know a lot of teachers who have asked, "I think so-and-so is gay. Should I just ask him? Wouldn't that help him come out?" It can be very scary to have someone tell you what they think they know—even if that person is right. A questioning child might not be ready to use a certain term; they might be thinking "I'm gay" and not "I'm non-binary," for instance. Or, one of their fears might be that others can "tell"— that they don't look or act "normal." In almost every situation, it is better to wait, to be a mirror and reflect back how the student sees themself.

guardians to community resources that offer—groups where families of LGBTQ+ kids get together for conversation and discussion. A lot of parents and guardians want to know, "What do I do if I think my kid is queer?" Beyond just the answer to that question, these groups can provide a sense of community—a sense that they aren't in this alone. And, of course, online forums, groups, and workshops are also available and can be advantageous for people in areas where in-person groups aren't happening as well as for anonymity.

The final sort of caregiver-oriented problem comes not from the parent or guardian who thinks that their child might be transgender or GNC, but from the parent or guardian who thinks that transgender and GNC students who attend school alongside their cisgender child are a problem or a danger. Most often, this takes the form of "that student shouldn't be allowed . . ." to use a facility (". . . in the girls' bathroom") or join a group (". . . on the field hockey team"). In those cases, the conversation needs to be referred to the right person: whether that is the principal or the dean of students, someone who knows the school's policies and has institutional authority should field this (whereas a coach or classroom teacher shouldn't be made to defend their student or player, for example). Throughout the process, the student's privacy needs to be respected. Additionally, the administrator handling the conversation should frame the issue in terms of students in general, not this one student in particular.

To the extent possible, the caregiver's concerns should be heard, understood, and responded to. They, too, should be directed to resources where they can educate themselves. The response to such parents/guardians needs to walk a fine line: the parent/guardian needs a clear understanding of what the school's rules are—particularly around inclusion and harassment—but also needs to not be completely shut down. Caregivers who feel they have not been listened to are more likely to act out or try to gather a group to resist the inclusion work of the school. If there is an ongoing community dialogue—whether that's a workshop, a book group, a forum, or another chance for conversation on school policy—make sure the parent/guardian knows about it (and then make sure the facilitators of the group are ready to handle disagreement). It is only through education and engagement that we will come to mutual understanding and lasting, effective change.

The work outlined in this section only takes on more importance in the current political climate. School boards across the country—some in very liberal states—have imposed restrictions on the sorts of supports, facilities, and accommodations a school can offer. In many cases, these policies are supported in the name of parental rights. This movement has made me feel even more strongly that schools should be doing work toward gender inclusion for *all* students and designing policies and practices for *all* students, doing away with reference to gender as much as possible. But that is a big leap for many schools to make.

What's a smaller step a school can take to support transgender and GNC students in this moment when parental rights are on the front page? As difficult as it seems, I'd say this is the time to engage students' families. To listen to them, to invite them to civil discourse. Talk about a range of topics, not just gender. Bring them in as partners. Don't wait for the reaction. There's never a good conversation when the person is already angry—and at this moment, many people in this country are angry. Whatever policies are in place that are under dispute, be open to discussing them, articulate their value, and put them in the frame of your mission and values for all of your students.

Unfortunately, this approach probably won't win over many caregivers who are entrenched in their beliefs. Right now, the dispute isn't truly over what rules should be in place for transgender youth—the dispute is over whether trans youth have a right to exist. Still, schools can model for all of their students what civil discourse, what discussion and community-mindedness, actually looks like.

SUPPORTING STUDENT ACTIVISM

One of the many detrimental outcomes of recent anti-LGBTQ+ legislative actions is the extensive silencing that follows their passage. For instance, Florida's "Don't Say Gay" law bans in-school discussions of "sexual orientation and gender identity"—an extremely broad set of topics. The result in many classrooms is educators playing it safe; teachers leave an extremely wide margin around anything that potentially could get them in trouble. The silence that creates a sense of (precarious) safety for the teacher or administrator creates real danger for queer youth: a lack of representation, self-understanding, hope. Even in these charged atmospheres—in fact, especially in these places—it is crucial for schools and educators to find ways to support student engagement and activism.

There are many ways to do this, depending on location, political climate, and the specific issues at hand for your school. Consider Nancy Garden's 1982 young adult novel *Annie on My Mind*, a book that has faced much scrutiny and censorship for depicting a positive romantic relationship between two high school girls. In 1994, after an Olathe, Kansas, superintendent unilaterally removed donated copies of *Annie* from schools in his district, one high school's student government unanimously approved a resolution to reinstate the book to their school library. At a second district high school, students took a more grassroots approach by creating and distributing leaflets that protested the book's removal.[a] In advocating for student agency and well-being, it's key to encourage youth to politically engage in ways that are attainable, that match the spirit of their concerns, and that respond meaningfully to circumstances affecting their school or greater community.

In truly embattled schools, the best option might be to connect students with state and local organizations that are involved in education, lobbying, and activism. Having class or club time that is devoted to discussing current events is another way to help students have a voice. In a state where anti-trans legislation is up for a vote, schools should be facilitating conversation about these potential laws. Educators can inform students about upcoming school board meetings, town meetings, or other places where a student might advocate on their own behalf.

Of course, this isn't possible for every student. Some may not be able to get transportation to meetings outside of school. Others may not feel comfortable speaking on topics of queer identity in public. It may be more plausible for a school to support student voices and activism in the school newspaper, for instance. Here, too, is a moment where supporting transgender students and advocating for transgender rights can be folded into the larger discussion of supporting all students and broader rights. Any school with a newspaper knows that protecting rights to free speech and freedom of the press is paramount. Giving transgender students and their allies space within those pages to articulate their positions is a great way to foster student activism. Encouraging political engagement and activism via student government, as the Kansas students undertook, is another option.

Although a distressing number of school districts and states now limit what topics can be discussed in the classroom, schools can and should look for ways to teach students that they have a voice and a right to formulate their own ideas. In every state where laws have been enacted along the lines of "Don't Say Gay," there are groups actively lobbying legislators to fight the bills or protesting publicly to show their dismay. Connecting students to these groups and to their own voices is a crucial way to support LGBTQ+ youth and prevent the feelings of isolation and hopelessness that silence can create.

WHEN THE KIDS AREN'T ALL RIGHT

It is sadly almost inevitable that bullying and harassment will occur at any given school. Therefore, all schools need to be prepared to respond productively and effectively to incidents of bullying. Many schools have a single approach to handling harassment—but bullying is not one size fits all.

Study after study shows that LGBTQ+ students (and students who are perceived to be LGBTQ+) are the victims of bullying and harassment at alarming rates. For instance, the CDC's 2019 Youth Risk Behavior Surveillance found that LGB youth in the US were almost twice as likely as their straight peers to experience bullying either on school grounds or online.[b] This reality, coupled with pervasive anti-LGBTQ sentiments in national discourse and politics,[3] has a deleterious effect on the mental health of queer youth. According to the 2021 National Survey on LGBTQ Youth Mental Health, conducted by the Trevor Project, "42%

---

3 As previously noted, in the 2021 Trevor Project survey, 94% of respondents reported that recent political activity in the US had negatively affected their mental health (note c).

of LGBTQ youth seriously considered attempting suicide in the past year, including more than half of transgender and nonbinary youth" surveyed—an alarming statistic perhaps partially explained by the fact that of the nearly 35,000 total respondents, almost half (48%) reported having been unable to access mental healthcare counseling in the past year, even though they'd wished to do so. Queer Black, Latinx, Native/ Indigenous, and mixed-race youth were especially prone to suicidal ideation and attempts, and rates of both generalized anxiety disorder and major depression disorder were especially high for transgender and non-binary youth (with 77% and 70% of this group of respondents suffering from those disorders, respectively).[4]

Bullies who target based on politicized identity (or perception thereof) are making very specific attacks on personhood. This isn't to suggest that other types of bullying—such as picking on a person based on their preferred clothing style or hair color or interests—aren't harmful but rather to say that if an LGBTQ+ student is harassed or bullied for their sexual orientation and/or gender expression, the response to that bullying needs to acknowledge and address the homophobia and transphobia of the offending student, i.e., the systemic foundation of their mistreatment of the targeted student. (The same goes for bullying based on other differences that are influenced by society-wide systems of power.)

For this reason, I would suggest that schools who are working on gender inclusion look into transformative justice.[5] As discussed in Chapter Six, transformative justice can be part of what is often considered the disciplinary process. Instead of suspending a student or setting a punishment such as detention or community service, transformative justice considers the specific wrong that was done, asks how that offense has affected the offender's community, and then weighs what the offender needs to do to rejoin the community in good standing. This process makes the specific nature of the offense crucial and asks the offender not just to sit in detention, "reflect," and perhaps, at most,

---

4 Many organizations collect information and statistics on bullying. The Pacer Center's website has well-organized and regularly updated information on bullying of a wide range of individuals, not just LGBTQ+.

5 This is also sometimes called restorative justice. I prefer transformative because I have often found that, particularly for victims, there often isn't trust to "restore"—it never existed in the first place.

write a letter of apology, but to actively work to mend the relationships and community values that they have harmed or broken.

This process takes more time, more energy, and more resources, but it also produces results that are often more long-lasting and impactful. I am neither an expert on nor a trainer in transformative justice, but I will offer a short synopsis of why I think it is a good system for transgender and GNC students in particular. I would urge members of a task force working on gender inclusion to undergo training in restorative justice together: It is an excellent professional development opportunity.

One of the central components of transformative justice is bringing the offender into mediated dialogue with the victim. Bullying and harassment strip away the sense of personhood; they leave the victim feeling exposed and vulnerable. Transformative justice gives the victim a voice in the process. Instead of an administrator handing out a punishment, the student who has been bullied has the chance to share how that harassment felt and to talk face-to-face with the person who caused that harm, all with the support of their school.

On the other side, the offender has to acknowledge the personhood, the worth and value, of the student they harassed. The dialogue continues until the victim feels satisfied that the offender understands and has come to terms with the harm they have done. Typically, the process includes counseling and education for the offender as well— they might attend support groups or read and discuss articles with a teacher or counselor. This education might pertain to a better understanding of transgender identity, or it might address some of the root causes of bullying in an effort to get the student to understand why they have fallen into this pattern of behavior.

There is much more to this process, and it will not be a good solution for every school. But I would encourage any school that is working on any topic of inclusion to consider looking into transformative justice training. Even if it isn't adopted as part of the disciplinary system, the modes of discourse and dialogue that it teaches can be extremely helpful in facilitating conversations between teachers and administrators, or the task force and the school board, or administrators and parents/guardians.

Because this is such a politically fraught moment for many transgender students, the process of transformative or restorative justice may need to be combined with robust mental health support. Certainly, counseling could be helpful for both parties, but it may be crucial for the transgender student to get that gender-affirming care to help handle the anxiety of engaging in conversations around their identity. Schools should identify counselors and social workers who have specific training in working with transgender youth to help support students as they process the trauma of harassment. And, even outside of navigating conflict, schools should do all they can to network with and hire practitioners who are comfortable and competent with topics pertaining to gender identity and sexuality, and to make students aware of these resources.

NEXT STEPS

REFLECT

1. Think and write about what is going on in your state, your school, or in the country right now in general. What have you read about? Have you heard stories from students or colleagues? What are your concerns and fears? Put them on the page and reflect on where your fears are coming from concretely.

RESEARCH

1. Investigate the way that power works and decisions get made in your school and/or district. Identify key players and bodies.

2. Brainstorm different ways that your school is able to support student activism.

ACT

1. Offer opportunities for parents/guardians to learn about gender identity and get involved in conversations about gender inclusion.

2. Connect with alumni, boards of trustees, and local school boards about the topic of gender inclusion and try to offer some informational or conversational sessions.

3. Train teachers and administrators on how to facilitate potentially difficult conversations with parents and guardians of LGBTQ+ students.

4. Publicize available resources for student activism so that students are aware of them.

5. Consider training in transformative justice and using that as part of the response to bullying and harassment.

NOTES

a. Casey Stepaniuk, "The Burning and Banning of *Annie on My Mind*," *Book Riot*, March 16, 2018, https://bookriot.com/annie-on-my-mind/.

b. "Youth Risk Behavior Surveillance – United States, 2019," *Center for Disease Control and Prevention: Morbidity and Mortality Weekly Report* 69, no. 1 (Atlanta: Centers for Disease Control and Prevention, August 21, 2020): 1–83, https://www.cdc.gov/healthyyouth/data/yrbs/pdf/2019/su6901-H.pdf.

c. The Trevor Project, "National Survey on LGBTQ Youth Mental Health," https://www.thetrevorproject.org/survey-2021/?section=Introduction.

CHAPTER ELEVEN:

GENDER IN LIBRARIES

Given only a quick glance, it might seem odd that libraries are such a profound site of queer and trans liberation. But many stories of queer self-awareness and many stories of queer community begin in public and school libraries. Sometimes it's a perceptive librarian who suggests books to a student or child who seems to not fit in with their peers. Other times it is just the shelves themselves—the quiet of them, the almost-privacy of them—and the titles that they offer. Even for the person—child or adult—who doesn't yet dare to take a book off the shelf, to make that gesture of interest or commitment, merely seeing a title like *Queer Bodies, Queer Selves* is enough to give them some hope.

And, for queer youth across the country, public libraries have often been safe harbors when schools and school libraries are not or cannot be. The late nineties and early 2000s saw a wave of banning Gay-Straight Alliances (GSA) from schools.[1] Some schools even went so far as to ban all clubs to prevent the GSA from meeting or existing. At the private day school in Florida where I taught from 2003 to 2006, the students asked me to help them form a GSA—the administration said no; in public they told the students they were concerned for their safety; they didn't want the students who attended to become targets. In private, to me and other adults, they said they didn't want the controversy, didn't want parents to be turned off from the school. Some of the students wanted to fight, to

---

1 The growth and development of GSA-style clubs at schools is a fascinating one—a good example of the expansion and then pushback against LGBTQ+ rights in schools/communities. Unfortunately, some current legislation is reviving this trend, such as Louisiana H.B. 466, which bans teachers, school employees, and any other "presenter" from discussing sexual orientation or gender identity "during any extracurricular academic, athletic, or social activity." (See note *a*.)

protest, and other students didn't want to be so public and visible. So, we rebranded as "Diversity and Tolerance," and the club gained approval . . . and frequent visits from the administration to make sure we weren't talking too much about homosexuality.

This case was fairly typical for a private school of that era. If I had been teaching at a public school, I probably wouldn't have been able to form the club, even under an alternate name. In many places, when bans and prohibitions like these went into effect, clubs to support queer and trans youth went underground or awkwardly merged with a legit group (more than one drama club has championed "Equal Rights for plays and thespians"). Others left school grounds altogether, frequently finding a home at the public library.

The public library, a place where community and privacy are beautifully blended, offers a respite for clubs like these to meet. Students I've worked with say that the library—whether the one at school or the one in town—feels like an oasis. Anyone might go there for any number of reasons, so people don't tend to be suspicious of why others might be entering. And there's gentle respect for a wide range of activities and behaviors—from the elderly person napping in a chair, to the teenager cruising the web, to the toddler banging on the cover of a picture book.

For these and other reasons, both public and school libraries are important places to consider when doing the work of supporting transgender students. No wonder libraries are under attack by conservative politicians and parents—they truly are places of self-discovery and empowerment. They have the power to connect people to others who are like them, to help them feel less alone through the pages of a book or the frames of a film—no matter how isolated they may feel in their day-to-day lives—and expose them to wholly new ideas of what their lives could become.

In 1990, Dr. Rudine Sims Bishop, a professor of education and scholar of children's literature, proposed her oft quoted metaphor for the different ways that books can connect readers, especially young readers, to the world and to themselves:

"Books are sometimes windows, offering views of worlds

that may be real or imagined, familiar or strange. These windows are also sliding glass doors, and readers have only to walk through in imagination to become part of whatever world has been created or recreated by the author. When lighting conditions are just right, however, a window can also be a mirror. Literature transforms human experience and reflects it back to us, and in that reflection we can see our own lives and experiences as part of the larger human experience. Reading, then, becomes a means of self-affirmation, and readers often seek their mirrors in books."[b]

This potential for connection is precious for everyone—especially so for people who are marginalized—and seeing oneself represented in literature truly does matter. Research in developmental psychology and media studies shows that children's self-esteem is enhanced by the existence of positively portrayed characters who share their identity, whereas the absence of media representation can lead to negative psychological outcomes for youth of underrepresented identities.[c] [d] In addition to the social and psychological benefits of representing diverse identities in literature, research shows that students learn how to read more competently and deeply when engaging with texts whose characters or subject matter reflect major aspects of their own lives.[e]

There are two main ways to think about how libraries can offer supportive mirrors and expansive glass doors for transgender students (and other transgender individuals): programming and collections.

OFFERING INCLUSIVE PROGRAMMING

Libraries have a long history of providing programming about books and programming going way beyond books. Whether they're arranging literary salons, hosting knitting clubs, helping seniors prepare taxes, or serving as cooling centers in the summer and warming centers in the winter, libraries are often the hubs of social services in their communities. At times, in my work with libraries, they have hosted explicitly queer reading groups and brought in queer authors to work with patrons. At other times—in conservative communities, or when libraries are operating in environments where funding is being threatened—the queer literary activities are a little more under the radar.

My first novel tells the story of an ancestor of mine who ran away from home, disguised herself as a man, and fought in the American Revolutionary War. When it first came out, in 2015, libraries would often invite me to come talk about it. A typical program poster featured the cover and a short synopsis, as well as a program title that made a general mention of gender: "Revolutionary Woman," or something of the sort. What the librarians would ask me for privately, in email or a phone call, was another story: They wanted a presentation on gender and transgender identity, and they made it clear that they would let their interested patrons know exactly what I was going to talk about; they just couldn't put it on the poster or website.

These conversations with librarians opened my eyes to just how much they know about the adults, kids, students, and communities that they serve. It was quite often that a librarian would say to me, "I'm calling because we just had a student come out at the junior high school, and their mother was wondering . . ." And then I'd hear the story of a parent who needed support, a school that was stumbling, or a child who wanted some community—all things that a library can help with, given the chance.

A library can also be a center for community education more broadly. Though many libraries (wisely) shy away from being places of political activity, they do often host events that develop civic engagement and awareness. This can be very powerful for those of us who do civil rights work. When you are working from a marginalized position, the question often is: How do I reach from the margins toward the center?

Libraries can help with this education. For instance, from 2017 to 2018, I was involved in the New Hampshire campaign to include protections for transgender people in the state's non-discrimination clause. A lot of the work we did involved traditional lobbying: lunches and coffees and meet-and-greets with politicians to explain who we were and what we wanted. But the other component was community outreach—trying to explain to the greater public why this was a fight they should care about and support. One of the main places we did this was in public libraries.

There were several types of programs that libraries hosted, and when we worked with libraries we were very careful to take out the politics, the lobbying, and to frame our sessions as education only. One typical type of workshop was a panel presentation called "Ask a Trans Person Anything." These were lively, and sometimes difficult, conversations in which we explained trans identity and tried to dispel commonly held misconceptions about being transgender. Audiences were curious and libraries were the perfect site for these presentations—it was all about learning and discovery, and we would often end the panel with a list of suggested reading. The audience could walk right over to the stacks and display tables and continue their education.

The other program we commonly offered was a "Drag Queen Story Hour." In the last couple of years, these sorts of programs have garnered a lot of headlines and have led to some defunding of library programming and even attempts to ban drag performances altogether in some states. The basic content of the program is to have a drag queen, in full regalia, read storybooks to an audience of children and adults. In the conservative media, this is portrayed as brainwashing, grooming, recruitment, and abuse. Even many adults who don't consider themselves conservative bristle a bit at the idea of drag queens and kindergartners, seeing drag as something inherently sexual. This misunderstanding just goes to show how much we need to think about and learn more about how gender works.

Drag is not the same as transgender. At all. In fact, you'll find many transgender people who distance themselves from drag—and with good reason. drag queens put on an occasional persona; transgender people live as who they are. drag queens wear flamboyant outfits; transgender people wear clothes. For me, the clearest explanation of the difference between these two categories comes from Marjorie Garber's 1992 classic text, *Vested Interests*, in which she writes that the drag queen wants to be looked *at* while the transgender person wants to be looked *through*.[2] The

---

2 Garber does not use the word "transgender" but "transvestite," a word now considered dated and problematic that was more in currency in the early 1990s, when she was writing.

drag queen wants to be a spectacle—that is the purpose of drag. All gender is performance, as Judith Butler has famously argued, but drag is an intentionally exaggerated performance of gender.

It is this exaggerated aspect that makes drag queens so perfect for children's programs. Drag queens are loud, colorful, engaging. Watch a child with a drag queen and you will see delight, curiosity, interest, maybe a little confusion. drag queens are doing something that many little kids like to do: they are dressing up, they are dancing, they are using their imaginations to project fanciful, temporary versions of themselves.

At most Drag Queen Story Hours, the queen will introduce herself and read some books, bantering with the children along the way. Gender tends to be the backdrop to these engagements, not the foreground. The queen might introduce herself, might comment on her outfit, might say that at other times she is an accountant named Dan— but there is no lecture on gender. Likewise, the chosen books are often children's literature staples. *Hansel and Gretel* is as likely to get read as something LGBTQ+-themed, such as *And Tango Makes Three*. Like any good story hour, there's a lot of engagement: animated storytelling, music, maybe dancing or a little lip-syncing.

When I hear critics complain about these events or try to ban them, the rhetoric used is often the same as for keeping transgender and queer topics (and teachers) out of classrooms of all ages: These events expose young children to dangerous ideas. Here, "dangerous" is code for "sexually explicit." Even more deeply, "dangerous" is code for "things that make me uncomfortable." I've been remarkably surprised and disappointed at how often I've heard the word "deviant" crop up in recent political discourse around such library events. Deviant, as in, "departing from the norm," as in, "there's a single right way to be and it cannot be veered from."

While drag may challenge some people's preexisting conceptions of gender, and even make them uncomfortable, the truth is, there's nothing inherently sexually explicit about a drag show. Yes, you can get an R-rated one at a nightclub. But just like a hypnotist or a comedian or any other performer, the drag queen is aware of her audience and pitches her content, music, jokes, and dance to that age group. Many groups will point to adult-oriented drag shows as examples of why this material doesn't belong in libraries and children's story hours, but the reality is that these shows can easily be made age- and venue-appropriate. Those who advocate against them are simply uncomfortable with drag.

And that is exactly why drag belongs in libraries. Libraries should contain ideas that are uncomfortable. To argue against this is to fail to understand the civic purpose of libraries (and education). Discomfort is not the same as harm. The community should have access to a wide range of ideas, presentations, images, and positions across a broad horizon of topics. A parent may make choices for their own children—but not for other people's children.

In addition to accusations of sexually explicit content, the other common complaint about these events—as well as the inclusion of LGBTQ+ content in class material—is that there is some effort at recruitment and conversion behind "exposing" children to such material.[3] Here, the argument seems to be that if you expose children to drag, they will start to behave in a similar fashion and want to try drag themselves. Or, to shorten it to the part that most concerns conservatives: After attending a Drag Queen Story Hour, a boy might want to put on a dress. This calls back to very old ideas about LGBTQ+ people being predatory, of queerness itself being dangerous.

Yet libraries and schools are in the business of teaching new language, new stories, new ideas; of giving students frameworks and concepts that help them make sense of a world that is sometimes overwhelming, often confusing, and generally interesting. It is true that after seeing a drag queen give a funny and entertaining story hour, or after reading a young adult (YA) book about a non-binary kid coming out, a child might decide that it would be fun or interesting to wear a skirt instead of pants or learn to tie a necktie. Similarly, when I was kid and read a children's version of *Huck Finn*, I went out to my backyard

---

3 The current term most readily used is "grooming," a term borrowed from language that has been used to describe how sexual predators cultivate their victims and prepare them for exploitation. As an educator, I've been trained extensively to recognize boundary crossing, boundary violation, and grooming behaviors. This understanding is powerfully important to keeping students safe from sexual misconduct. I find it particularly repugnant that a term like grooming has been appropriated and misapplied to the situation of queer adults merely existing around children; it weakens the impact of language in an area where clarity, precision, and understanding are crucial.

and built a raft, determined to float down a river on it. Libraries, class-rooms, and literature ought to open up new ideas, create possibilities, inspire us to try new things.

Likewise, children's primary job in life is to grow and learn, to follow their curiosity where it takes them on the way to figuring out what kind of person they want to become. Caregivers and educators are meant to support and encourage that curiosity. The idea of a child being inspired by a Drag Queen Story Hour or queer-themed novel is only disturbing if one finds queerness itself disturbing. As I said in the introduction to this book, it is anti-educational to only allow students to pursue the self-dis-covery and -education deemed acceptable to those in power.

It's also true that queer programming and materials aren't only beneficial for LGBTQ+ youth, but all youth. That kid who feels an inkling of confusion alongside their excitement at seeing a drag queen read *Chicka Chicka Boom Boom* may have just had their conception of gender productively—and wholesomely—expanded, in ways that will stay with them forever. And that can be true regardless of how that child might eventually end up identifying, or how they might one day spend their time. After all, cis people—adults and kids—also gain from internalizing a sense of freedom, variety, and expansiveness when it comes to gender expression.

Those who oppose Drag Queen Story Hours and other queer library programming out of hand may not have considered the pos-sibility that their discomfort is indicative of something, that their notions of gender, sexuality, and identity may be due for a shake-up. Discomfort can be a great teacher, but the older we get, we often grow more intolerant of investigating and unpacking it—which is all the more reason that youth's curiosity should be protected. In doing the work of gender inclusion and gender education, it is crucial to remem-ber that everyone has a gender identity and gender expression(s). And that all of us change that self-understanding and expression of gender throughout our lives. This isn't just a topic of discovery for children and adolescents. Perhaps that is part of what is so frightening and dis-comforting to conservative adults.

As recent political action and legislation have ramped up, I've seen mainstream LGBTQ+ groups cede ground on Drag Queen Story Hours—that is, agreeing with conservative opponents that these programs are too "out there" for public libraries. Drag has always been a bit on the edge of the community, just like transgender has always hung a bit awkwardly on the margin of lesbian and gay identity. Yes, drag queens are flamboyant and loud and make a spectacle of themselves. They are outwardly queer and not part of the "norming" trajectory that the mainstream gay civil rights struggle has followed over the last decades. By this, I mean the tendency to politically organize around assimilationist or even conservative standards of social respectability, like marriage and joining the armed forces, instead of standing for queer liberation independent of the norms and expectations of cis, heterosexual dominant culture. In other words, is the end goal to ensure and then prove that LBGTQ+ people can fit into society as it stands, or is the end goal to ensure that all queer people are free to live openly as they see fit?

My hope is that the LGBTQ+ community will rally behind events like Drag Queen Story Hours not because everyone in the community loves drag but because everyone in the community loves and values libraries, places of public civic engagement, places where activities and ideas can be shared and discussed—even when (especially when) you don't fully agree with those ideas. But for many libraries, particularly school libraries, the larger, "showy" events like Drag Queen Story Hours aren't possible or perhaps even desirable. To support LGBTQ+ students in these school library spaces, the programming and presence should be more subtle. Years ago, I worked with a private school to update their library collection to include more queer titles and resources. A very well-intentioned librarian bought some rainbow stickers and affixed these to the cover and spine of each of these books to make sure students would know what to look for. Sadly, the outcome of this action was to keep those books firmly on the shelf. Not so many students were willing to walk around with a book that was blatantly labeled as queer.

For school libraries that are operating in hostile environments, or even in neutral ones, I suggest threading the topic firmly into the mainstream curriculum. Yes, certainly make queer texts and resources available. Definitely put together that display table for Pride Month or Transgender Day of Visibility. But more powerful and effective is to pull the texts that are currently taught at the center of your school's curriculum and put together resource and study guides, posters, and pamphlets, that help students understand the material—and include the queer presence in those texts.

I'll use *The Great Gatsby* as an example, since this book is currently taught in a majority of high school English classes and is generally accepted as an American classic. If a librarian curated resources to help English students prepare for the AP exam or write an essay on this text, they might put together a handout that included symbolism (the green light) and prominent themes. Gay attraction would be one of them: Nick Carraway ends up looking at Mr. McKee's photographs while the other man is lounging in bed in his underwear. And gender, too, from Jordan's "tomboy" presentation to Tom Buchanan's hyper-masculinity.[4]

The goal is to make people realize that many texts—from *Othello* to *Frankenstein*—contain themes of sexuality, gender, and queerness, including those that are considered canonical. Instead of having libraries address queerness at the margins, bring it right to the center. In addition to constituting a more honest and academically rigorous engagement with the texts, this approach will show students—LBGTQ+ and otherwise—that queerness and gender expansiveness have always been part of literature and, by extension, the human experience.

PROTECTING COLLECTIONS FROM CENSORSHIP

Censorship is not a new topic for school libraries. Restrictions on the type and content of books in schools go back decades and decades. Regardless of the specific content under attack, the narrative of censorship remains the same: Certain ideas are dangerous and corrupting; books are the vehicles for these ideas. In this narrative, libraries occupy a sort of gatekeeping function for social norms, and those who wish to dictate what can and cannot be on library shelves position themselves as fighting moral corruption and maintaining standards of decency.

---

4 I will also note that such a handout should include themes of race and class. Oftentimes, in discussing *Gatsby*, the symbolism of the green light and the eyes of Dr. Eckleburg are the focus points. These are "safe" topics.

Words like "obscene" and "inappropriate" often bubble up in these conversations. The particulars vary. At times, the fight is over depictions of underage drug use in novels; at other times, it is stocking books that explain Communist ideology.

For those who wish to control and limit what books are available, libraries are places of narrowly defined wholesomeness. They function in an assimilative role, providing texts that support the maintenance of mainstream social norms. For the LGBTQ+ community—among many others—libraries play a very different role. The relationship between the reader and a text is a private and intimate one. For most readers, engaging with a text is a solitary activity, a very personal act. For queer readers, particularly young queer readers, books can provide the first chance to connect to someone like themselves. Libraries provide the opportunity to create a community and sense of self in a place where that is not easy. Gender-inclusive books are essential for LGBTQ+ students' development in a multidimensional sense.

To quote Dr. Bishop again: "When children cannot find themselves reflected in books they read, or when the images they see are distorted, negative, or laughable, they learn a powerful lesson about how they are devalued in the society of which they are a part."[f] Efforts to censor texts that represent queer identity harm LGBTQ+ youth. Not only do they limit access to texts that will help them understand who they are, but the rhetoric around censorship further marginalizes queer youth, positioning their identities as dangerous, harmful, and even criminal. This criminalization has recently been extended to librarians and educators: In nineteen states so far, a spate of laws has been passed, have been considered, or will be considered which would enable librarians and educators to be fined or imprisoned for circulating media deemed "sexually explicit," "obscene," or "harmful" according to state law. The harshest of these, passed as Oklahoma state law in 2022, states that "school employees and public libraries could face up to $20,000 in fines or ten years in prison for providing 'indecent exposure to obscene material or child pornography.'"[g] In many of these laws, the question of who gets to decide what counts as "obscene" is left vague, perhaps intentionally so.[5]

---

5 Some librarians are seeking to overturn these laws on the basis of First Amendment rights

School libraries have come under particular attack in the last year or two, with organized actions by parents, school boards, and other governing bodies to remove LGBTQ+-themed (and particularly trans-gender-themed) texts from shelves. The American Library Association (ALA) compiles an annual list of the "most banned books," and the report from 2022 is quite revealing. The top titles are *Gender Queer, All Boys Aren't Blue, The Bluest Eye, Flamer, Looking for Alaska, The Perks of Being a Wallflower,* and *Lawn Boy.* With the exception of *The Bluest Eye,* all of these books are named for having LGBTQ+ content and being sexually explicit.[b] These are also all books that are geared for the young adult audience, readers age thirteen and up. Indeed, between June 2021 and June 2022, 41% of books banned in American class-rooms and libraries featured LGBTQ+ themes and characters.[i]

Dating back to at least the mid-1800s, when Walt Whitman's *Leaves of Grass* was pulled from all but one public library in the US due in large part to its homoerotic content,[6] queer books have been targeted by cen-sorship efforts of various kinds.[j] When it comes to school and classroom libraries, claims of age inappropriateness can act as circumventions of the First Amendment, which prohibits the censorship of materials based on one person's (or group's) dislike of the material's ideas. However, the definition of appropriateness is inherently subjective, leaving LGBTQ+-themed texts vulnerable to homophobic affront.

For example, in Escambia County, Florida, *And Tango Makes Three* was banned by the local school board on the basis of "sexual innuendo" deemed inappropriate for the book's target age group—but if that was really the problem, wouldn't any book about a new baby in a family be likewise inappropriate?[k] There is nothing age-inappropriate about *Tango,* a picture book adaptation of the true story of two male chinstrap pen-guins living in the Central Park Zoo that formed a pair bond. Together, they raised a chick that the zookeepers named Tango. Labeling such a story as somehow prurient speaks to the way that heterosexuality, includ-

6 Whitman was working as a governmental clerk when Secretary of the Interior James Harlan found a copy of *Leaves of Grass* on the poet's desk. Harlan's complaint that Whitman was "wrong, was a free lover, deserved punishment, &c." was eventually reported and cost Whitman his job. (See note *j*).

ing in the implicit context of family formation, is deemed acceptable and wholesome for all ages, whereas even chaste representations of same-sex unions—or, as in the case of this book, families that include a queer relationship—are deemed inherently hypersexual and inappropriate.

There are state- and national-level conservative organizations behind these censorship attempts, distributing lists of texts and talking points and sharing videos that misrepresent the intent of the literature and exaggerate how explicit the content is. The ALA reports that most censorship attempts are part of coordinated, multi-title efforts by such lobby groups.[1] When I've worked with schools that are trying to address concerns around censoring library collections, I frequently find that no one involved in making the complaints has actually read the texts in question. This makes conversation very difficult.

There are also anti-censorship organizations that coordinate counter-efforts to this work, producing guides that debunk conservative misrepresentations of hot button books. One of my favorite resources is Common Sense Media, which has a clear and visually accessible website that explains the content of many books. Another resource is the National Council for Teachers of English, which produces meticulous guides for explaining the content and importance of frequently banned or challenged books. I have read several with great interest and appreciation. Unfortunately, these guides are often utterly useless because the topic of debate is not the content of any given book; it is the abstract idea of the book itself.

Considering the case of *Gender Queer*, a graphic memoir by Maia Kobabe, gives a feeling for how these debates have rolled out recently and how a school might thoughtfully address a push to censor library collections. *Gender Queer* tells the story of the author's coming-of-age and coming-of-gender.[7] It discusses and presents in illustrations gender dysphoria, body dysmorphia, puberty, sexual attraction, and a host of other topics related to gender and identity. Parent groups that have lobbied for this book to be banned in school libraries often come armed with certain pages from the memoir, calling them pornographic. Graphic novels and memoirs are particularly vulnerable to

---

7 Kobabe uses the neopronouns e/em/eir.

censorship campaigns because parent groups often refer to a "picture book feel" that invites younger readers to engage with the text. It is true that Kobabe's memoir contains illustrations of menstruation, masturbation, and other subjects that are deeply personal and related to bodily function. Groups arguing for censorship pull individual pages or panels and hold them up as sexually explicit and pornographic.

For a school that wants to engage in a conversation, it is crucial to insist on putting pages or images in context, to consider the work as a whole. Asking why the author wants to (needs to) depict menstruation in a graphic manner requires the lobbying group to address not just one piece but the merits of the entire work. If a school can facilitate a discussion with a parent group around a book like *Gender Queer*, a good outcome might be the realization that while the images and topics are not age-appropriate for very young readers, those same images and topics are entirely appropriate for teenage readers, whose bodies and minds are going through (some of) the same experiences that the memoir depicts.[8]

Sadly, many school districts and even many private schools that have faced complaints about *Gender Queer* have completely removed the book from their stacks or have put it behind the circulation counter, available by request only. A better compromise solution is to put a large sticker on the cover that indicates age-appropriate content and guides teachers, librarians, students, and parents to material that is geared to a developmental stage. This is a measure that can be done for all books in a library.

In truth, though—and the media accounts of schools' treatment of *Gender Queer* bear this out—the real goal of most of these censorship efforts isn't to get rid of any particular book but rather to control and limit all of the reading material and curricular content, paring it to the comfort of a vocal minority. Very quickly, these conversations or legislative actions go from being about one text to being about creating a blanket policy or procedure for any book to be approved in a library

8 Kelly Jensen's May 2023 *Book Riot* article about *Gender Queer* analyzes attempts to censor the book from eight school districts in Maine. In several of those cases, school board and other committee members moved to retain the book after reading the entire text, encountering cherrypicked images and language in their proper context, and feeling empathy for the author and for the transgender, GNC, and questioning young readers to whom the book might speak. (See note *m*.)

or classroom—thereby shifting the locus of curatorial control from librarians and educators to outsiders with vested interests.

Given that reality, what can help? In the case of private schools, it is very helpful to have a statement or policy in place that covers diversity, expansive thinking, consideration of a range of topics and opinions, and the belief in broad exposure filtered through a critical lens. Schools can articulate their values—much in the same way I suggest in Chapter Two, in the section on institutional missions—so that when parents point to a particular text, the schools can move the argument away from that book and back onto the terrain of "what it means to get an education here" or "what it means to be a scholar here." Schools should be able to articulate their goals, ideals, and guidelines about learning, thinking, and community in such a way that censorship is clearly not tolerated. Putting that policy out to students, trustees, and families in the advance of a school year and taking the time to review it in family sessions as well as in work with students, will help not only to explain the reason for these values (reasons that extend far beyond preventing censorship)—it will also help students absorb and embody the ideals the school strives for.

I also find that it helps, in both public and private contexts, to be proactive and clear in establishing the goals and purposes of a library. As I've highlighted elsewhere in this volume, having a mission, sharing that mission, and aligning action with that mission is crucial in supporting transgender students. That's true in a library as well. Does your library have a policy and goals around how it grows its collection? Is that shared widely? Does the library have a statement of its values and purpose? Is that posted? Have librarians spent time with teachers, students, and parents, discussing, exploring, and explaining the role of a library in a school and in society? Stepping back from the specific issues of race, sex, and gender that are inflaming the current moment, libraries can quietly and clearly assert the reasons for their existence, and then rely on that mission and values to help them articulate their response to certain books or programs being banned.

At many public and private schools, I've seen celebrations of banned books. These can be wonderful ways to shed some light on texts that have been censored in the past and present. At a school that tends toward the liberal, such programming can be not only informative but galvanizing, a call to action for students to address the censorship that might be happening not at their school but in the broader community. However, in a state or district or school where matters are already inflamed—and particularly in states like Texas, Iowa, and Wyoming where there are campaigns fueled and funded by national organizations—sponsoring and celebrating banned books can actually be counterproductive. Sadly, many instances of events that were designed to elevate and publicize censored titles have just fed into the rhetoric of "obscene" and "inappropriate" material being shared in schools. Individual texts or even passages within those texts have become the focus of the debate, shifting the attention away from the larger issue of speech, censorship, and the purpose of libraries.

Instead, I'd suggest that libraries in such climates set up programs that look beyond the specific books and instead dive into the history of censorship, or the history of intellectual freedom, or even a deep consideration of the first amendment as it applies to libraries. The first amendment is a concept that applies to every citizen and using it as a gateway into the conversations around specific texts can take the pressure off the marginalized population in these conversations. As other sections of this book suggest, supporting transgender students is most effectively and durably done from the center, not the margins. Find the values and rights that are shared or universal and articulate your position from there.

Librarians, teachers, and school administrators are increasingly having to face hostile parents or community members. There have been recent cases of LGBTQ+ and anti-censorship student groups presenting to school boards and being heckled, jeered, and insulted by adults for their views. In this moment, one way of supporting transgender students looks like modeling how to navigate a hostile environment and fostering community for those who no longer have access to texts and resources in a public school.

One way to do this is to set up a clear and consistent way for parent concerns to be raised. Asking for and receiving feedback is seldom easy, but librarians and administrators can set up sessions or provide forms to invite feedback. Provide space for discussion within a clear set of guidelines for behavior, format, and decorum. Similarly, all community members should know how to lodge a complaint about a book and be able to fill in a form to start that process. There should be a clear set of steps taken after this complaint is lodged. A review committee, a library board, or some other group should meet to go over the complaint. Wherever possible, include a student representative or multiple in the review process. It's important to involve a multiplicity of constituencies and perspectives in order to accurately reflect the community's priorities and to counter bias.[9] In the case of public schools, where the particulars of the complaint process are likely district mandated, this could look like diligently following the procedure with community oversight instead of cutting corners to "keep the peace" or keep the process private.

Establishing a transparent, multi-level procedure and then walking through it not only makes the complainant feel heard but also allows for a fairer and more well-considered process. A major challenge at the moment is that schools feel under attack and respond in an ad hoc manner, making decisions on the fly. In fact, a 2022 study conducted by PEN America found that of the more than 1,500 book bans studied, 98% "involved departures of various kinds from best practice guidelines designed to protect students' First Amendment rights," often in direct violation of schools' own established book reconsideration policies.[o] In the Escambia County example, for instance, the school board overrode the recommendation of "a district-mandated review committee made up of administrators, teachers, parents, and community members" when it banned *And Tango Makes Three.*[p]

Overall, schools and libraries need to think of this moment of attack as a small part of a larger whole. Right now, the vulnerable group is transgender people. Two years ago, critical race theory, and so implicitly Black, Brown, and Indigenous books and authors, was the focus

---

9 For instance, in 1993, a Kansas superintendent overrode district librarians' acceptance of donated copies of *Annie on My Mind*, the previously mentioned YA novel about a lesbian high school romance. The superintendent only rejected the donated books but also unilaterally drafted and implemented a "Book Donations Guidelines" document for the district to use. This roughshod (and homophobic) approach eventually led to the ACLU suing the school district on the grounds of First Amendment rights violations—and winning. (See note *n*.)

(not that that focus has entirely gone away).[10] And before that, it was the gay agenda, and before that, it was something else. It certainly isn't wrong to address the issue head-on—there are many good arguments to be made specifically for including texts about transgender individuals. But educators and librarians and administrators will find themselves playing an endless game of whack-a-mole as they advocate for one text, address one topic, and then have to repeat again and again as another book and another idea is contested. Rather, schools and libraries should look at the big picture of book banning and censorship and address the problem at its root. Doing so not only will lead to better outcomes in the volumes on the shelf but will educate patrons and students in the process.

Of course, if public and school libraries are denuded of LGBTQ+-themed texts by force of law, it becomes even more important for caregivers and community organizations to provide those texts and resources for transgender youth. In their survey of queer-centric YA American literature published between 1969 and 2004, Michael Cart and Christine A. Jenkins cite their shared "continued belief in the power of books to help teen readers understand themselves and others, to contribute to the mental health and well-being of GLBTQ youth, and to save lives—and perhaps even to change the world—by informing minds and nourishing spirits."[q] Whatever the legal circumstances at play, protecting and sharing the power of literature is a key part of advocating for transgender and GNC youth and for youth in general.

As unpleasant as the media representations can be around the censorship of texts, this coverage can be an effective springboard for conversations between caregivers and transgender youth. Go out and purchase the book that's being censored. Read it and discuss it. Talk about how the book is presented in the media accounts. Learning to read, analyze, and respond to media narratives about LGBTQ+ people is a crucial skill for any transgender person. Sadly, at this moment in many states, it feels like making lemonade from lemons is the best that can be done to support transgender students.

---

10 40% of books banned in American classrooms and libraries between June 2021 and June 2022 featured prominent characters of color.

NEXT STEPS

REFLECT

1. What visibility, if any, does queerness currently have in your school's library?

RESEARCH

1. Does your school's library have a mission statement or other declaration of goals and values? If so, is it clearly posted? When was the last time it was updated?

2. What is your school's library collection policy? Is it publicly accessible? What about the procedure for contesting or reconsidering a book? When is the last time it was updated, and how carefully is it constructed?

3. Have there been any contestations of books in your school's library, recently or historically? What was the reasoning? How did the cases turn out? Was the established policy for book contestation followed?

4. Have any LGBTQ+-themed books been relegated to a "special shelf" or removed from your library altogether?

5. Are librarians in your state impacted by new censorship laws, such as the one passed in Oklahoma? If yes, how can you or your school support resistance efforts?

6. What are some popular or perennially taught texts at your school that the library can create queer-inclusive study guides and other resources for?

7. If your school's library is constricted in its engagement with queer literature and programming, what are some ways you can connect students with similar resources at the public library?

ACT

1. Attend and otherwise support Drag Queer Story Hours and other LGBTQ+-themed library programming.

2. If you can't attend yourself (for example, if your kids have aged out of story time), drop your public library a comment in support of the programming and encourage them to keep it up. If they don't or have never had a Drag Queen Story Hour, request one.

NEXT STEPS

3. Request that your school library add new and classic queer titles that are missing from their collection.

4. Suggest LGBTQ+ authors who could speak at your/your student's school.

5. Consider what type of program addressing the history and reality of censorship would best fit your school and organize its execution.

6. If applicable and possible, organize a revision of your school library's book contestation forms and procedure.[11]

---

11 See Jensen's May 2022 *Book Riot* article for further tips on how to approach this (note *r*).

NOTES

a. Provides relative to discussion of sexual orientation and gender identity in public schools, H.R. 466, LA State Leg. (2023).

b. Rudine Sims Bishop, "Mirrors, Windows, and Sliding Glass Doors," *Perspectives: Choosingand Using Books from the Classroom* 6, no. 3 (Summer, 1990): ix–xi, https://scenicregional.org/wp-content/uploads/2017/08/Mirrors-Windows-and-Sliding-Glass-Doors.pdf.

c. L.M. Ward, "Wading Through the Stereotypes: Positive and Negative Associations BetweenMedia Use and Black Adolescents' Conceptions of Self," *Developmental Psychology* 40, no. 2 (2004): 284–94, https://doi.org/10.1037/0012-1649.40.2.284.

d. Riva Tukachinsky, Dana Mastro, and Morgan Yarchi, "The Effect of Prime Time Television Ethnic/Racial Stereotypes on Latino and Black Americans: A Longitudinal National Level Study," *Journal of Broadcasting & Electronic Media* 61, no. 3 (August 8, 2017): 538–56, https://doi.org/10.1080/08838151.2017.1344669.

e. Yvonne Freeman and David Freeman, "Connecting Students to Culturally Relevant Texts," *Personalizing Literacy* (April/May 2004): 7–11, accessed July 17, 2023, https://s3.amazonaws.com/scschoolfiles/819/personalizing_literacy-culturallyrelevantreadings.pdf.

f. Sims Bishop, "Mirrors, Windows, and Sliding Glass Doors," ix–xi.

g. Hannah Natanson, "School librarians face a new penalty in the banned-book wars: Prison," *The Washington Post,* May 18, 2023, https://www.washingtonpost.com/education/2023/05/18/school-librarians-jailed-banned-books/.

h. American Library Association. "Top 13 Most Challenged Books of 2022," Banned & Challenged Books, accessed July 17, 2023, https://www.ala.org/advocacy/bbooks/frequentlychallengedbooks/top10.

i. Amy Watson, "Share of book titles banned in school classrooms and libraries in the United States from July 1, 2022 to December 31, 2022, by subject matter," *Statista*, last modified 2023, accessed July 17, 2023, https://www.statista.com/statistics/1342868/book-titles-banned-us-schools-by-subject-matter/.

j. Paul Berman, "Poetic Justice," *The New York Times,* October 18,1998,https://archive.nytimes.com/www.nytimes.com/books/98/10/18/bookend/bookend.html.

k. Brooke Leigh Howard, "Florida School District Bans a Book on . . . Penguins," *Daily Beast*, February 22, 2023, https://www.thedailybeast.com/and-tango-makes-three-florida-school-district-bans-a-book-on-penguins.

l. "Censorship by the Numbers," *American Library Association*, accessed July 17, 2023, https://www.ala.org/advocacy/sites/ala.org.advocacy/files/content/Censorship-By-the-Numbers-Who.png.

m. Kelly Jensen, "Why Are Schools in Maine Keeping *Gender Queer* on Shelves, Despite Challenges? A Case Study in What Makes a Difference," *BookRiot*, May 31, 2023, https://bookriot.com/gender-queer-in-maine/.

n. "Banned in the USA: Rising School Book Bans Threaten Free Expression and Students' First Amendment Rights (April 2022)," *PEN America*, April 2022, https://pen.org/banned-in-the-usa/#policies.

o. Randy Meyer, "Annie's Day in Court: The Decision From the Branch," *School Library Journal* (April, 1996): 22–25, https://m.moam.info/annies-day-in-court-irls520paternalcensorship_59cec9931723dd81fff0dd9c.html.

p. Howard, "Florida School District."

q. Michael Cart and Christine Jenkins, *The Heart Has Its Reasons: Young Adult Literature with Gay/Lesbian/Queer Content, 1969–2004* (Lanham, Maryland: Scarecrow Press, 2006), xviii.

r. Kelly Jensen, "How to Update Your Book Challenge Forms (With Template): Book Censorship News, May 6, 2022," *BookRiot,* May 6, 2022, https://bookriot.com/book-censorship-news-may-6-2022/.

CHAPTER TWELVE:

THE ONGOING WORK OF INCLUSION

I hope that over the course of this book, I have convinced you that gender inclusion is a necessary aim for every educational institution. I hope I have also convinced you that making progress toward gender inclusion is absolutely possible—even if it can't be school-wide, even if it isn't systemic, even if there are legal restrictions you have to operate within. Meaningful change, change that supports and empowers students and supports learning, can happen even in the most transphobic and hostile environments. And I suspect that I have also shown you that working toward such change is not a one-and-done process. Little can be ticked off a neat to-do list with an accompanying sigh of, "Well, we don't have to worry about that anymore."

Even small changes, small victories—like altering the signage on single-user restrooms to read "all-gender" instead of "family bathroom"—will soon cease to be hallmarks of inclusion if the ongoing concomitant education and training doesn't occur. Signs, posters, even clubs and affinity groups can become so much wallpaper to schools: They are there, present, but so familiar that they hardly get noticed.

If a school wants to be inclusive—whether around gender or race or religion—it needs to be an active and ongoing engagement. Throughout this book, I have urged two angles that I believe are crucial to continuous inclusivity work. The first is training and education, and the second is the use of focus groups. Training and education keep the content fresh, present, and relevant. Focus groups allow for feedback and reflection, making sure that the training and education is having the intended impact.

Here, I want to lay out what some aspects of that training and education might look like in more detail, how a school year could be shaped (though you want this to last far beyond a year!), and lastly, how focus groups come into play.

TRAINING (THROUGH) THE TASK FORCE

Let's start with the gender inclusion task force. This group is the petri dish in a sense, the incubator, where training for wider audiences can be tried out, adjusted, and modified.

When I described how to form a task force in Chapter Three, I suggested that it's often good to include people who are interested in working for gender inclusion but who don't know much about gender. Why? Because having people for whom transgender identity is a new concept will make the task force slow down and go over basic concepts in detail. The people who are learning this material for the first time will have questions and concerns that will be important to address—and that will be heard later from other constituents over the course of the inclusion work. These conversations provide a rehearsal and a chance for the task force to refine its messaging as well as its in-group understanding.

What might this task force training look like? It could be the group taking a trip to an LGBTQ+ conference or watching a webinar. The group could read a book and discuss it or have a movie night. Or the task force could invite a speaker, or even a panel, to address them. The form the training takes depends on budget and time; the core element is that there is some outside expertise that everyone is taking part in. No one person on the task force bears the responsibility of being the group's expert. They are all learning together.

Of course, a lot of the education will come from the process of doing: Simply running the gender audit will bring up lots of questions and the chance to learn more. Talking to focus groups of transgender and gender non-conforming (GNC) alumni will be enlightening. But on-the-job training isn't sufficient; there should be a more deliberate group engagement outside of the task force's real-time work.

In some cases, a school might decide to hire an outside consultant to work on gender inclusivity with the task force. If this is the case, the consultant should be able to provide some of this initial training, as well as guidance on how to proceed. But many schools won't have the willingness or budget to work with a consultant, so the task force will usually need to furnish its own education.

Once those self-training plans are in place, training and education for other constituencies need to be built into the timeline that the task force creates. There should be opportunities for students, for faculty, and for families. If it is possible to reach out to trustees, school boards, or alumni to offer educational opportunities, so much the better. Each of these constituencies will need a slightly different approach.

Let's start with students—they are the easiest in some ways (at least for me as a teacher myself: I am used to thinking about how to educate them). The task force should consider the entirety of the academic year. Don't try to cram this topic into Pride Month or, worse, National Coming Out Day. The educational opportunities need to be spread out throughout the year and need to build on each other so that the conversation develops rather than stagnates. Again, school culture will dictate whether these opportunities can be required for students or if they should be optional. But if they are optional, then the advertising for them—the posters and the social media posts—should serve some educational function as well.

A task force might decide that addressing four "touchpoint" topics as a school, one per academic quarter, is a good place to start. They might want first to consider the topic and category of gender broadly, not just transgender, and perhaps start with patriarchy, misogyny, and gender norms. Maybe there's a speaker or a panel presentation, with the opportunity for a follow-up conversation (or a required conversation in homeroom or advisory). The next touchpoint could be on transgender identity, introducing terminology, in small group sessions run by the task force and other trained faculty members (learning to run this could be part of the faculty educational process). And so on.

As usual, the form and the content will depend on where the school culture is, what general level of education around gender exists, and what budget is possible. The crucial elements are to create space for the presentation of new ideas and then space for individuals to discuss, question, and explore these new ideas. Too often, schools hire an expert speaker, who delivers a gorgeous lecture and then is promptly forgotten. The follow up matters as much as, if not more than, the "sage on the stage."

The task force might also consider running special training sessions for student leaders. Whether these are student council members, the heads of clubs, or team captains, working with student leaders can be a very effective way to start to shift school culture and to get feedback on what sort of educational programs have the most impact. In working with schools, I've often found that the culture of student leadership is sort of passive. Students are elected or appointed to office and then . . . expected to lead. The task force might therefore be stepping into a space that is largely a vacuum and could form a meaningful partnership with coaches and club advisors to develop a curriculum addressing what it actually means to be a leader. One angle of training student leaders that I've found to be really helpful is "upstander" training: teaching them how not to be a bystander when they see or hear or witness a problematic encounter (and to center the needs of whoever is being targeted while doing so). Gender inclusion might be just one topic that these leaders are trained on, but it could be crucial to helping them be educated in other areas, such as consent and bullying.

For faculty involved in the work of gender inclusion, much of what I'd suggest follows the pattern outlined above and what I've described earlier in the book. Part of the education should be the chance to review and discuss proposed changes to school policy, spaces, and practices. Bringing in three potential new restroom signs and letting the faculty consider the merits of each is a great way to have low-key conversations about gender and get people to be aware of the changes that are coming. More formal training might look similar to that of the students, with a speaker making a presentation and then following up with small group work. When I lead such trainings, I like to give faculty the time to talk through potentially tough situations—the moments where they fear they will slip up or not know what to say. Faculty training should focus on buy-in and building comfort, competency, and confidence.

As discussed in the previous chapter and throughout the book, families should be offered the chance to participate. I am huge fan of schools offering book clubs for families on a variety of topics. I am also a big fan of having faculty give presentations on what they are teaching, so that families get a window into the classroom. If a biology teacher has recently added a section on being intersex, or a history teacher is covering the first wave of feminism in a new way, letting families know what is being taught is a great way to include them in their student's education while also signaling the school's values. There will also be times when a school might want to bring in an outsider to do the parent or guardian education. Sometimes it feels safer and more effective to have an expert present on a topic and facilitate a conversation, especially if that conversation could be controversial. But just as with the other constituencies, families should be given the opportunity to have repeated encounters with the topic of gender inclusion, so that they can engage, consider, reflect, and engage again. That's how growth and in-depth education happen.

Lastly, I would say that to the greatest extent possible, the educational work should be fun and center on community-building. Something as simple as showing a movie, or a clip, can give students (and adults) the chance to relax and absorb. The programs don't need to be elaborate or expensive—there's a wealth of material that is available for free online. The crucial element, which takes time and intentionality rather than money, is making sure that your facilitators (whether faculty or students) are well-trained and prepared to handle difficult follow-up conversations. Frequent, low-stakes opportunities are the best way to educate both students and adults in the community. The goal is to make gender a comfortable topic, to reduce anxiety around asking questions and to handle situations that arise.

GENDER INCLUSION'S PLACE IN THE LARGER WORK OF INCLUSION

When I arrived at Harvard in the fall of 1996, I was the first openly transgender student in the school's history. The freshman (since renamed "first-year" to be gender inclusive) dean's office was welcoming and worked with me on dormitory placement, selecting a single room on a men's hallway that had a small, shared bathroom with good privacy barriers in place. I had changed my name legally that summer, a few days after my eighteenth birthday, and the deans were very helpful in making sure that the change was registered on all my forms. I was ready to begin college as Alex Myers, man.

As I stated earlier in the book, like many young trans people, I was eager for this experience. I wanted to be in a new place, where no one had known me before, where I would have a chance to just live as a guy, without always having to explain this whole transgender thing, over and over again. Though my high school had been supportive and encouraging, and though I didn't think Harvard would be any different, I wanted to be more than just "the transgender kid."

Within the first two months of school, I was over it. In that short span of time, I missed the community and understanding of other LGBTQ+ people. I had already heard so many homophobic and misogynistic comments from the guys in my dorm that I felt like a coward for not being open about who I was and calling them on their remarks. For those two months, I had passed as a guy—no one had given me a hard time about the bathroom or the shower, or anything else—but I had moved around with a sense of doubt and fear: *When would they find out? How would they react?* I didn't want to be scared. I wanted to be out.

So, I came out—and pretty soon found myself swept up in the LGBTQ+ community at Harvard and then in Cambridge and Boston. The trans community was just getting going at that time, and I joined a wonderful group of people—mostly transgender women—who were organizing to change the city of Cambridge's non-discrimination clause to include the words "gender identity." I worked with them and, simultaneously, started a similar push within Harvard College. As I said earlier, the work this change was adopted quickly in Cambridge, but Harvard College didn't change its language until 2010.

For me, that battle felt like an eternity. In the intervening years, between when I graduated in 2000 and when Harvard finally made the addition, I stayed in intermittent contact with the transgender student groups on campus. The administration's argument remained the same: "Sex" covered "gender identity," and the college would respond swiftly to any charge of discrimination against a transgender person—so there was no need to change the language. But we kept on pushing. Even if it was largely symbolic, it was an important shift. Having language that accurately reflects reality—that gender and sex are not the same thing—is crucial to promoting understanding and fair treatment of transgender individuals.

When the college finally changed the non-discrimination clause, it was a huge victory. It took a lot of hard work from students and alumni. I share this story because I want to draw two very important conclusions from it. First, real change can take a while. It is necessary to be persistent. It is necessary to hear a resolute "no" from people in charge and then continue to work with them. It is necessary to work toward a long-term goal and also work on short-term goals at the same time. It is necessary to shift and compromise and adjust and also to keep pushing for change.

Second, though it felt to me like this change took a while to accomplish, the pace was actually incredibly fast. 1997 to 2010. Look at the pace of many of the civil rights gains for LGBTQ+ people—whether that's marriage equality or employment non-discrimination. Very, very quick. This is not to say that it was easy. This is not to say it came fast enough. But major milestones have been reached in a struggle that's not much over fifty years old.

I had cause to reflect on this when, in 2017, Phillips Exeter approved its first all-gender dorms. I'd graduated from the school in 1996 and joined the faculty in 2015. Soon after, I started working with a task force to develop a plan for all-gender housing and, within a year, we were approved to open two dormitories.

At the faculty meeting where we voted to approve the dorms, a Black colleague spoke up during the discussion period. He said: "I have nothing against these dorms, I think they'll be great. But I want to know, I've been here as Black faculty member for years, and there have been decades and decades of Black faculty and Black students pushing this school for fundamental changes around classes and policy and hiring and housing for students and faculty of color. How come this change—these all-gender dorms—happened so fast, but we haven't made any substantial changes around the demands made by Black students?"

The answer to his question is quite simple and quite unfortunate:

White privilege. Being LGBTQ+ is a marginalized identity, for certain. But being LGBTQ+ can also intersect with privilege. A family tree of straight, White, well-to-do people can abruptly have a branch that includes a gay man or a transgender woman. Just by coming out as queer, the rest of that privilege doesn't disappear.

The movement for LGBTQ+ rights has proceeded at a quicker pace than the movement for Black civil rights because the mainstream sector of the LGBTQ+ movement has been able to leverage White privilege and the relative economic privilege that often goes with it. Too often, I've seen this be a source of tension, of resentment and misunderstanding, especially when the most visible parts of the LGBTQ+ movement concentrate on objectives that don't benefit the most marginalized people in the community—particularly transgender women of color.

Statistics quoted throughout this book have shown, for instance, queer Black and Brown youths' increased vulnerability to mental health issues and the especially high rates of sexual assault against transgender women of color.[a] The 2015 Transgender Survey, further, shows that Black, Latinx, Asian, and Indigenous trans people in the US are likelier than their White counterparts to be living in poverty; that these racial groups along with multiracial and Middle Eastern trans people were likelier than White trans people to face unemployment; and that Indigenous, Black, Middle Eastern, and multiracial trans women faced the highest rates of homelessness compared to other races, with 59%, 51%, 49%, and 51% of respondents in those racial groups, respectively, facing homelessness at some point in their lives.[b]

There's a real disconnect between these fundamental, material concerns and the more bourgeois agendas of many White-led, mainstream LGBTQ+ civil rights initiatives, which historically have focused on the concerns of LGBTQ+ people who are already privileged by their race and class identities. To take an example from recent memory, prior to the 2015 Supreme Court decision that legalized same-sex marriage throughout the US, prominent queer rights organizations adopted marriage equality as their rallying cause. While this was indeed an important political goal, it is also incommensurate with the means of basic survival, such as access to affordable housing and healthcare—issues that are urgent for the most vulnerable members of the LGBTQ+ community. In other words, who's thinking about whether they can get married if they don't have a safe place to sleep? Yet, because of the way that privilege operates, these latter issues might not even be perceived as specifically relevant to LGBTQ+ advocacy work.

This is not a call to abandon the work toward expanding LGBTQ+ rights but rather to make sure that the leadership and goals of any organization fighting for these rights are robustly inclusive. An intersectional lens must be applied to emergent activism as well as to the way that history gets recorded and interpreted. For instance, the complete story of the fight for LGBTQ+ civil rights clearly shows how artists and activists of color have been downplayed in and erased from dominant retellings of the history. The truth of Stonewall is that Black and Brown drag queens and transgender women led the charge. But their stories have been shunted aside in favor of a more "mainstream" narrative. The Mattachine Society and the Daughters of Bilitis, two early American gay rights advocacy organizations founded in the 1950s, both championed a performance of queer identity that was White, upper-middle class, binary, and palatable to straight, cisgender society. Both trans and non-White people were largely unwelcome in these spaces.[1]

All of this is to say that identity-based power dynamics concerning race, as well as other vectors such as class, dis/ability, and religion, exist and must be reckoned with within LGBTQ+-focused activism and inclusion work, and that true inclusion means grappling with these dynamics and their various permutations and complexities. Too often, when I work with queer groups—whether that is in affinity or with allies—and the topic of race comes up, there's a defensive reaction from White members: "We've suffered too!" But being marginalized doesn't enter you into some bizarre Oppression Olympics. It doesn't free you from the responsibility to honestly reckon with your blind spots and sources of privilege. And it doesn't give you permission to further enact and perpetrate injustices. You can be queer and suffer from the effects of transphobia and still have implicit bias and gain

---

1 For more on the history of these groups and the history of LGBTQ+ rights and activism more broadly, see Susan Stryker's *Transgender History: The Roots of Today's Revolution.*

advantage from a White supremacist institution. Acknowledging that and working for racial equity along with queer rights and inclusion is the way forward. If we do this work well, it makes schools better places for all students. It can take a while, and it can be a frustrating struggle. But the end results are well worth the effort.

*   *   *

In the few years that have intervened between the publication of the first edition and this second edition of *Supporting Transgender Students*, a lot has shifted in the work for gender inclusion in schools—and, too often, nothing has shifted at all. In addition to all the legislative action, the restrictions, and the political work to demonize trans people, there have also been deeper studies of and work towards understanding and supporting transgender youth. States that don't face legislative hurdles have found themselves acting as safe havens for transgender youth and their families: As one state bars medical intervention for trans youth, another state finds its doctors speaking up and speaking out about the necessity of this care.

Recent events make me uncertain what the next few years, let alone the next decade, will bring for transgender students. The things I know for sure—the high rates of depression, anxiety, suicidal ideation, and suicide attempts—don't make me overly optimistic. In the face of growing and deepening economic inequality in our country, some leaders seem ever more inclined to use identity politics as a distraction—and trans people have proven to be a very effective distraction.

I try to find comfort in the work I can do. This work is not on the national stage and not in the political arena. It is in schools and classrooms and libraries, often in liberal states, that see themselves as a refuge. That understand the comfort and solace and support they can provide and know that it is life-changing and life-saving. I tell myself that going to these schools and meeting with trans youth is important and makes a difference—and it does. Lately, I've been noticing a few things that remind me of how important this work is.

First, on a very small level, I've paid attention to the trans kids I meet with individually. Often, schools will hire me to speak to the faculty or the whole student body. And then, when my talk is done, they'll arrange for a private room and have the one or two trans students there to talk with me, sometimes along with a school counselor or an out teacher. The phrase the students most often say has come to haunt me: *You're the first real trans person I've met.* There they are, seventeen, fifteen, twelve years old—some of them have been out since second grade, some with supportive families, many with supportive teachers or peers—and they haven't ever met an adult who is out as trans. Our queer students need more role models in the flesh. They need to see transgender lives being lived in the day-to-day.

Second, I've noticed a rising convergence of transgender identity and individuals on the autism spectrum. There are studies that look into this linkage,ᶜ but outside of the autistic community, schools are just starting to pick up on it and wonder what's going on as they struggle to figure out how and what to support: Is the gender queerness or uncertainty part of the autism expression? Or what?

While I don't have the depth of knowledge or expertise on autism to answer this, what I have heard repeatedly from students who are autistic and identify as trans or non-binary is that, to them, gender simply doesn't matter. They don't see it, feel it, or process it as part of who they are. Many of them struggle to explain this to teachers and peers who are constantly seeing and thinking about gender. Yes, this is a small subset of transgender people, but I highlight this as a topic that more schools ought to pay attention to—and more researchers, too—as we try and understand how gender works socially and psychologically for a broad variety of people.

Lastly, I stand by the conclusion to the first edition as pertains to race and the need for the LGBTQ+ community to center the experiences of Black people, Indigenous people, and other people of color. In the wake of the Black Lives Matter protests, many schools stepped up their education and efforts around racial justice. As I continue to move through schools and do the work of gender inclusion, I am seeing those efforts fade. Sometimes, it is simply the school's attention being caught by something new and urgent. More often, there are voices on the board, from students' families, or within the alumni that are calling for an end to what they claim to be indoctrination.

We rise together and we fall together. The voices clamoring against racial justice are the voices clamoring against transgender inclusion. We need to fight our fights and stand up for each and with each other. We will do this together, or we will not do it at all.

NOTES

a. The Trevor Project, "National Survey on LGBTQ Youth Mental Health," https://www.thetrevoproject.org/survey-2021/?section=Introduction.

b. James et al., *The Report of the 2015 U.S. Transgender Survey*, http://transequality.org/sites/default/files/docs/usts/USTS-Full-Report-Dec17.pdf.

c. Kate Cooper et al., "The lived experience of gender dysphoria in autistic adults: An interpretative phenomenological analysis," *Autism* 26, no. 4 (May 2022): 963–974, https://www.ncbi.nlm.nih.gov/pmc/articles/PMC9014767/.

Suggested Supplemental Reading

What's Your Pronoun? Beyond He and She by Dennis Baron. New York: Liveright, 2021.

Gender Trouble: Feminism and the Subversion of Identity by Judith Butler. New York: Routledge, 1999.

Safe Spaces, Brave Spaces: Diversity and Free Expression in Education by John Palfrey. Cambridge: MIT Press, 2018.

Normal Life: Administrative Violence, Critical Trans Politics, and the Limits of Law by Dean Spade. Durham, NC: Duke University Press, 2015.

Transgender History: The Roots of Today's Revolution by Susan Stryker. New York: Seal Press, 2017.

Covering: The Hidden Assault on Our Civil Rights by Kenji Yoshino. New York: Random House, 2007.

Bibliography

American Library Association. "Top 13 Most Challenged Books of 2022." *Banned & Challenged Books*. Accessed July 17, 2023. https://www.ala.org/advocacy/bbooks/frequently-challengedbooks/top10

American Psychiatric Association. "What is Gender Dysphoria?" *American Psychiatric Association*. Accessed March 4, 2024. https://www.psychiatry.org/patients-families/gender-dysphoria/what-is-gender-dysphoria.

Associated Press. "Principal resigns after complaints on 'David' statue nudity." *The Associated Press*, March 24, 2023. https://apnews.com/article/florida-censorship-david-statue-nudity-michelangelo-84bba40d47339eff7770ec58fcb23dd1.

Bagagli, Beatriz Pagliarini, Tyara Veriato Chaves, and Mónica G. Zoppi Fontana. "Trans Women and Public Restrooms: The Legal Discourse and Its Violence." *Frontiers in Sociology* 6 (March 31, 2021). https://www.ncbi.nlm.nih.gov/pmc/articles/PMC8022685/.

"Banned in the USA: Rising School Book Bans Threaten Free Expression and Students' First Amendment Rights (April 2022)." *PEN America*, April 2022. https://pen.org/banned-in-the-usa/#policies.

"Bans on Transgender Youth Participation in Sports." *Movement Advance Project*, last modified January 24, 2024. https://www.lgbtmap.org/equality-maps/youth/sports_participation_bans.

Basile, Kathleen C. et al. *The National Intimate Partner and Sexual Violence Survey: 2016/2017 Report on Sexual Violence* (Atlanta: National Center for Injury Prevention and Control, Centers for Disease Control and Prevention, June 2022). https://www.cdc.gov/violenceprevention/pdf/nisvs/nisvsReportonSexualViolence.pdf.

Bauer, Sydney. "A Day in the Life of Three Transgender Athletes: What it Takes to Be Elite." *Teen Vogue*, July 19, 2021. https://www.teenvogue.com/story/transgender-athletes-what-it-takes-to-be-elite.

Berman, Paul. "Poetic Justice." *The New York Times,* October 18, 1998. https://archive.nytimes.com/www.nytimes.com/books/98/10/18/bookend/bookend.html.

Binkley, Collin. "Biden administration proposes rule to forbid bans on transgender athletes but allow limits." *PBS NewsHour*, April 6, 2023. https://www.pbs.org/news-hour/politics/biden-administration-proposes-rule-to-for-bid-bans-on-transgender-athletes-but-allow-limits.

Bishop, Rudine Sims. "Mirrors, Windows, and Sliding Glass Doors." *Perspectives: Choosing and Using Books from the Classroom* 6, no. 3 (Summer, 1990): ix–xi. https://scenicregional.org/wp-content/uploads/2017/08/Mirrors-Windows-and-Sliding-Glass-Doors.pdf.

Bodo, Peter. "Follow the money: How the pay gap in Grand Slam tennis finally closed." *ESPN*, September 6, 2018. https://www.espn.com/tennis/story/_/id/24599816/us-open-follow-money-how-pay-gap-grand-slam-tennis-closed.

Boren, Cindy. "Transgender wrestler Mack Beggs wins second Texas state girls' championship." *The Washington Post*, February 25, 2018. https://www.washingtonpost.com/news/early-lead/wp/2018/02/25/transgender-wrestler-mack-beggs-wins-second-texas-state-girls-championship/.

Brown, Anna. "About 5% of young adults in the U.S. say their gender is different from their sex assigned at birth." *Pew Research Center*, last modified June 7, 2022. https://pewrsr.ch/4d8XtNU.

Cart, Michael and Christine Jenkins. *The Heart Has Its Reasons: Young Adult Literature with Gay/Lesbian/Queer Content, 1969–2004.* Lanham, Maryland: Scarecrow Press, 2006.

"Censorship by the Numbers." *American Library Association.* Accessed July 17, 2023. https://www.ala.org/advocacy/sites/ala.org.advocacy/files/content/Censorship-By-the-Numbers-Who.png.

Cole, Devan. "Former Connecticut high school athletes urge appeals court to revive their challenge to state's trans-inclusive sports policy." *CNN*, March 23, 2023. https://www.cnn.com/2023/03/23/politics/connecticut-transgender-sports-lawsuit-appeal/index.html.

Cooper, Kate et al. "The lived experience of gender dysphoria in autistic adults: An interpretative phenomenological analysis." *Autism* 26, no. 4 (May 2022): 963–974. https://www.ncbi.nlm.nih.gov/pmc/articles/PMC9014767/.

DeChants, Jonah et al. "Homelessness and Housing Instability Among LGBTQ Youth." *The Trevor Project*, November 23, 2021. https://www.thetrevorproject.org/wp-content/uploads/2022/02/Trevor-Project-Homelessness-Report.pdf.

"Definition of Affirmative Consent." *SUNY*. Accessed February 20, 2024. https://system.suny.edu/sexual-violence-prevention-workgroup/policies/affirmative-consent/.

Draper, Kevin. "Finally, the N.B.A. Comes to Charlotte." *The New York Times*, February 15, 2019. https://www.nytimes.com/2019/02/15/sports/nba-charlotte-bathroom-bill.html.

Freeman, Yvonne, and David Freeman. "Connecting Students to Culturally Relevant Texts." *Personalizing Literacy* (April/May 2004): 7–11. Accessed July 17, 2023. https://s3.amazonaws.com/scschoolfiles/819/personalizing_literacy-culturallyrelevantreadings.pdf.

Gamble, Justin. "Jackson State University debuts first NCAA Division I female kicker at an HBCU." *CNN*, October 16, 2023. https://www.cnn.com/2023/10/14/us/leilani-armenta-jackson-state-university-reaj/index.html.

Gessen, Masha. "The Movement to Exclude Trans Girls from Sports." *The New Yorker*, March 27, 2021. https://www.newyorker.com/news/our-columnists/the-movement-to-exclude-trans-girls-from-sports.

"Girls Are As Athletic As Boys, Study Says." *Huffington Post*, June 7, 2012. https://bit.ly/4azFrCG.

GLAD Law. "Sarah Huckman, featured speaker at GLAD's 2018 Spirit of Justice Award Dinner." *YouTube*, 8:44, video, October 16, 2018. https://www.youtube.com/watch?v=-V57D3Hv8zvw.

Golodryga, Bianna, Ben Church and Henry Hullah. "Caster Semenya says she went through 'hell' due to testosterone limits imposed on female athletes." *CNN*, November 6, 2023. https://www.cnn.com/2023/11/06/sport/caster-semenya-totestosterone-limits-world-athletics-spt-intl/index.html.

Grannan, Cydney. "Has Pink Always Been a 'Girly' Color?" *Encyclopedia Britannica*, August 30, 2016. https://www.britannica.com/story/has-pink-always-been-a-girly-color.

Hasenbush, Amira, Andrew R. Flores, and Jody L. Herman. "Gender Identity Nondiscrimination Laws in Public Accommodations: a Review of Evidence Regarding Safety and Privacy in Public Restrooms, Locker Rooms, and Changing Rooms." *Sexuality Research and Social Policy* 16 (July 23, 2018): 70–83. https://doi.org/10.1007/s13178-018-0335-z.

Hashemi, Danial. "Examining the Tennis Pay Gap." *Washington Square News*, September 16, 2019. https://nyunews.com/sports/2019/09/16/tennis-pay-gap-problem/.

Howard, Brooke Leigh. "Florida School District Bans a Book on . . . Penguins." *Daily Beast*, February 22, 2023. https://www.thedailybeast.com/and-tango-makes-three-florida-school-district-bans-a-book-on-penguins.

Huckman, Sarah Rose. "Sarah Rose Huckman: As transgender athlete, I oppose HB 1251." *The Conway Daily Sun*, February 12, 2020. https://bit.ly/4aUp03t.

"Identity Document Laws and Policies." *Movement Advance Project*, last modified February 28, 2024. https://www.lgbt-map.org/equality-maps/identity_documents.

International Olympic Committee. *IOC Framework on Fairness, Inclusion and Non-Discrimination on the Basis of Gender Identity and Sex Variations* (Lausanne, 2021). https://stillmed.olympics.com/media/Documents/Beyond-the-Games/Human- Rights/IOC-Framework-Fairness-Inclusion-Non-discrimination-2021.pdf.

ISNA. "How common is intersex?" *Intersex Society of North America*. Accessed July 10, 2023. https://isna.org/faq/frequency/.

James, Sandy E. et al. *The Report of the 2015 U.S. Transgender Survey* (Washington, DC: National Center for Transgender Equality, December 2016). https://transequality.org/sites/default/files/docs/usts/USTS-Full-Report-Dec17.pdf.

Lee, Jennifer and Karthick Ramakrishman. "From Narrative Scarcity to Research Plenitude for Asian Americans." *RSF: The Russell Sage Foundation Journal of the Social Sciences* 7, no. 2 (2021): 1. https://doi.org/10.7758/rsf.2021.7.2.01.

Jensen, Kelly. "How to Update Your Book Challenge Forms (With Template): Book Censorship News, May 6, 2022." *BookRiot*, May 6, 2022. https://bookriot.com/book-censorship-news-may-6-2022/.

Jensen, Kelly. "Why Are Schools in Maine Keeping *Gender Queer* on Shelves, Despite Challenges? A Case Study in What Makes a Difference." *BookRiot*, May 31, 2023. https://bookriot.com/gender-queer-in-maine/.

Kansas Women's Bill of Rights. S.B. 180, Kan. State Leg. (2023).

Karni, Annie. "House Passes Bill to Bar Transgender Athletes from Female Sports Teams." *The New York Times*, April 20, 2023. https://www.nytimes.com/2023/04/20/us/politics/transgender-athlete-ban-bill.html.

Killermann, Sam. "Edugraphics." *It's Pronounced Metrosexual*. Accessed March 5, 2024. https://www.itspronouncedmetrosexual.com/edugraphics/.

Kliegman, Julie. "Lawmakers Say Trans Athlete Bans Are About Protecting Women's Sports . . ." *Sports Illustrated*, January 25, 2022. https://www.si.com/golf-archives/2022/01/25/luc-esquivel-trans-sports-ban-boys-and-mens-teams-daily-cover.

Klosterboer, Brian. "Texas' Attempt to Tear Parents and Trans Youth Apart, One Year Later." *ACLU*, February 23, 2023. https://www.aclu.org/news/lgbtq-rights/ texas-attempt-to-tear-parents-and-trans-youth-apart-one-year-later.

Lavietes, Matt. "Utah official faces calls to resign after falsely suggesting teen girl is transgender." *NBC News*, February 8, 2024. https://www.nbcnews.com/nbc-out/out-news/utah-official-faces-calls-resign-falsely-suggesting-teen-girl-transgen-rcna137903.

Macmillan, Carrie. "Expertise with Kids Questioning Their Gender Identity." *Yale Medicine*, January 23, 2019. https://bit.ly/49BLhlI.

Meyer, Randy. "Annie's Day in Court: The Decision From the Branch." *School Library Journal* (April, 1996): 22–25. https://m.moam.info/annies-day-in-court-irls520 paternalcensorship_59cec9931723dd81fff0dd9c.html.

Murchison, Gabriel R. et al. "School Restroom and Locker Room Restrictions and Sexual Assault Risk Among Transgender Youth." *Pediatrics* 143, no. 6 (June 2019): 1–10. https://doi.org/10.1542/peds.2018-2902.

Natanson, Hannah. "School librarians face a new penalty in the banned-book wars: Prison." *The Washington Post*, May 18, 2023. https://www.washingtonpost.com/education/2023/05/18/school-librarians-jailed-banned-books/.

Padawer, Ruth. "When Women Become Men at Wellesley." *The New York Times*, October 15, 2014. https://www.nytimes.com/2014/10/19/magazine/when-women-become-men-at-wellesley-college.html.

Parental Rights in Education. H.B. 1557, FL State Leg. (2022).

Pendharkar, Eesha. "Pronouns for Trans, Nonbinary Students: The States With Laws That Restrict Them in Schools." *Education Week*, June 14, 2023. https://www.edweek.org/leadership/pronouns-for-trans-nonbinary-students-the-states-with-laws-that-restrict-them-in-schools/2023/06.

Perry, Sophie. "Kansas' new anti-trans bill is so extreme some cis women could be banned from toilets." *PinkNews*, April 28, 2023. https://www.thepinknews.com/2023/04/28/kansas-trans-lgbtq-bathroom-bill-ban/.

Provides relative to discussion of sexual orientation and gender identity in public schools. H.R. 466, LA State Leg. (2023).

Relative to participation in school sports programs for female student-athletes. H.B. 1251, NH State Leg. (2020).

"Restorative Practices in Schools." *International Institute for Restorative Practices*. Accessed February 8, 2024. https://www.iirp.edu/resources/restorative-practices-in-schools-k-12-education.

Seldin, Melissa and Christina Yanez. *Student Reports of Bullying: Results From the 2017 School Crime Supplement to the National Crime Victimization Survey* (Washington, DC: NCES, Institute of Education Sciences, U.S. Department of Education, July 2019). https://nces.ed.gov/pubs2019/2019054.pdf.

"State Action Center." *National Center for Transgender Equality.* Accessed July 10, 2023. https://transequality.org/state-action-center.

Steer, Daymond. "Kingswood athlete speaks out in support of bill." *The Conway Daily Sun*, June 13, 2018. https://bit.ly/4aWE4xw.

Stepaniuk, Casey. "The Burning and Banning of *Annie on My Mind.*" *Book Riot*, March 16, 2018. https://bookriot.com/annie-on-my-mind/.

"The Criminal Justice System: Statistics." *RAINN.* Accessed February 6, 2024. https://www.rainn.org/statistics/criminal-justice-system.

The Given Name Act. H.R. 81, LA State Leg. (2023).

The Trevor Project. "National Survey on LGBTQ Youth Mental Health 2021." *The Trevor Project*, last modified 2021. Accessed February 23, 2024. https://www.thetrevorproject.org/survey-2021/?section=Introduction.

Tukachinsky, Riva, Dana Mastro, and Morgan Yarchi. "The Effect of Prime Time Television Ethnic/Racial Stereotypes on Latino and Black Americans: A Longitudinal National Level Study." *Journal of Broadcasting & Electronic Media* 61, no. 3 (August 8, 2017): 538–56. https://doi.org/10.1080/08838151.2017.1344669.

Wadler, Joyce. "The Lady Regrets." *The New York Times*, February 1, 2007. https://www.nytimes.com/2007/02/01/garden/01renee.html.

Ward, L.M. "Wading Through the Stereotypes: Positive and Negative Associations Between Media Use and Black Adolescents' Conceptions of Self." *Developmental Psychology* 40, no. 2 (2004): 284–94. https://doi.org/10.1037/0012-1649.40.2.284.

Watson, Amy. "Share of book titles banned in school classrooms and libraries in the United States from July 1, 2022 to December 31, 2022, by subject matter." *Statista*, last modified 2023. Accessed July 17, 2023. https://www.statista.com/statistics/1342868/book-titles-banned-us-schools-by-subject-matter/.

Wills, Matthew. "Doctors Have Always Been Against High-Heeled Shoes." *ITHAKA*, May 11, 2020. https://daily.jstor.org/doctors-have-always-been-against-high-heeled-shoes/.

"Youth Risk Behavior Surveillance – United States, 2019." *Center for Disease Control and Prevention: Morbidity and Mortality Weekly Report* 69, no. 1 (Atlanta: Centers for Disease Control and Prevention, August 21, 2020): 1–83. https://www.cdc.gov/healthyyouth/data/yrbs/pdf/2019/su6901-H.pdf.

Index

American Library Association (ALA), 220–21

American Psychiatric Association, 15

anatomical sex, 3n3, 13–17, 18n21, 51, 53, 69

And Tango Makes Three (Richardson and Parnell), 214, 220–21, 225

Annie on My Mind (Garden), 202, 225n9

anti-censorship groups, 221, 224

application forms, 56, 57n11, 165–67, 166n6

Arizona, 22

Arkansas, 22, 133, 139n14

Armenta, Leilani, 134n7

Asian and Asian American people, 56n10, 239

"Ask a Trans Person Anything" programming, 213

asserting identity, 7, 10–11, 54–55

assumptions, 16–17, 18n21, 24n28, 55–56, 58–59, 67, 73–74, 96–97, 109, 163, 169–70, 170n8

athletics, 129–47

audit. *See* gender audit

autism, 242

awareness, 6n7, 24–25, 32, 54–55, 58, 69, 212

Bagagli, Beatriz Pagliarini, 106

banned books, 218–26, 226n10

Baron, Dennis, 10n13

bathrooms, 28–29, 104–26

   all-gender bathrooms, 69, 70n8, 83, 116n8, 122–23, 232

   bathroom bills, 52n8, 104–8, 117

"test runs," 161–62

visitation policies, 167–72

drag queens, 240

Drag Queen Story Hours, 213–17

dress codes, 30–32, 57, 73–79

driver's licenses, 24n28, 56n9

DSD (Differences of Sexual Development), 137n12

dysphoria. *See* gender dysphoria

Earnshaw's Infants' Department (trade publication), 78n14

"effeminate" men, 18, 18n22

elementary school classrooms, 10n16, 18–20, 85

empathy, 72

English departments, 99

Escambia County, FL, 220–21, 225

estrogen, 140

ethnicity, 145n24

expected conduct, 118–19, 118n11. *See also* behavior(s); conformity

external genitalia, 13–14, 51. *See also* anatomical sex

facilities. *See* bathrooms; dormitories; locker rooms

faculty. *See* teachers and administrators

family bathrooms, 70n8, 232

family involvement, 65, 67–68, 163–65, 175–76, 195–201, 235–36

feedback, 115, 163, 167, 224–25, 235

field trips, 172–77, 175n13

faculty training, 235

family involvement, 163–65, 195–201

gender binary, 152–57

gender-segregated spaces, 106–7

homosexuality, expectation or accommodation for, 152n1

N.H. Interscholastic Athletic Association (NHIAA), 142, 142n19

rooming situations and off-campus trips, 172–77

single-gender institutions, 185–90

transgender athletes, 136–45

visitation policies, 167–72

See also institutional mission and values; law and legislation

policing behavior or identity, 75–76, 118, 120, 144

politicized identity, 204

polling and focus groups, 161–62, 166–67

power, 116–17

preferred names. *See* chosen names

Primetime Live, 2–3

privacy, 89, 111, 112, 113–15, 115n6, 119, 123, 142n20, 161, 162, 171, 174, 195–96, 200

private schools, xviii, 68, 71, 141, 209–10, 222–23

privilege(s), 80, 116–17, 172, 189n4, 237–40

professional development, 72, 205

programming, inclusive, 211–18

programming and censorship, 223–24